'Greg Sheridan is a gifted and uniquely talented writer. To embark on writing a book on "Christians" is a daunting task but one that Greg has undertaken cleverly, passionately and insightfully. However, it's not surprising that Greg would write about Jesus when Jesus is still one of the most significant figures throughout history who has changed hundreds of millions of lives. Greg beautifully expresses that to the point that you feel like you have met Jesus. I wholeheartedly endorse this book as a must read.' **Russell Evans, Senior Pastor, Planetshakers International Church**

'Who could have predicted that one of Australia's most seasoned journalists would emerge as one of the country's most compelling public Christians! Sheridan is widely read, judicious and witty on virtually every page. With simplicity of insight and expression, he cuts through much of the modern nonsense about the Bible and Christianity peddled by professional scholars like me and invites readers to make their own common-sense judgements about Jesus of Nazareth, Paul of Tarsus, Mary, angels and the rest. The result is a forthright defence of what Christians (generally) agree on, that somehow manages to remain cheerful and secularly accessible. The numerous personal stories throughout inspire both the intellect and the emotions. If there is ever going to be a renaissance of Christian belief to save us from the dreariness of much secular humanism, it will come from a book like *Christians*. I will be buying it and giving it away to believers and sceptics alike.' **John Dickson, author, historian, Distinguished Fellow at Ridley College and host of Undeceptions podcast**

'The story of the Christian faith, and its enduring good for our world, will always be best heard when proposed, not imposed. In his new book, Sheridan makes such a proposal for belief in Jesus of Nazareth in readily accessible words and with warmth of expression. Through personal narratives and interviews with Christian witnesses, the Christian message is told by those who have talked and walked the Way. It is a good read about Good News. At the heart of the Christian story is the truth about the life of Jesus as witnessed to by his friends, and what his life brings to our lives today. At the heart of this book is an attentive look at this truth, those friendships and that gift.' **Peter Comensoli, Catholic Archbishop of Melbourne**

'We will always need the intelligent and admired intellects like Greg Sheridan to topple the "tyranny of experts" whose claim to fame is their "debunking" of faith without ever getting close enough to the wellsprings of it to discern the profound truths it holds in its sources, its deep and stirring paradoxes and most of all in its people. Greg has done all that, and manages to bring the reader along in what was clearly a hugely enjoyable rediscovery of the people who inhabit the gospels, most especially Jesus, while giving the heave-ho to some popular but improbable theories about who he was. Greg brings the reader along in an enjoyable discovery of the contentious scholarly debates and the extraordinary people in whom the living faith moves today. Mirroring the very human dilemmas in the gospel stories, their faith, like Greg's, is both great and humble, and reflects the continuing relevance of Christianity today.' **Rachael Kohn, author of *The Other Side of the Story* and former long-time host of ABC Radio National's *The Spirit of Things***

'This insightful book is an invitation to discover or rediscover Christianity through a variety of access points: the historicity of the claims made by the early Christians, the persons and personalities of the Gospels, and the inspiring witness of the "ordinary" Christians living amongst us today, expressing their faith in the service of others. Greg Sheridan's masterful work offers something to engage and edify every reader, whatever their stage of belief or non-belief.' **Monica Doumit, columnist, *The Catholic Weekly***

BY THE SAME AUTHOR

God Is Good for You
When We Were Young and Foolish
The Partnership
Cities of the Hot Zone
Asian Values, Western Dreams
Tigers: Leaders of the New Asia-Pacific
Living with Dragons

CHRISTIANS

CHRISTIANS

THE URGENT CASE
FOR JESUS
IN OUR WORLD

GREG SHERIDAN

ALLEN&UNWIN
SYDNEY•MELBOURNE•AUCKLAND•LONDON

Allen & Unwin
83 Alexander Street
Crows Nest NSW 2065
Australia
Phone: (61 2) 8425 0100
Email: info@allenandunwin.com
Web: www.allenandunwin.com

A catalogue record for this
book is available from the
National Library of Australia

ISBN 978 1 76087 909 9

Internal design by Midland Typesetters, Australia
Set in 11.5/17 pt Sabon by Midland Typesetters, Australia
Printed in Australia by McPherson's Printing Group

10 9 8 7 6 5 4

The paper in this book is FSC® certified.
FSC® promotes environmentally responsible,
socially beneficial and economically viable
management of the world's forests.

For Jessie

CONTENTS

PART 2: CHRISTIANS AND THEIR NEW WORLDS

Why this book,
called *Christians*?

This book is about the compelling, dramatic, gripping characters you meet in the New Testament. Above all, it is the search for Jesus. It seeks to meet him directly, in the New Testament, and in history, and to meet him indirectly through his friends, both his first friends, and some of his friends today.

Christians came about partly because a friend remarked to me that my last book, *God is Good for You*, was all well and good, but he didn't get a strong sense of the living Jesus from the Gospels, the complex, extraordinary figure who changed all of history initially by changing the lives of the people closest to him.

That led me to spend a year or two inside the New Testament. What fun it was. What a happy assignment. There's a lot of fun in the New Testament, just as there is in the Old Testament. In some ways, it suffers from both its good publicity and its bad publicity. People don't read the Bible enough with a sense of fun. They don't read it in the round. Think of it as long-form journalism that you expect to be true. There is Peter, ultimately heroic but several times broken along the way, wisely telling his followers, after Jesus is gone, that, yes, Paul can be a bit hard

1

to understand but he is a 'beloved brother' and his writings are to be considered as Scripture.

There is Paul in all his irascible, magnificent human strength and heroism, so annoyed with the followers misleading the Galatians, as he sees it, that he wishes that they might all go and castrate themselves.

This is not meant to be flip. The New Testament is also full of the moral beauty of the Sermon on the Mount, of the passion and agony of the crucifixion, and all the teaching and narrative celebrated in Christian history. Much of it is awe-inspiring. But it is also filled with pulsating, activist, sometimes confused figures of history.

There is Mary, so dynamic, so full of agency. There she is at the cross, with several other women and only one man, John, standing by Jesus as he dies. And surely this death of God, even though it's transcended in Jesus' resurrection, is the most radical thing in the universe.

And what about the angels? They are all through the New Testament, as indeed they're all through the Old Testament, God's messengers, humanity's friends, God's secret agents, as a great man once called them.

And it's all so immediate. The human passion of the New Testament calls out to us, demands our attention, across nearly two thousand years. The characters pulsate with life and purpose and brilliant, brilliant humanity in all its blood and thunder, all its quiet moments and its storms.

But this is not just a story, it's a true story. The whole modernist project of the last couple of centuries has crumbled partly in the face of archeology and modern historiography. The old modernist project, extant for the last two hundred years or so, held that the Christian scriptures had been written perhaps hundreds of years after the time they described, made up by scheming Church officials to retroactively fit up Jesus with orthodox religious views. Jesus, the modernists said, may or may not have existed at all. Certainly, they concluded, he was not God, nor did he claim to be.

But it turns out everything about the modernist project was wrong. Fragments of the Gospels were found that were much earlier than the modernists had thought possible. A fragment of John's Gospel, the last of the Gospels to be written, was found in Egypt and confidently dated at the end of the first century or early in the second century. The other Gospels, and all of Paul's letters, were written decades earlier than that, decades earlier than the end of the first century.

Other archeological discoveries showed us the New Testament accurately described Jewish society at the time of Jesus. Things that were once thought to be anachronisms in the Gospels turned out to be accurate history. And this process keeps unfolding as we discover, detail by detail, fragment by fragment, more about the ancient world. The New Testament is not exactly a historical record, but it is historically reliable, in the way that any human testimony by eyewitnesses, and the close friends of eyewitnesses, is historically reliable. Once you accept that the New Testament is the work of eyewitnesses, and reporters who spoke to eyewitnesses, then Jesus becomes the most richly documented figure of the ancient world.

There are historical references to Jesus beyond Christian writings, but merely accept that the contemporary Christian writings had something to say about the real Jesus, and all of a sudden we are bursting with testimony and historic knowledge.

And yet, it's still more important for people to know God than to know about God, to experience the friendship of Jesus than to know about the theoretical possibility of the friendship of Jesus.

As the first Apostles died out, the people who had known Jesus directly during his lifetime also began to die out. And then even the people who knew the people who knew Jesus directly, they too died out. But Christianity kept spreading. Paul, one of the giant figures of human history, but also in his countless stubborn contradictions and burning passion, one of the most appealing, makes the epic claim: 'The life I now live in the flesh I live by faith in the Son of God, who loved me and gave himself for me.'

Thus Paul is a startlingly modern figure. Paul was not there with the twelve Apostles when Jesus walked the streets of Jerusalem or the green fields of the Galilee. Assume for a moment, as modernism has for so long, that Christianity is all baloney. This Jesus must nonetheless have been an astonishing person to inspire this reaction in Paul, even though Paul was not there when Jesus was teaching.

The influence of Jesus, the presence of Jesus, doesn't stop with Paul. That's what the second half of *Christians* is about. Jesus seems somewhat less alive in the popular culture now than a few decades ago. But even here there is plenty of Jesus to see in contemporary culture.

More important than that are the lives of Jesus' good friends today. What about these Christians who just keep giving, whose love of others is a consequence of their love of Jesus? They form a striking unity of outlook with the first Christians. They are in the same 'head space', as Paul and Mary and John, two thousand years apart.

The same is true of those faithful Christians in China, true to the person and message of Jesus through all the difficulties and spasmodic persecutions they face. And what do Jesus' life and teachings, and his friendship, have to offer to those who would be our leaders, and to those who lead the Christian churches?

This book tries to offer partial answers to those questions.

Now let me introduce you to Jesus and his first friends . . .

PART 1

JESUS AND HIS FIRST FRIENDS

PART 1

JESUS AND HIS
FIRST FRIENDS

CHAPTER 1

The death of Jesus Christ

I heard a man say once that Christians worship sorrow.
That is by no means true. But we do believe there is
a sacred mystery in it.

Rev. John Ames, in Marilynne Robinson's novel *Gilead*

Anybody living in the strength of Christ's baptism
lives in the strength of Christ's death.

Dietrich Bonhoeffer

Because no other could do it, he himself went to the greatest
distance, the ultimate distance, the infinite distance. This
infinite distance between God and God, this incomparable
agony, this marvel of love, is the crucifixion.

Simone Weil

We proclaim a Christ crucified.

Paul, in the First Letter to the Corinthians

Can God die?
Western culture has been doing its best to kill God for a couple of hundred years. It's behind the times. It should know that this has been done once already. But that's not the end of the story. Christianity is surely the only religious sensibility in human history that has encompassed the death of God in its own central teachings.

Can God die?

Can the living God feel pain? Suffer? Weep? Almost despair?

The gods of polytheism, of myth and romance, can sometimes suffer these indignities—Zeus can fall out with Thor, as the Marvel franchise has reminded us—but the all-powerful, ever-knowing, eternal God of monotheism, can he be humiliated?

The most radical idea of Christianity, unique in all human history, is perhaps not finally the resurrection of Jesus, but the death of Jesus.

The death of Jesus. The death of God.

How can it be that God died? Physically died. And what does it mean? The world's most famous atheist, Richard Dawkins, once remarked in a television debate: 'Who would follow a God who would do this to his son?'

Yet as Dawkins might attest, we are all going to face death. We can't remember anything of our birth. We can't imagine our physical resurrection, if we believe in it. Of the three great events commemorating the signposts of Jesus' life—Christmas birth, crucifixion death and Easter resurrection, it's only death that we can contemplate for ourselves. How would we want to face it? What meaning does it have?

The whole of Christianity centres on the person of Jesus Christ. He is the Christian hope, the key to, the embodiment of, the Christian faith. He is the reason Christianity is generally so cheerful. From the outside, Christianity can sometimes look forbidding, dour or old fashioned, or bound by too many rules. But that's not its heart. It's a bit like when Frodo first meets Aragorn, the true and hidden king, in *The Lord of the Rings*. Frodo concludes that Aragorn is for real, and is good. If not, the shrewd hobbit observes, Aragorn would look fairer but seem fouler. On the inside, Christianity is full of feast days and family, full of fellowship, full of friendship. And everyone is welcome, surely never more so than at Christmas. It's full of care for the sick and the elderly, and for infants. It's full of sport and play, hard work and rest. It's full of good music and laughter, happy rituals and lots and lots of food (it's very big on food). It is the principle of human solidarity. It is the search for decency. It's a conversation with each other and with God. As John Denver might have put it, in Christianity you routinely speak to God and rejoice at the casual reply.

But there's another side, of course. Christianity also deals with the hard things, and death is generally the hardest of all.

Jesus' short human life of just 33 years or thereabouts embraced times of quiet, periods of sustained human attachment, the deepest regard for Mary and Joseph, and also for his disciples, and for every person who came his way. Especially for the sick and the poor, the lepers and the outcasts, the beggars and the marginalised. But there were also times of drama, as well as episodes of shocking savagery of the type in which the ancient world had particular expertise.

Most of the time, Jesus was good to be around. He got on well with his parents. You never went hungry in his company. He was always making new friends, happy to mix with anybody—tax collectors and prostitutes, poor and rich, beggars and pillars of respectability—happy to eat and drink with people of all backgrounds. He'd cook breakfast for the apostles when they were out fishing. He made sick people well. He lightened the burden of those with a heavy conscience, forgiving their sins and telling them to go in peace—to go in peace—and sin no more. If you brought your troubles to him, he'd help. Just knowing him somehow made you a better person. People wanted to be near him. He could be emotional. He wept, never hiding his tears.

There were times, too, when he was scary. There were times when he'd tell you things you didn't like to hear, times when he'd challenge you, especially the authenticity of your commitment. Sometimes people so badly wanted to harm him that they'd harm you just for being his friend.

Jesus' short life had three astounding pivot points.

The first is his birth. The first Christmas Day was the moment when eternity dramatically announced its intervention in time. The immense and the everlasting pierced the thin curtain of the moment. It's as though humanity went to sleep in a tent in the middle of a desert and woke up the next morning, stepped out of the tent and found itself in a tropical rainforest.

What just happened? All of life and nature transformed in the blink of an eye.

The circumstances of the first Christmas were surely as modest as any could be. Mary and Joseph were on the road. Soon, after the birth of Jesus, they would become refugees, fleeing the murderous persecution of Herod. On the night Jesus was born, they found only rough shelter. But for all that, the birth of any baby is happy.

The miracle of human life is infectious. Remember Mother Teresa, when she picked up a tiny infant in Kolkata, in circumstances so daunting that birth at all was a miracle: 'See! There's life in her!'

And yet in the physical poverty of Bethlehem there was splendour too, with the appearance of the Magi, the wise men (three in number according to tradition), bearing gifts, though we don't know when exactly they showed up. Christmas remains the most unambiguously happy festival all over the world. The other tradition of Christmas is that everybody is welcome. I have listened, transfixed with joy, to Christmas carols sung in hotel lobbies in Muslim Kuala Lumpur and Hindu Delhi and Shinto/Buddhist Tokyo, and in cities and towns and the countryside all over the world.

As Charles Dickens suggests in *A Christmas Carol*, you can tell something about a person, and their culture, by their attitude to Christmas. In 2018 the Chinese city Langfang decided to abolish Christmas altogether, to make decorations and celebrations for the feast illegal.

That may reflect the formal antipathy between communism and religious belief, but it was an uncharacteristic move for post-Mao China. The commercial potential of the Christmas feast means it normally gets a pass in almost every country. Only the real outliers like North Korea, societies all but cut off from normal international interactions and obsessed with an obscure ideological purity, ban Christmas altogether.

So while part of its wide appeal is commercial, Christmas is as near to a universal human festival of good cheer and good hope as our divided human race has produced. The world understands something at least about Christmas.

The other great Christian festival, Easter, celebrates the victory of Jesus over death in his resurrection. This is generally seen as the defining moment of Christ's drama. The early Christians passionately believed and taught the resurrection. This is a theological fact, and a historical fact. Paul, in Corinthians, proclaims: 'If Christ is not risen, your faith is futile' (1 Corinthians 15:17), then shortly after goes on to say:

'But in fact Christ has been raised from the dead, the first fruits of those who have died . . . for as all die in Adam, so all will be made alive in Christ.'

Paul's First Letter to the Corinthians was written only about 20 years after Jesus' death. Clearly from Paul's letter, even by then, the resurrection was the established belief of Christians, the people Paul was writing to. Paul was not explaining to the Corinthians something they had never previously heard of. He was reaffirming their established Christian faith. Indeed, Paul himself says that he received the news of Jesus' resurrection years before that, when Jesus appeared to him and he had his own conversion experience.

So belief in the resurrection—that Jesus, in his body, rose from the dead and, glorified in a body made new, walked again among the disciples, taught them and inspired them—was held by Christians from the earliest times following Jesus' life and death.

Easter is a big deal wherever in the world there is a community of Christians. Nonetheless Easter is not nearly as global a celebration as Christmas. This is partly because Easter has more fully maintained its God content. Everyone can rejoice at the birth of Jesus; not everyone can accept the resurrection of Jesus. Most of humanity does not believe in the resurrection.

This book will argue (in more detail in the next chapter) that Christmas and Easter are historical events. They really happened. The evidence for them is strong. Of course, it's not on the basis of the historical evidence that people believe. But here's the rub—nor is it on the basis of the historical evidence that people disbelieve.

Believing that Christmas was the birth of the Son of God, and Easter was the resurrection of the Son of God, is more reasonable and consistent with the facts than any other belief, unless of course you start your inquiries with the view that the miraculous is impossible.

But Christians must also be clear and honest about the limits of the historical evidence. History certainly does not prove that Jesus was God and that he rose from the dead. It is similar to the question of whether to believe in God at all. It is reasonable to believe in God and it is reasonable not to believe in God. Some of those who disbelieve in God, however, argue that science has taken a stand against God, that science has rendered God literally unbelievable. This is profoundly and extravagantly untrue. Science itself has nothing at all to say directly about God. Belief in God certainly fits most easily with all the facts, all the scientific facts and all the human facts. It requires less magical thinking, fewer leaps of faith, than conscientious atheism. But you cannot prove God by reason alone.

However, belief in God is entirely reasonable, entirely consistent with reason. Most of the things we actually believe in life are reasonable but not proven.

The same basic pattern applies regarding belief in the Gospels. There are no established facts at all which contradict the Gospels in fundamental ways, but the facts of history likewise do not prove the Gospels are true. Nor does history prove the opposite, that Jesus did not rise from the dead. Belief in miracles, or disbelief in miracles, is a matter of faith and judgement.

But here's the thing: faith in Jesus is not against facts, against evidence, against science. It's not irrational, it doesn't contradict any established facts.

Where does that leave us with the agonising death that the historical man, Jesus, experienced in the crucifixion?

Ironically, unlike Christmas and Easter, there is no real historical controversy about the crucifixion. It is recounted in all four Gospels and in the letters of Paul. Other non-Christian historians of the ancient world record that Jesus was executed. No one seriously challenges it historically. Those who give Jesus some serious thought but reject absolutely the Christian idea of Jesus as the second person of the Holy Trinity—Father, Son and Holy Spirit—which is God, tend to fall into one of several broad schools. They see Jesus either as a familiar Jewish holy man who never meant to transcend Judaism, or primarily as a prophet, or an exorcist, or as a radical preacher with strong ideas about the end of the world, or as a kindly social reformer who administered free health care through no-fee home-visit miracles, or lastly, and most absurdly, as a political revolutionary. There is a tiny cohort of anti-Christian writers who think that Jesus never existed at all, which is surely the most eccentric conclusion of the lot. Something like denouncing drunkenness while claiming that the existence of alcohol is a myth.

And then there is a school of thought, among them a very small number of well-known Christians, who see Jesus as the Christian leader alright, but deny his divinity (no Christian church holds that view, but some famous Christians have). For these Christians, Jesus was an inspired man rather than the Son of God. That position is the opposite of a common mistake in the first centuries of Christian belief, during which some saw Jesus as certainly divine, but denied his true humanity (though of course there were other early heresies that denied his divinity). Councils of the early Church ultimately decided that view was heresy. The Council of Nicaea, in 325, codified previous widespread belief into the doctrine of the Holy Trinity. It reaffirmed Jesus' divinity. It affirmed that Jesus was fully human and fully divine. But in any event it's there, clear and plain, in the New Testament.

I don't think any of the modern interpretations which deny Jesus' divinity square easily with the historical facts, or square at all with the Gospels, or with the life and character of the early Christian community, the people who knew Jesus. But that's not really my point here. It's that even these folks, with all their different interpretations, generally accept that the crucifixion of Jesus took place (except obviously those few who think that Jesus never lived).

The crucifixion—we know that really happened. We know that as a fact of history.

It is a unique event, so shocking to contemplate that even after 2000 years we seldom think of it in any detail. More than anything else, it is the crucifixion which offers us the greatest and most accessible insight into the personality of Jesus. For there is no faking who you are in that kind of death.

The death of Jesus was ugly, vicious, prolonged and excruciating in its violence and humiliation. Mel Gibson's film *The Passion of the Christ* was criticised for its extreme violence. There is too much violence for my taste in a number of Gibson's films. But in this case, the uncompromising savagery was realistic.

The ancient world was a violent place, red in tooth and claw, although Jesus lived under a certain, limited Pax Romana. Paul's status as a Roman citizen sometimes helped him in his many brushes with the law. The Romans did deliver some order. But the ancient world was still routinely rough and violent and unpredictable. Slave owners did what they liked with their slaves. Aristotle, the most enlightened man of Greek antiquity, thought most slaves were 'natural slaves' and should be considered living tools or animated machines. Christian teaching on sexual morality was one of the first provisions which offered protection for the physical person of the slave, although there had been general edicts, especially in Jewish life, for masters not to be gratuitously cruel to slaves.

Crucifixion was a type of death typically dealt out to slaves, in part to make sure they never contemplated revolt. It was carried out thousands and thousands of times. King Herod, fearing the rumour of a new king born in Bethlehem, had all the male children in the Bethlehem area under the age of two slaughtered. There is nothing remotely unbelievable about that. Killing potential pretenders to the throne is almost core logic for absolute monarchs with paranoid tendencies throughout history. It's the way North Korea's dictator, Kim Jong-un, has dealt with his own family in the 21st century. John the Baptist was beheaded because Salome danced lasciviously for her stepfather, Herod Antipas (son of Herod the Great who ordered the baby boys killed in Bethlehem). He promised her anything she wanted as a reward. She demanded he kill John the Baptist and present her with his head, so that's what he did, feeling only the mildest regret at the excess of her request. Although the killing of such a famously good man as John the Baptist outraged his Jewish followers, such casual killing was not even remarkable among all the killings in Herod's family. (It was said that it was safer to be a pig than one of Herod's sons, because all the brothers were constantly plotting against each other.)

The Roman Empire imposed some order, but it was no democracy. Fathers all but owned their children and all but owned their wives. Slaves, childless widows, foreigners— there were a lot of marginalised people in the ancient world. Nothing was more savage than a Roman crucifixion. It could have only one end; no one escaped from it. And it was intentionally structured to take a long time. Humiliation was mixed with pain. Terror, the power to frighten, the example set to others of what could happen to them—these were part of the design.

Crucifixion was a contemptible punishment. It declared that its victim was the lowest point of humanity the ancient world could imagine or create. The idea that God himself would be crucified was simply inconceivable.

The sheer physical details of Jesus' crucifixion are enough to startle us even today. Pontius Pilate, the Roman governor, is scared of executing Jesus but also scared of letting him go. Jesus' fate at one point is left to the crowd. They don't want him released. Pilate, who rules Jerusalem in tacit alliance with local community leaders, much as the British East India Company once ruled large parts of India, orders Jesus to be whipped and then taken for crucifixion. After Jesus is condemned, the soldiers take him out to the crowd. They mock him as the king of the Jews, strip him of his own clothes and dress him in a robe of purple to mimic and ridicule his kingship. They beat him over the head, spit on him, abuse him, fashion a crown of thorns and stick that on his head. Just think of this action, rough and hard and prolonged.

Then Jesus is paraded through Jerusalem, and the crowds encouraged to mock him. He must carry the cross and he falls under its weight. There are those in the crowd moved by pity, especially, as ever, women, who weep for him. There is a tradition, though it is not mentioned in the Gospels, that one woman, Veronica, ran forward to wipe Jesus' face. But not many in the crowd want to stand up for Jesus, or stand against the crowd itself.

Stumbling and falling, he must make his way to Golgotha, the Place of the Skull, where he will die.

It is nine o'clock in the morning when the process leading to his crucifixion begins and he doesn't die until three in the afternoon, after three full hours on the cross. The human body is stubborn. It clings to life. The crucifixion is mimicked in modern torture techniques which employ so-called 'stress positions', where the mere act of breathing becomes increasingly painful. On the cross, his feet nailed to the post and his arms to the cross beam, Jesus' body slumps on itself. Each breath requires a physical effort to rise up and take a gulp of air. This goes on for hours. He develops a terrible thirst, as well as a terrible fatigue. The only complaint of pain wrung from him is the shocking: 'I thirst'. A sponge dipped in vinegar and water is thrust at his mouth. There is no defence against ravenous birds, growing more aggressive, more confident, as they realise that this dying man cannot fight back. He dehydrates. Slowly, his body grows colder.

This death seems inaccessible to us. We don't want to think about it. Even to imagine it happening to us, or to someone we love, is beyond us. We hope and pray we don't have a death anything like that. Yet in certain limited ways we had to confront one element of the terror of Jesus' kind of death in the time of COVID-19. That element was the enforced, physical isolation of the dying from friends and family.

The last act of human solidarity is to sit by the bedside of someone you love and hold their hand as they die. Christianity has a long expertise in comforting the dying. Yet COVID, as it killed its millions of victims around the world, waged a war against this most elementary mercy in death. It waged war on the Christian way of death. COVID has been the enemy of human solidarity, while Christianity is the principle of solidarity. COVID imposed a way of death which in its physical isolation recalls Jesus isolated on the cross from his family and his friends.

And the COVID victims too, like Jesus, they struggled for each breath.

Because COVID is so infectious, many people have had to die almost alone, cut off from the people whom they love most and who most love them. To die with no partner or friend, or even kindly stranger, to hold your hand, to pat you gently on the shoulder, to encourage or console with touch or kiss, that is not what we want. The last sight for many of the legions of the COVID dead was a heroic health worker behind heavy layers of protective gear, looking something like a robot in an old science fiction movie.

Perhaps at the last such a patient sees only the distant eyes of a nurse, caring or distracted, doing their best.

Albert Camus, in his viscerally affecting novel *The Plague*, an allegory of Nazi occupation of France, observed: 'The chief source of distress, the deepest as well as the most widespread, was separation.'

The death of Jesus, while more violent than a hospital death, has about it nonetheless something of the COVID death. At the foot of the cross were his mother, Mary; a couple of other women, including Mary Magdalene; and his beloved disciple, John. Most of the men who cared about him were not there. So often in the Gospels the men betrayed Jesus, or denied him, or fell asleep when he asked them to stay awake with him in his night of troubles, or just failed to show up. But the women were there, braver, more faithful. And later they were the first to see him risen, the first apostles of the risen Christ. But before that, they shared his agony.

Most of the very few things Jesus was able to say on the cross do not readily remind you of an all-conquering, all-powerful god of the type the ancient world was very familiar with, and a facsimile of which so many people try to become today, as they deny the place of the living God in their lives.

Jesus' words instead suggest a man, a human being, bearing the unbearable, which in some sense is the fate of all human beings in death.

Some of Jesus' last words recall to me things I have heard family members and friends say as they lay on what turned out to be their death beds in hospitals, and once or twice in hospices.

Everyone I have known approaching death is concerned for the people closest to them, who they will leave behind. And the concern most often is not just sentimental, but also practical. With my wife I once went to a hospital to visit a dying woman we knew, half of a couple who were dear friends, though we had known them only a few short years. Our dying friend asked to see my wife and me alone. We went to say goodbye, and tell her we loved her. She was not scared, she said, but just wanted to go. But she had one request of me: you'll keep in touch with my husband won't you? You'll stay friends? Meet up for a coffee now and then?

She was about to die, but she was thinking only of her husband.

On another occasion a beloved uncle lay dying, a former policeman, a strong, tough man, a migrant to Australia, a war veteran who had faced more challenges and difficult circumstances in his life than I could really imagine, and uttered almost his last words: 'Won't you get my wife a cup of tea?'

The last words Jesus spoke to friend or disciple from the cross were these two injunctions. He looked down on his mother, standing next to John, in what must have been the deepest distress of her life, and he said to her: 'Woman, this is your son.' And to John: 'This is your mother.' And from that day, so the Gospels tell us, Mary lived in John's home as a member of his household.

Christians see all kinds of theological meaning in all of Jesus' words, particularly, perhaps, his words when he is dying. But forget theology, doctrine and teaching for a moment. Surely there is a powerful human import in Jesus' last words to friend or family. He cares for his mother and he asks his most devoted disciple, his best friend you might say, to look after her.

Earlier, as his cross was being set up and the crucifixion beginning, Jesus prayed for the men killing him: 'Father, forgive them, for they know not what they do.'

Viktor Frankl, the Austrian Jewish psychiatrist who survived Auschwitz and other Nazi camps, and wrote the piercing book *Man's Search for Meaning*, suffered many beatings at the hands of camp guards. He wrote about his experience that the worst element of a beating was the implied insult, the humiliation. Jesus' experience on the cross involved insult and humiliation at every turn.

Many people in such circumstances dream of revenge on their tormentors. Jesus, in his selfless love, prays for them.

His last words to his disciples concerned the care for his mother. But he spoke to God the Father out loud twice more. Shortly before his final death, Jesus cried out in Aramaic, *Eli, Eli, lama sabachtani*, which means: My God, my God, why have you abandoned me?

Almost, almost, almost Jesus feels despair. I am not saying something revolutionary about Jesus here. I am certainly not meaning to doubt his courage or his faithfulness or his confidence in his Father. He fully accepted his death on the cross. But Jesus was also fully human, a flesh-and-blood man. He experienced the alienation and loneliness of extreme suffering.

Jesus was fully human all the way through the Gospels. Luke (2:52) tells us that as a child Jesus grew in wisdom, age and grace. What does it mean for God to grow in wisdom? It means he was a fully human child while he was also fully divine.

Fully human, fully divine.

Jesus could experience temptation, he could face temptation. The two ways to sin against hope, to deny hope, are presumption and despair. The devil had previously tempted Jesus with a form of presumption, in the desert where Jesus had fasted for 40 days. The devil offered him kingship, sovereignty over a nation much greater than Israel. Jesus rejected the temptation and dismissed him.

Struggling to breathe on the cross, his body growing colder and colder as death approached, watching his mother suffer at the foot of the cross, surely any human being would be tempted to despair.

But to be tempted is not the same as succumbing to temptation. There is no fault in temptation. No sin in it. Being tempted involves no stain on virtue at all. Jesus ultimately did not despair. One reason Jesus lived as a human being was to show us how to live, how to face the temptation of despair.

Finally came the most searing cry from Jesus, his last words on the cross: 'Father, into your hands I commend my spirit.'

Frankl also observed that there is one final freedom which no human being ever loses completely when conscious, and that is the choice about how to respond to whatever circumstance he finds himself in.

This is Jesus' last response. His cry 'Father, into your hands I commend my spirit' is the culmination of his human life before the resurrection. The essence of this moment is Jesus' complete surrender of his human will to the Father and his complete reliance on the Father.

'Into your hands I commend my spirit.' I can do no more. I can say no more. I have no more solutions, no more agency, no more action. Father, I am yours.

In one Gospel account, Jesus says: 'It is finished.'

If this seems superhuman, I think it is actually close to the attitude every believer tries to take to death: thank you for this life, please look after the people I love, I am sorry for my wrongs (Jesus didn't need to say that), please let this suffering pass, now I am yours and I rely on you absolutely. That is how

Jesus fulfills and also transcends his humanity, by surrendering absolutely to God the Father.

In the crucifixion Jesus reveals again the fullness of his humanity. Yet still in this crucifixion there is a moment when Jesus also reveals his glory, and acts with the authority of the divine king of creation. Often the problem with thinking of Jesus is to understand that he was always fully human, and he was always fully divine. Being divine didn't shield him from all the hardship and uncertainty, all the pain and change, the growth and decay, the forever shuddering uncertainty of human life, it didn't shield him from the human condition. But at the same time, being human did not strip him of his divine status, his role as the second person of the Trinity, who, as John says, in the beginning was with God and was God.

Jesus is crucified between two thieves. One mocks him and continually abuses him. He taunts Jesus in language similar to that which the devil used in the desert. If you are the Christ, save yourself and save us as well.

The other thief rebukes this man. We got the same sentence as Jesus, the good thief says, we deserve our sentence. But Jesus has done no wrong. Finally the good thief has an intuition about Jesus, an understanding, a revelation of faith, and he says to Jesus: remember me when you come into your kingdom.

There are sorrow and repentance and faith in the good thief. Jesus replies to him: Truly I tell you today you will be with me in paradise.

Normal human beings cannot guarantee each other, with authority, that they will meet God in paradise. But Jesus can. Because as well as being a human being, he is God. Of course, the resurrection within three days shows us that Jesus has conquered death, that Jesus is the Son of God. But Jesus knew that already—he was still God when he was a man dying on the cross, and he offers mercy and reassurance and salvation to the good thief.

Similarly, the cry of Jesus, 'My God, why have you forsaken me?', is a quotation from the start of Psalm 22. And it is true that this psalm begins in isolated lamentation and ends in a declaration of triumph. But this doesn't mean that Jesus uttered these words only for their educative or allusive quality, that it was not what he was feeling. Jesus knew the Old Testament intimately. Religious people in the most extreme moments always have scripture running through their heads. Jesus grew up steeped in the knowledge of the Jewish scriptures.

I think Jesus' cry of desolation is both what he was feeling at that moment and also an allusion to the psalm in its fullness. For he had both human feeling and divine inspiration.

I have a friend, a former politician, who was gravely ill for many months in the intensive care unit of a Sydney hospital. Her prayer all the way through her ordeal was Jesus' prayer in the Garden of Gethsemane: Not my will be done, Lord, but yours. She was praying by reciting Scripture, which is a very normal Jewish and Christian way to pray. She was also praying those words because they perfectly expressed her feelings.

In some certain ways, being divine might have made Jesus' job of being human even more taxing. For Jesus clearly foresaw his own death and suffering. He prophesied it more than once.

It was in the Garden of Gethsemane that the cost to Jesus of this knowledge is made clear, especially in the gritty, gripping account provided in Mark's Gospel. Jesus knew what was coming for him. Surely the contemplation of such a fate is psychologically almost unbearable.

On the night before the crucifixion, Jesus took his disciples to the Garden of Gethsemane. He wanted to pray. So often when he prayed he took himself apart from others so that he could pray directly and undistracted to God the Father. Yet he asked the disciples to stay nearby. He needed solitude to pray, yet he also asked for the solidarity of his friends nearby. So, from among the disciples, he took Peter, James and John with him. Here is something almost unique in the New Testament. Mark tells us that a sudden fear came over Jesus, and that he was in great distress. Jesus tells Peter, James and John that he is deeply grieved, even to death. And he asks them to stay awake.

Three times he comes back to his closest disciples and, having asked them to pray, he finds they are asleep. Jesus' prayer in Gethsemane to his Father is the prayer anyone might make. Abba, he calls the Father, the intimate family name, for you everything is possible. Please take the cup (of suffering) away from me. Jesus is in acute distress at these moments. In Luke's Gospel, the sweat pours from Jesus like drops of blood. Plainly, Jesus' holiness and courage and unity with God the Father did not exempt him from the human suffering as his ordeal approached.

But the second half of the prayer Jesus makes is in a different tone: Not my will be done but yours. Jesus has accepted his death on the cross, but he still wishes that it wouldn't happen, that somehow there's a way to avoid it. Jesus' prayer in Gethsemane takes a long time. Jesus uses prayer to become more fully in communion with his Father. At the human level he uses it to steady himself. He has regained complete possession of his composure when he is finished. But it takes a long time to do this, time enough for his closest apostles, strong men, to fall asleep, against their will, again and again. Several times in the Gospels Jesus tells his followers to persevere in prayer, to stay the course, to continue to pray no matter what, even if it seems their prayers are unanswered. Though himself divine, Jesus experiences a familiar human benefit of prayer, a calming of the spirit.

Jesus' life is of course much more than the crucifixion. It is all the teaching and miracles and fellowship and meals and feasts and everything else. And, triumphantly, it is the resurrection.

Why was Jesus crucified? The Gospels tell us that when, in anger, he overturns the tables of the money lenders and traders in the temple, the temple leaders decide to take action against him. But it was more than this. They are alarmed at his raising Lazarus from the dead. They are alarmed at the miracles he performs, especially on the Sabbath. They are particularly alarmed at the way he claims to forgive sins, when the authority to forgive sins lies only with God. They are alarmed at the way he interprets the traditional law of the scriptures, to give effect to its spirit while overturning the letter of the law as they have been interpreting it. In a religious culture obsessed with rites of purification, they are alarmed at the way he touches lepers to cure them. They are alarmed altogether about the company he keeps.

Then they are doubly alarmed about his triumphant entrance into Jerusalem. They are further alarmed by the large crowds that have come to Jerusalem for the Passover feast, for they fear that in some manner Jesus might gain their support.

Finally, when Jesus is accused before the Sanhedrin, the council of city elders in Jerusalem, the main charge against him is blasphemy, because he has continually referred to himself as though he were the equal of God.

His accusers seem to have lost interest in the incident of his overturning the tables in the temple. Instead they focus on his alleged blasphemy in equating himself with God.

In Mark's Gospel (14:61) the high priest asks Jesus is he the Christ, the son of the Blessed One? And Jesus replies: 'I am! And you will see the Son of Man seated at the right hand of the Power, and coming with the clouds of Heaven.'

The high priest instantly condemned this as blasphemy and all his colleagues agreed.

As you spend more time in the Bible, you are struck by just how accessible it is, how much it speaks for itself, how much you get out of it without any homework in advance, so to speak. But one small challenge for the modern reader is to bear in mind how completely Jewish was the context of Jesus' life and teachings. They were universal teachings and they were intended for the whole of humanity, but their context was Jewish and they grew entirely out of Jewish soil.

Certainly the New Testament is richer if you have an idea of its Jewish background. Jesus frequently refers to himself as the Son of Man, which is a somewhat enigmatic term. Yet in places in the Old Testament, certainly in the Book of Daniel, it is a term used to describe a figure who sits on a throne beside that of the Father in heaven, with his own kingly status.

And many times in the Old Testament, when God talks to humanity he comes 'with the clouds of Heaven'. For Jesus to use these words describing himself is a strong statement of his divine status. This is critical in understanding who Jesus was and claimed himself to be, which is in turn essential in understanding why he was crucified.

In John's Gospel, Jesus' declaration of his own divinity is completely clear. And the claims of Jesus' divinity are present throughout the writings of Paul and in the other books of the New Testament.

The character of the first three Gospels (the Synoptic Gospels), Matthew, Mark and Luke, is different from that of John, and in the declaration of Jesus as God, a little more complex. As evident in the figurative and allusive stories he tells, Jesus is a superb literary artist. He is also a master teacher. Except when he is being cross-examined by temple leaders, he doesn't generally go in for close scriptural argument and contests of logical flow and the like. Instead, he teaches mainly through stories, especially parables. When asked a question, he often replies with a question, not to be smart but to get his questioner to follow him down a line of reflection. He teaches men and women, which was not altogether common in the ancient world. His disciples clearly include women. He more or less abolishes all social classes.

But he does not seek or have a public profile at all for the first 30 years of his life. And he then follows a plan of gradual disclosure of himself, just as the disclosure of God and his true nature is gradual and progressive through the course of the Old Testament. When Jesus asks Peter who Peter thinks he is, Peter replies 'You are the Christ, the Son of the living God' (Matthew 16:16). Jesus blesses Peter for this insight of faith. At other times when the disciples proclaim Jesus the Messiah, he doesn't disagree with them but tells them not to tell others. He makes his full identity clear in his own time.

And as his life goes on, he makes evident that he is the spiritual Messiah for all humanity, not the political Messiah for Israel's conflict with Rome. Of course, Jesus was a faithful Jew and honoured his Jewish inheritance. (All Christians should honour the Jewish religion.) In the Christian view, Jesus fulfilled that inheritance.

Some of Jesus' contemporaries thought he was a political threat, or alternatively a political hope, because of the magnetism of his personality and the crowds he commanded. But at no stage did he propound a political program for the reform of society from the top down. And his kingdom, as he said, was not of this world (at least as presently constituted). And the charge for which he was condemned and handed over to Roman authorities for execution, was blasphemy, in effect, in the authorities' view, claiming to be equal to God, or even more scandalous, to be God.

This is important because it is sometimes argued that in the first three Gospels, Matthew, Mark and Luke, Jesus doesn't claim to be God, but only does so unambiguously in the fourth Gospel, John, which is generally thought to be the last of the Gospels to be written. This argument can lead to a high-falutin' version of the conspiracy theory mindset of Dan Brown's nonsensical *The Da Vinci Code*, that the whole idea of Jesus as divine was a much later invention by scheming Church authorities.

The problems with this preposterous but popular idea are endless. For a start, the divine Jesus is present in many places in Paul's writings, and these pre-date John's Gospel. So this was a conspiracy of Church authorities apparently hatched long before John's Gospel was written. In fact it is pretty confidently thought that Paul's letters also pre-date the other Gospels as well, so if the Church was in on a conspiracy through Paul, it started very early. Which leads to the obvious question—if the conspiracy was already hatched before the other Gospels were written, why not just include some other, explicit claims about Jesus' divinity in the Synoptic Gospels? But as we have seen, the divinity of Jesus is in any event strongly suggested in the Synoptic Gospels.

Folks who hold the conspiracy theory that the early Church invented the idea of Jesus' divinity long after the event also generally hold that most or all of Jesus' miracles were added to the Gospels later. But if that's true, and the people who added in the miracles also dreamt up Jesus' divinity, then why not just put in some clear doctrinal statements about Jesus' divinity in Matthew, Mark and Luke?

Like all conspiracy theories, the reasoning is circular and ultimately mad.

For it is also the case that the first three Gospels do disclose Jesus' divinity. Mostly they do this in a way that is not absolutely explicit, but can lead only to that conclusion. On the cross Jesus promises the good thief that he will see him in paradise. He forgives sins as only God can. He raises people from the dead on his own authority. He expels demons in his own name. He miraculously feeds large crowds as God did for the Israelites in the desert. He accepts the designation of the Christ, the son of the living God. He tells his accusers they will see him 'coming in the clouds of heaven'. The Synoptic Gospels (for example, Matthew 17) all also recount the Transfiguration of Jesus, when he and Peter, James and John walk up a mountain to pray.

Jesus is transfigured, his face shines like the sun. Moses and Elijah appear beside him and a voice from the cloud says: 'This is my Son, the Beloved: with him I am well pleased, listen to him!'

Jesus' accusers, though naturally they didn't know of the Transfiguration, understood in some measure what Jesus was claiming. They were scandalised by it, or perhaps scared by it, or perhaps both.

So that's why the authorities decided they wanted Jesus crucified. That's the human explanation of why the crucifixion took place.

Now we come to the much bigger question: what was the divine purpose of Jesus' death and resurrection?

Countless libraries full of books have been written, by the most brilliant people who ever lived, to answer that question. But like most key Christian beliefs, it is at once very simple, and yet involves a degree of mystery.

Jesus died for the love of us, for the love of all human beings. The idea of the immortal, omniscient and all-powerful God suffering humiliation and death for human beings is difficult to grasp. Paul called the crucifixion a stumbling block for Jews and a folly for Gentiles. It was so radically at odds with everything the ancient world thought of God, or of gods. We've had 2000 years to get used to the idea and it's still strange.

Along with Jesus' many parables and teachings, however, it is the reason Christian churches, Christian communities, Christians generally, have always tried to help in solidarity with suffering.

It is worth recalling, in this time of COVID, that one of the reasons the early Christian movement expanded so rapidly was because of the power of its example during the plagues which regularly beset the ancient world. Christians didn't run away during plagues. A lot of them stayed to help. They followed Jesus' example on the cross, of maximum solidarity with suffering humanity. Cyprian, a third-century bishop of Carthage, who was later himself martyred, wrote the main historic description of the plague that ravaged the Roman Empire in his time. Historians speculate it may have been an influenza pandemic. At its worst there were 5000 people dying per day in Rome. This was accompanied by all manner of barbaric and ruthlessly selfish behaviour. Cyprian wrote that the plague 'searches out the justice of each and every one and examines the mind of the human race; whether the well care for the sick, whether relatives dutifully love their kinsmen as they should, whether masters show compassion for their ailing slaves, whether physicians do not desert the afflicted.'

This is why the Rev. John Ames, Marilynne Robinson's lead character in *Gilead*, recalls that people think that Christians worship sorrow. This would certainly be more true if the crucifixion were not followed by the resurrection.

But still, to say that Jesus died for the love of all people is not enough. Paul says in 1 Corinthians (15:3) 'Christ died for our sins in accordance with Scripture' and in Romans (6:8) 'If we have died with Christ, we believe that we will also live with him.'

If you believe that God is good, then you don't even need to be a Christian to see that humanity is in constant rebellion against God. Not only that, each human heart struggles against itself every day to be good and to do good.

The Christian teaching is that humanity put itself at odds with God, first through Original Sin, and then through the many ways of human evil. And that without divine help, we weren't able fundamentally to put the relationship right again. Jesus becoming man and dying on the cross atones for all our sins and puts us in good standing with God.

Romans 3:21 says: 'It is the same justice of God that comes through grace to everyone, Jew and Gentile alike, who believes in Jesus Christ. Both Jew and Gentile sinned and forfeited God's glory, and both are justified through the free gift of grace by being redeemed in Christ Jesus who was appointed by God to sacrifice his life so as to win reconciliation through faith.'

Why do I say the doctrine is at once both simple, and a mystery?

Here's the simple part. Jesus became a man, lived and taught and was crucified and died, and then rose from the dead three days later, to bridge the unbridgeable gap between God and man, to make up for our Original Sin and all our continuing sins. He came to share in our life, and that meant sharing in our suffering. A fully human life has its share of suffering, and Jesus was fully human. He came to expose the fraudulent glamour of evil and to show us the true nature of goodness. He came to show us what a perfect human life looks like. He also came so that we might share in his life. By becoming a human being, Jesus in a sense makes the whole of human nature divine, in that he shows that human nature is grand and magnificent enough to carry the divine personality.

Of course as we try to work this out in all its fullness, we are like children staring at the stars. Our parents have told us a bit, but we don't know and can't understand everything.

As usual, C.S. Lewis is a very helpful friend. On the simple bit, he says: 'The central belief is that Christ's death has somehow put us right with God and given us a fresh start.'

Don't feel too downcast about the element of this doctrine which is involved in mystery. Rowan Williams, the former Anglican Archbishop of Canterbury, in a sermon on atonement, quotes Corinthians again: 'No one comprehends what is truly God's except the Spirit of God.'

Williams counsels that we should stand: 'in contemplative wonder before the pure and unconditioned self-consistency of God's being, and also in contemplative gratitude before the fact of grace at work—and there is no other rational place for the Christian to stand—[then] you will begin to see it was necessary for the Christ to suffer and so enter into his glory.'

Pope Benedict XVI, when he was merely Cardinal Joseph Ratzinger, wrote: 'In the Bible the cross does not appear as part of a mechanism of injured right; on the contrary in the Bible the cross is quite the reverse: it is the expression of a life that is completely being for others . . . This is truly something new, something unheard of—the starting point of Christian existence . . . God does not wait until the guilty come to be reconciled; he goes to meet them and reconcile them. Here we can see the true direction of the incarnation, of the cross.'

Exactly how atonement works in what we might term the divine economy of the Blessed Trinity is something on which mainstream Christian traditions sometimes offer different interpretations, and on which many accept that we don't know everything.

It is worth listening to C.S. Lewis again. Here is how he thought about that mysterious element of atonement, and how the death of Jesus on the cross puts us right with God and gives us a fresh start: 'Theories as to how it did this are a different matter. A good many different theories have been held as to how it works; what all Christians are agreed on is that it works.'

A good many different theories—these theories address the mystery. But true faith always involves this tantalising and ineluctably human paradox—a certain, clear, simple truth, which anyone can understand, is set against a mystery so profound and majestic that the proper response is awe. The simple truth can only be understood next to the great mystery, which itself is only a great mystery because it accompanies an essential, arresting and simple truth.

As Les Murray wrote about another aspect of Christian belief in his brilliant, short poem 'The Knockdown Question': 'The answer to that is not in the same world as the question.'

We believe, and we believe we know the truth, but we don't know everything about the truth.

The image of the cross was first used to mock Christians, as a symbol of the failure and humiliation of their God. It took 300 years for Christians to readily use the cross as their own symbol. And it was nearly a thousand years after the death of Jesus before European artists felt comfortable depicting Jesus on the cross. And yet, from the start, the cross was central to the Christian story.

Greater love has no one than this, that they lay down their life for their friends. We all have our cross. A perfect life looks perfect only from a distance. Flaws in a life invisible from far away are evident from close by, and may be overwhelming for those inside the life. But whatever the flaws, we all also have the unbreakable promise of the new life that the One Cross has brought us.

CHAPTER 2

Jesus is history, living and true

If modern scholars, progressive-minded clerics and the docile
public all surrender to this critical erosion of the (Christian)
Scriptures, the last group of defenders who will obstinately
maintain that there is a living Jesus at the central core of the
Gospels will be made up of artists and creative writers, for
whom the psychological evidence of style carries much
more weight than philological arguments.

**Pierre Ryckmans, writing as Simon Leys, in the introduction
to his translation *The Analects of Confucius***

The Gospels were written within living memory
of the events they recount.

Richard Bauckham, *Jesus and the Eyewitnesses*

On the first Easter Sunday, only the women attended the
tomb of Jesus. As so often, the men were elsewhere.
The first Christians were terrified and near despair. The radical
and charismatic and loving teacher they had followed, their
Jesus, had been crucified and humiliated and mocked.

The best of them still had faith. But this was the time of
maximum trial. Mary Magdalene found to her horror that the
tomb of Jesus was empty. Later she met Jesus himself. At first
she didn't recognise him. It's striking that she was the disciple
who first saw the risen Christ.

This is the story the Christian Gospels tell. The resurrection, 2000 years ago, whether you believe it happened as the Gospels recount or not, was the pivotal moment in human history. It has shaped the lives and beliefs, the deepest intuitions, of cumulatively billions of people. As I write these words, there are approximately 2.5 billion Christians in the world.

Christianity is expanding rapidly in Africa and Asia and finding new life and energy in Latin America.

If the resurrection didn't happen, then it's all based on nothing, it's all an illusion.

In the West—North America, Western Europe, and Australia and New Zealand—religious belief has been in serious decline in recent years. The loss of faith is part of a broad movement in the culture. It is also partly, just partly, related to a shocking loss of knowledge. This represents a bleeding wound of loss for Western civilisation.

Christianity is a universal faith and the Bible is a universal book. Christianity is available to everyone—absolutely everyone is welcome in Christianity—and the majority of Christians alive today are not located in the West. But the Bible is also the central book of Western civilisation (this is an accident of history, but also a reality of history), just as the *Analects of Confucius* is the central book of Chinese civilisation. The West is a culture willing itself into amnesia and ignorance, like a patient carefully requesting their medical records and then burning them, so they and their physicians will have absolutely no knowledge of what made them sick in the past, and what made them well.

This is a weeping pity from every angle. If you believe, as I do, that the Bible is true, this is our society wilfully depriving itself of the truth. But it's a cultural and human deprivation even if you don't believe the Bible is true. The most militant and famous of modern atheists, Richard Dawkins, argues in *The God Delusion* that Bible literacy is vital for the culture. Julia Gillard, our former prime minister, made a similar case when she spoke with goodwill and empathy of her own conscientious atheism, and said that she nonetheless believed in the importance of Bible literacy and was grateful that she learnt a lot of Christian Scripture at school.

But this chapter is not concerned primarily with the cultural value of the New Testament. Rather, there is one question about it that counts more than any other: is the story of the Gospels true?

History cannot answer this definitively. Ultimately, religious belief requires faith. But there is nothing in history to convince the believer, or indeed just the fair-minded inquirer, that the Gospels are not true.

The pendulum of scholarship has swung back to regarding the Gospels as history based on the testimony of eyewitnesses. Of course, Biblical scholarship is now such a huge field that any generalisation is easily contradicted. But more serious scholars are coming to the view that the Gospels represent eyewitness testimony, or at least writings by people who interviewed eyewitnesses. Every archeological discovery we make bears out the broad historicity of the New Testament. Yet think how widespread the view now is that the New Testament was written many decades or even centuries after Jesus, that countless false claims were made up by scheming church authorities a hundred or more years after Jesus' life to support the claim of Jesus' divinity, that scholarship and science have proven the Gospels false.

All this is spectacularly, wickedly untrue. A few years ago, I undertook a systematic reading of the New Atheists—Dawkins, Christopher Hitchens et al.—and found nothing new, or convincing, or even persuasive, about them at all. It was the same familiar old nineteenth-century arguments accompanied by a lot of irrelevant science, as though merely pointing out that the universe is 14 billion years old is somehow an argument against the existence of God. Whereas it strikes me as absolutely characteristic of God that he would spend 14 billion years preparing a beautiful gift for us. What the New Atheists are really trying to do is bluff Christians, and potential Christians, out of their beliefs by mobilising the commanding heights of the culture to deliver a false message: science has declared against God. Science has done no such thing, and in any event is incapable of doing any such thing.

The same is true of Biblical scholarship. Authentic Biblical scholarship has not declared against the historicity of the New Testament. Instead a good portion of it is swinging back to favour their broad historicity. At the same time, we mustn't put too much store in trends in Biblical scholarship, even when they favour the historicity of the New Testament and therefore, indirectly at least, favour belief.

Let me be clear about what I mean by historicity. No historic inquiry can prove that Jesus rose from the dead, that he was the Son of God, that he worked many miracles. But to deny absolutely the resurrection on historical grounds, as opposed to merely being unsure or unconvinced, you have to go well beyond any evidence. Among other things, you must assume that Paul was lying about the people who saw the risen

Christ (1 Corinthians 15:5–8), including the 500 people he cites 'many of whom are still alive'. And there needs to be a satisfactory explanation for why the apostles, too scared even to attend the crucifixion, scared out of their wits in fact when Jesus was killed, were transformed into the most courageous truth defenders, ready to lay down their lives for the truth of the Gospel, including the resurrection.

But historicity—that is to say the serious examination of historical evidence—can prove, and I think substantially has proved, that Jesus Christ was a real man, that he lived at the time the Gospels say, that he was crucified and that the broad course of his life follows the Gospel story. Historicity can also prove that the Gospels, in their background stories and incidental events, accurately describe the Jewish society, with its Roman and Greek influences, which formed the background to Jesus' life. Similarly, it can prove that the earliest Christians held their distinctive doctrines about Jesus and that these were not added in, many years later.

If this is true, then the whole modernist project of the last 200 years or so of discrediting the Gospels has been a big mistake, fraudulent at worst, self-indulgent and lacking in rigour, and simply wrong, at best.

First, let's distinguish what different types of scholarship and research can tell us.

There has been a bit of a rebellion against the tyranny of experts in recent years. This can be anti-intellectual and even anti-rational if we are just saying any expertise which doesn't fit our prejudices is wrong. But a certain distrust for the certitude of experts, when the certitude is mistaken or claims more certainty than really exists, is warranted.

Consider it this way. If we sent a spaceship to Mars and it picked up some rocks and brought them back and they turned out to be a completely new kind of mineral, different from anything we had ever seen before, that would be a new fact. Contrast, say, an economist who predicts a certain cataclysmic recession when, say, a goods and services tax is to be imposed. That's a speculation, an analysis, based on expertise. It might turn out to be wrong. You're entitled to disagree with that, and disagreeing is not a sign of irrationality.

Ordinary Christians are entitled to be wary of Biblical scholarship which does not uncover incontrovertible new facts. They needn't dismiss such scholarship, nor do they need to have their faith blown off course by it. Not having their faith blown off course by the claims of a self-confident scholar, or even a trend in scholarship, is rational.

I am somewhat arguing against the case I'm going to make in this chapter—don't be absolutely governed by Biblical scholarship—because the trends in scholarship have recently moved back towards supporting the historicity of the Gospels. So in this case, I think the scholarship is right.

But be aware there are many different sorts of scholarship. We are dealing here, in shorthand, with very different types of research, discovery, deduction and scholarship, and it's important to keep the differences clear.

The type of research which has often had the greatest impact on our understanding of the Bible is archeological discovery. This is not Biblical scholarship as such, but it can produce new facts which every Biblical scholar has to take account of. In 1947, the first of the Dead Sea Scrolls were discovered in the Qumran Caves on the shore of the Dead Sea. More of them were discovered over the next few years. They included books of the Hebrew scriptures—what we know as the Old Testament—and religious writings from the community of Jews who lived there. The documents were written in Hebrew, Greek, Aramaic and other ancient languages. At least a fragment of each of the books of the Old Testament except Esther was found as well as a complete copy of the Book of Isaiah. Their dating is not precise but it's believed they cover a period from a couple of hundred years before Jesus to several decades after his birth. They were a unique, almost *Raiders of the Lost Ark* type discovery, including more than 800 separate documents or scraps of documents.

They don't mention Jesus, and they have no characters in common with the New Testament stories, other than characters referred to in the Old Testament. There is no particular reason they should mention Jesus or his disciples. The community at Qumran were probably Essenes, one of the four major tendencies in Jewish life at the time. The Essenes were very strict in their observance of Jewish law and were eagerly awaiting the coming of the Messiah for the nation of Israel.

The Dead Sea Scrolls don't challenge any historical fact in the New Testament, but they are hugely significant for the New Testament in two ways. First, because of their detail, they provide us with much greater knowledge of the Jewish background against which the New Testament took place. That knowledge offers us a more nuanced way to understand how certain writings in the New Testament would have been received by a Jewish audience.

Second, in sketching Jewish life at the time of Jesus, they help us judge whether the Gospels provide an accurate picture of that period. In much revisionist opinion about the New Testament, it was often alleged that the Gospels were written much later, sometimes much more than a hundred years later. By then Christianity had moved out of the rural Jewish setting Jesus was familiar with and into the towns and cities. Trying to fictionally recreate the Jewish life that Jesus knew would have been difficult for second-century impostor Gospel authors. It turns out that the Gospels accurately describe Jewish life at the time of Jesus. Typical religious debates covered in the Dead Sea Scrolls, and in the New Testament, include things like whether you should rescue an animal, or a child, on the Sabbath if it should fall into a well. After all, you're not meant to work on the Sabbath.

Similarly, there were substantial discussions about who it was proper for observant Jews to eat with. The sorts of things described in Jewish society in the New Testament are also described in the Dead Sea Scrolls.

That's a big tick for the broad historicity of the New Testament. In so far as they bear on the historicity of the New Testament, the Dead Sea Scrolls support the New Testament. Yet the very romance and exoticism of discovering so many new documents tend to create the sense that something radical and shocking has been uncovered, something that disrupts the Christian narrative.

As a result, there is a kind of faux scholarship cum conspiracy mindset that has used the Dead Sea Scrolls in a basically dishonest way. Because they provide such a rich context, you can find points of Jesus' life which correspond to that context and then construct a fantasy argument that has it that Jesus' involvement with the Essenes is the deep truth about Jesus.

That's not only fraudulent, it is all but meaningless. At the very best it is entirely speculative and without real, serious evidence, but a lot of feeble Jesus scholarship and popular narrative is constructed that way.

Something like this did happen with the Dead Sea Scrolls. A theory was popular for a time that Jesus himself was an Essene, perhaps the 'Chief Priest' mentioned in the Scrolls. Another line of speculation is that he somehow escaped crucifixion to live at the Qumran community. There is not one speck of evidence for anything like that. There were plenty of Essenes around in Jesus' time and he surely knew some of them and may well have been influenced by some, just as he knew other Jewish groups and individuals, such as Pharisees, Sadducees and Zealots.

There are a few similarities between Jesus' teachings and Essene teaching, such as the need for human beings to seek forgiveness from God. But there are also radical differences and contradictions between the beliefs of the Essenes and those of Jesus. The Essenes had a strict, puritanical and ritual idea of purification. Jesus, on the other hand, viewed purification as essentially a spiritual question. Essenes were hypervigilant about the detailed implementation of laws which Jesus reinterpreted so radically that in effect they did not apply any more. Jesus took the view that purification came from within, occurred within, rather than being a result of physical ritual. Nothing could more thoroughly contradict Essene teaching. Similarly, Essenes were very particular about who they came into physical contact with, avoiding lepers in particular. Jesus was free and easy about who he came into contact with, and touched a leper to heal him. Essenes were a closed group, Jesus was open to outsiders.

This fad of seeing Jesus as a Qumran Essene, secretly sheltering there after surviving the crucifixion, has had its undeserved day in the sun and is now gone. But it demonstrates how easily such nuttiness, nuttiness derived from Biblical scholarship but vastly exceeding any realistic scholarly conclusion, can gain a wide audience and, for a moment, or longer than a moment, is in vogue.

This sort of stuff is quite damaging because it can teach ordinary people things about Jesus that are just untrue, or it can teach them the equally wrong lesson that nothing reliable can be known about Jesus. So long as you regard the Gospels as having almost no historical accuracy, but nonetheless still regard Jesus as a somehow unique and important figure, you can create any fantasy version of Jesus you like. Back in 1970, when space travel and UFOs were all the thing, Erich Von Daniken made a big splash with *Chariots of the Gods*. The book and related film, which were commercially successful, had it that religion, including the Bible, resulted from visits by aliens from outer space who taught humanity new technologies. As space travel failed to live up to its Moon-landing promise, this especially wacky scenario was happily retired, though with science fiction's great return in recent times I wouldn't rule out its getting another run, its ineffable silliness securing another season of inane popularity.

Being utterly ludicrous, of course, didn't stop *Chariots of the Gods* being a huge success. Dan Brown does just this kind of thing with *The Da Vinci Code*. He has it that Jesus was married to Mary Magdalene, and that they had a line of descendants running right down to present times. Not only that, *The Da Vinci Code* claims that until the Council of Nicaea in 325 AD, Christians had not believed that Jesus was divine. It should go without saying that this is all complete baloney. In a way, it doesn't amount to much. But the book sold millions of copies and the film grossed several hundred million dollars. What this means is that an audience who knows almost nothing about Jesus was told relentless lies about him, and the implication was that these lies were the truth. The film makers refused even to add a disclaimer that their film was fiction.

Part of Brown's fantasy is based on the Gnostic gospels and epistles of the second century AD. Gnosticism was a breakaway movement from mainstream Christianity that denied the most central truths of Christianity. This happens from time to time, when a group distorts a teaching, or focuses on one aspect of a teaching without all the balancing aspects, or thinks up its own derivations of teachings. The Bible scholar John Barton, in *A History of the Bible*, writes that: 'Gnostics taught that the world and everything in it is evil, and that only extreme asceticism is an adequate human response to this.' The Gnostic gospels were fictional accounts written long after the real Gospels. They were never accepted by anyone of consequence in the early Church. Sometimes they purport to disclose sensational things such as Jesus instructing Judas to betray him, or telling Mary Magdalene that he valued her more highly than the male disciples. Because they are exotic, discovered late and attack the Christian idea of Jesus, from time to time they acquire a vogue, like other flamboyant ideas about Jesus.

The only document from this group that anyone regards as possibly having some direct relationship to the time of Jesus is the Gospel of Thomas, which is a collection of Jesus' sayings, some of them found in the real Gospels, some of them not, and some of them completely undecipherable. The early Church worked very hard to establish which of the early writings—the Gospels and the Epistles—were reliable and essential and therefore canonical, part of the true Bible. The Gospel of Thomas was never included.

Surely it's only a matter of time before a 'scholar' with a deep attachment to Green metaphysical speculations 'discovers' that Jesus was an emanation of Gaia (the term in Greek mythology for the personality of Earth), sent by Gaia to remind us to care for the environment. Hollywood has already given this treatment to Noah, in the Russell Crowe film, which managed to tell the tale of Noah and his ark without mentioning God at all.

But I digress. Archeological discoveries like the Dead Sea Scrolls are very rare. But there are many, many lesser archeological discoveries. It is particularly important when a physically ancient part of a text is discovered. The original physical documents of the ancient world tended not to last physically. The Dead Sea Scrolls were a special case—sealed in jars, many preserved from the air. Most of the documents we know from the ancient world are copies of copies of copies and generally our oldest physical copy of any document is centuries removed from the original composition of the text. Nobody seriously doubts the autobiographical writings attributed to Julius Caesar. Yet the oldest physical text we have for this work dates from 900 years after its composition. The earliest physical copies of the Gospels that we have are much earlier.

A clearly recognisable fragment of John's Gospel was discovered in Egypt in the twentieth century. The fragment is confidently dated to the early part of the second century at the latest. Every single Biblical scholar has to take account of that discovery. It obviously puts a limit on the date that John's Gospel was written. It shows that Christianity had spread very quickly to Egypt, and the whole of John's Gospel, plainly already considered a sacred text, had been circulated there. It will be fascinating to see if more such fragments are found and if they keep pushing the latest dates at which the Gospels might have been written ever earlier.

It is exceptionally rare that archeology turns up something as explosive as the Dead Sea Scrolls. But literally hundreds of lesser archeological discoveries have reinforced the historicity of the New Testament. In his extremely useful book *Is Jesus History?*, the Australian Bible scholar and historian John Dickson lists a number. Israeli archeologists discovered a Jewish tomb containing ossuaries, or stores of bones. An inscription showed that one of the ossuaries contained the bones of a father and son who had been crucified then buried. This establishes beyond any doubt that some crucifixion victims were buried, whereas the common practice was to throw the remains of the crucified into a pit. The bone of the dead man's foot showed that an iron nail had been used to crucify him. In other words, the method of crucifixion that the Gospels described was accurate and it was also by no means unreasonable that Jesus might have been buried, as recorded in the Gospels.

Similarly, an inscription which once adorned an ancient building demonstrated that the Gospels had the title of Pontius Pilate correct, while the Roman historian Tacitus had it slightly wrong. Archeologists have discovered the remnants of building types which correspond to buildings described in the Gospels. And, as Dickson shows, archeology also establishes that

Greek was widely spoken by a large minority of the Jewish population in Jerusalem and surrounding areas. These are real and incontrovertible facts. None of them proves that Jesus was the Son of God and rose from the dead, but they do establish that the Gospels faithfully recorded the society of the time, and must surely have been written within living memory of the events they describe.

Much Biblical scholarship, beyond archeology, is a species of academic literary criticism. Some of it is immensely valuable. Men and women of great goodwill, deep learning and prodigious energy have studied the Bible for hundreds of years and much that they have produced is tremendously valuable. But given how comprehensively it all contradicts itself, how much scholars disagree, and how different periods of scholarship disagree with other periods, you must logically conclude that most such scholarship is ultimately mistaken in its conclusions.

All of it, even the bits believers find highly agreeable, is pretty speculative. I don't believe the scholarship, even the speculations, is worthless. But I do believe they should never be represented as being the plain truth, or that to disagree with any of these speculations means you're a fundamentalist, or you're ignoring the facts or the 'science'.

People need to be free, confident even, intellectually as well as spiritually, to read the Gospels for their plain meaning.

A.N. Wilson is an entertaining and often wise British author who has written extensively on the Bible. He was a Christian, then went through an anti-Christian phase, then returned, relieved, to Christian faith. He now believes Jesus was real, as he discloses in his lovely meditation *The Book of the People*. However, his intellectual view of the debate about the historical Jesus has never been very optimistic. In his anti-Christian phase, he wrote a book, *God's Funeral*, explaining why Christian belief has fallen away in the West. In it he comments favourably on another commentator's conclusion that: 'There is very little evidence when these matters are in question, and that anything people say about the Gospels is likely to reflect what they already believe rather than what they have discovered as a result of research.'

This is too sweeping a statement, but there's more than a grain of truth in it. It also reflects Wilson's frame of mind when he wrote the book in 1999, which was to exclude almost entirely the Christian writings, the New Testament itself, as historical evidence. But it also recognises that the repudiation of mainstream Christianity arising from certain lines of Biblical scholarship is also, in Wilson's view, without objective foundation. Or, to use the more technical term, it's flim-flam. It's windy theorising, it doesn't embody conclusions from hard evidence.

It is substantially true that over the last 300 years the dominant views in Biblical understanding and scholarship have tended, naturally enough I suppose, to reflect whatever the prevailing outlook, the worldview, the intellectual fashion, generally was in any particular society at a given time.

However, it is in any age an unreasonable position to exclude the Gospels as historical sources. It's like investigating the fire at Notre Dame Cathedral in 2019, but, for the sake of objectivity, making sure to exclude all French reports from the time of the fire. The Christian sources are pro-Jesus, but they are still profoundly valuable historical sources.

The big assault on the historical reputation of the Gospels came in the nineteenth century in Germany, and was based in part on the work of Georg Wilhelm Hegel. This intellectual movement held that religion was a kind of folk myth mainly passed on by word of mouth. It held that if you were investigating the historical circumstances around any religious figure or belief, the last thing you gave any real historical credit to was the religious records, because these would be unreliable folk memories passed on by word of mouth, with ever growing inaccuracies and exaggerations and later interpolations. This approach shaped the facts to fit the theory. It didn't rigorously compare the Gospels, for example, with other biographies of the ancient world, which is the sort of document they most resemble. And it assumed very late authorship of the New Testament books themselves.

John Barton, in *A History of the Bible*, offers a sympathetic, updated but still broadly liberal view of the Bible. He is an Oxford scholar of high renown, a believing Christian, but does not hold that all of Scripture, even all of the New Testament, is 'inspired', much less, as the Evangelicals would say, 'inerrant', or free from error. I disagree with him on these conclusions. but whatever your views, his book is a valuable guide to Biblical scholarship.

He summarises the scholarly consensus on the dating of the New Testament. The earliest documents in the New Testament are the letters of Paul, which, he writes, began 'within a couple of decades of the crucifixion . . . in the 50s CE.' (Instead of CE, I shall use the notation AD, except where it's in direct quotes.) All of Paul's letters were completed before the first Gospels were written, he reports. He provides the mainstream scholarly range for dating the Gospels. Some think Mark was written before the fall of Jerusalem in the war with Rome in 70 AD. Barton thinks Mark was probably written some time after 70. Matthew, Luke and John are thought to come after Mark, with John commonly thought to be written in the 90s or even in the very first years of the second century. The dates for the Gospel of John, Barton says, are highly contested. John is regarded generally as the Gospel written last. Some scholars put it as late as the beginning of the second century, some put it much, much earlier, as early as Paul. Barton is an attractive, useful writer partly because he honestly and fairly reports lines of scholarship he disagrees with.

The original reasons for dating John so late have more or less disappeared, and it is possible therefore that John is much earlier than the scholarly consensus holds.

Nonetheless it has been the established view that John was written last for so long that it has acquired a kind of authority of tradition within Biblical scholarship (now there's an irony for you). Barton, while summarising the scholarly consensus on Gospel dating, is also honest enough to say that no one knows the actual decade in which any particular Gospel was written.

John was regarded as the last Gospel partly because it is, as we will examine in Chapter 3, a highly theological Gospel, with a high view of Jesus' divinity. This was once seen as being an evolution of the earlier Synoptic Gospels. But, as I argue in Chapter 3, John's Gospel is in fundamentals consistent with the Synoptic Gospels. More important, Paul, writing before any of the Gospels, shares the same high view of Christ's divinity as John.

John Dickson provides his own assessment of the historical consensus thus: 'Most date Mark to the late 60s, Luke and Matthew to the 70s and 80s, and John to the 90s.'

In his magisterial work *Jesus and the Eyewitnesses: The gospels as eyewitness testimony*, Richard Bauckham, formerly the professor of New Testament Studies at St Andrews University, strongly makes the case which his book title indicates, that is, that the Gospels rely, accurately enough, on eyewitness testimony. Barton, though sceptical of the attributed authorship of the Gospels and inclined to date them a bit later than Bauckham, nonetheless also thinks they record eyewitness testimony about Jesus, though this was conveyed by the second generation of Christians, in his view, rather than the first.

There is no unanimity on Biblical studies, but an impressive array of scholars follow Bauckham's lead or came independently to similar conclusions, among them the highly influential N.T. Wright and James Dunn. The former Pope Benedict XVI provides a masterly Catholic overview of the scholarly debate also seeing the Gospels as eyewitness testimony.

In *Jesus and the Eyewitnesses*, Bauckham argues that even if you accept the majority scholarly consensus for dating the Gospels, they were written within one long lifetime of Jesus' life and relied on eyewitness testimony. Bauckham writes: 'I take the Gospels to be substantially based on the testimony of eyewitnesses who had known Jesus in his lifetime.'

Now, no one should believe in Christianity just because Bauckham, splendid scholar that he is, and a trove of other scholars, now believe the Gospels are the testimony of eyewitnesses. But if Bauckham and fellow like-minded scholars are right, then much of the whole thrust against the historicity of the New Testament over the last 200 years is wrong, was really a waste of time.

The dominant type of this Biblical scholarship is known as 'form criticism'. This examined what it believed was the literary pattern of individual parts of the Scriptures and it further argued that these originated with, and were passed on by, oral transmission.

Other historical approaches argued that significant inaccuracies were added to Scripture, sometimes by accident and sometimes intentionally, to bolster a particular theological interpretation. Oddly enough, the Dead Sea Scrolls themselves tend to count against this as a way of understanding even the Old Testament. The Book of Isaiah which is preserved in the Dead Sea Scrolls is not a rough antecedent of the next available physical copy 1000 years later. It is the same text with some variations. In other words, once a classical scriptural text was written down and regarded as sacred, it tended to stay pretty stable.

Bauckham points out that for form criticism to apply even minimally to the Gospels, then all of its chief characters would have needed to die almost straight after Jesus did. Otherwise in the period after Jesus' death the memory of him would surely be sustained, and in a sense governed, by those eyewitnesses who saw him and heard him and knew him. We know that many of the eyewitnesses to Jesus did not die for decades after Jesus. And we know that that was quite a large group of people. A number of them beyond the most intimate disciples are named in the New Testament. Therefore the whole idea of an oral tradition widely changing and accruing many adds-on over the years just doesn't wash for the Gospels.

The Gospel authors were in direct contact with eyewitnesses of Jesus, or were eyewitnesses themselves. Bauckham concludes that the Gospel of John was indeed written by John, as the Gospel itself asserts, that is, written by an eyewitness. Bauckham is in a minority of scholars here. But the scholars have no real authority on this matter.

Biblical scholarship is not like the science of bridge building. If the science of bridge building becomes detached from reality the bridges will either never be constructed or will fall down. On the other hand, Biblical scholarship can wander down many fanciful false roads with no immediate consequence. The long-run consequences, though, are dire. If the fantasies are accepted in Biblical scholarship and replace the reality, it is not a bridge but the whole of society that might ultimately fall down.

Most believing Christians probably more or less ignore Biblical scholarship. One of its most doleful consequences over the last century has been to contribute to people reading the Bible less, but perhaps reading about the Bible, or hearing about it anyway, a bit more, and in completely unreliable ways.

Cardinal Ratzinger (later Pope Benedict XVI) made an argument like this way back in the Erasmus Lecture he delivered in 1988. Incidentally, surely the silliest element of the film *The Two Popes* was its depiction of Benedict as lacking a sense of humour. Almost everything he writes is full of wit and sagacity. He begins by conjuring a scene in which the anti-Christ is notable for holding a theology doctorate from a German university and having written a work recognised as 'pioneering in the field'.

But I digress. Concerning the historical-critical method of studying the Bible, Benedict wrote:

Gradually, however, the picture became confused. The various theories increased and multiplied and separated one from the other and became a veritable fence which blocked access to the Bible for all the uninitiated. Those who were initiated were no longer reading the Bible anyway, but were dissecting it into the various parts from which it had to have been composed. The methodology itself seems to require such a radical approach: it cannot stand still when it scents the operation of man in sacred history. It must try to remove all the irrational residue and clarify everything. Faith itself is not a component of this method, nor is God a factor to be dealt with in historical events. But since God and divine action permeate the entire Biblical account of history, one is obliged to begin with a complicated anatomy of the scriptural word. On the one hand there is the attempt to unravel the various threads (of the narrative) so that in the end one holds in one's hands what is the 'really historical', which means the purely human element in events. On the other hand, one has to try to show how it happened that the idea of God became interwoven through it all. So it is that another 'real' history has to be fashioned in place of the one given. Underneath the existing sources—that is to say, the Biblical books themselves—we are supposed to find more original sources, which in turn become the criteria for interpretation. No one should really be surprised that this procedure leads to the sprouting of ever more numerous hypotheses which finally turn into a jungle of contradictions. In the end, one no longer knows what the text says, but what it should have said, and by which component parts this can be traced back through the text.

So the result of hyper-sustained, speculative Biblical scholarship is that no one any longer reads the Bible, including the Biblical scholars themselves. And those who do read it don't trust it, and they don't trust it for all the wrong reasons. Least of all does anyone read it open to its natural meaning. Every great piece of literature should be read first for its natural meaning. With the Gospels, which are highly accessible and the crux of the Christian faith, this allergy to reading the Bible is a particular tragedy.

A more attractive approach is a movement sometimes called 'post-critical', which focuses on the final form of the text of the New Testament especially. This is the text that the early Church used. The four Gospels in the New Testament were powerfully present throughout Christian life by the beginning of the second century. They are the bearers of Christian teaching and inspiration. It is much more important to read those texts and to contemplate their meaning than it is to try to deconstruct them in a way which is intrinsically speculative.

There is a literary aspect to this as well. Much of the New Testament is sublimely beautiful as literature. Apart from its religious significance, it justifies reading for aesthetic pleasure, as well as literary appreciation and scholarship.

None of this is meant to devalue the good work of many Bible scholars. The best of them expand our understanding of the Bible and its background. But almost everything they say concerning the provenance and authorship and even dating of the Scriptures, and certainly anything new they say, is limited and speculative, unless it proceeds from a major archeological find. A lot of what many of them have said is plain wrong, and some of it weirdly and bizarrely and demonstrably wrong. The best Bible scholarship often reflects the inexhaustible riches of the Scriptures when scholars work at the task of trying to think through what the Gospels in particular say, and how they relate to other parts of the Bible.

To get a sense of just how fallible, and how wrong, historical-critical methods—which seek to discover 'the world behind the text'—can be, think what they might look like if applied to events today. Let me give you two examples, one real, one hypothetical. Neither is of the slightest intrinsic significance. I offer them, in the spirit of scholarly inquiry, as controlled laboratory experiments, to suggest the limits of reverse engineering historical truth on the basis of decoding written documents. This is quite different from reading documents as they are intended, and listening to and weighing testimony.

I began my full-time journalistic career in 1979 at *The Bulletin* magazine. Now defunct, it was once a powerful weekly news magazine (in the style of *Time* or *Newsweek* combined, perhaps, with *The Spectator*), owned by Kerry Packer, who also owned Channel 9. My first cover story—entirely insignificant now—was a big deal in my life. It concerned the regulation of children's television by the Broadcasting Tribunal which was then headed by Bruce Gyngell.

Gyngell is mostly forgotten now but occupies an honourable place in the history of Australian television, being the first face Australians saw on their screens when TV began in Australia in 1956. He was a friend of Kerry Packer's. I was 22 when I wrote that cover story. It made the cover because, in a pure fluke which reflected my lifelong tendency to do things late,

I rang the Tribunal at the end of its day. Miraculously, Gyngell answered the phone himself. In principle he wasn't giving interviews, but he answered all my questions.

The piece appeared as a feature article but I also expressed a view. That view was that Gyngell was being needlessly heavy handed and over-regulating the industry (was that view justified?—who knows?). Although not a personal attack, the piece annoyed Gyngell, who rang Packer to whinge. Packer rang *The Bulletin*'s editor, the formidable Trevor Kennedy, who double-checked with me that all the facts were right. So Packer was modestly unhappy with the story criticising his friend but quite properly took no action about it.

A couple of weeks later a journalist at *The National Times*, another now-defunct weekly paper, wrote a piece saying that my cover story represented a clear breach between Packer and Gyngell, and was a sign of their estrangement. My piece, he said, showed that Packer had turned on Gyngell and was a conscious attack on him. It was nothing of the kind. My piece had struggled to make it into *The Bulletin* at all and had been held out at least two weeks in a row. It just scraped through as a cover story because of Gyngell's interview with me, which was entirely fortuitous. The whole thing was chancy and contingent, like most journalism.

I later became quite matey with *The National Times* journalist involved. The point is that here was a perfectly competent journalist at *The National Times*, whose office was just a couple of kilometres from that of *The Bulletin*, who was operating in the same culture at the same time, with a good understanding of politics. But in attempting to infer causality and facts, sequence and purpose, not by reading what was written but by trying imaginatively to go behind what was written, he got the matter completely wrong.

Now consider a more extravagant hypothetical example. Bob Carr was premier of New South Wales for more than ten years, finishing up in 2005, the longest premiership in NSW history. I got to know him well at *The Bulletin*, where we were journalists together (though he was a big fish and I was a tadpole). Bob is clever, erudite, funny and a great friend. He is the person least interested in sport of anybody I've ever met in my life. He believes the only good thing about any sporting event is that it ultimately comes to an end. As premier he once had to attend a beach volleyball match at Bondi Beach and for the whole time listened, on his headphones, to a lecture about James Joyce.

Now imagine it is 2000 years into the future. Australian civilisation has been lost and found, transformed and redis-covered a dozen times in these two millennia. Imagine if historical-critical scholars in the year 4025, based in Istanbul and Cairo, want to locate 'the historical Bob Carr'. Sport fell out of fashion in the third millennium and there is, in the 4020s, a new movement in Istanbul and Cairo to reconnect to what was believed to be the state religion of sport in NSW. A new theory has emerged that Carr's record period of rule in Sydney was enabled by his being the high priest of the NSW sport religion.

In 2000 years, there have been wars and revolutions in Australia many times over. Almost all the historical records have been lost. Researchers come upon a scrap of paper, a profile I've written about Carr that says he had no interest in sport. Immediately they stand this against the historical context they know well. Australians in this historical period loved sport. It was a key to popularity among political rulers. There is growing scholarly consensus that it was the NSW state religion, probably the official religion of all Australia.

There is powerful contextual evidence. There are historical suggestions of another 'Bob' leader, Prime Minister Bob Hawke, declaring a temporary cessation of work because of a boat race. Another leader, John Howard, was known to worship cricket, describing himself as 'a cricket tragic'.

And then, while the records of NSW politics are scattered, scant and fragmentary, it is known that Carr presided over, and built the infrastructure for, the Sydney 2000 Olympics, which were the greatest sporting festival in human history up to then. These were held at the mid-point of Carr's ten-year reign as premier, a point full of symbolic consequence. Is it really possible that it was coincidence that the greatest sporting event in history marked the mid-point of Bob Carr's rule?

But wait. Here's what excites the scholars most. A cache of front pages from Sydney's *Daily Telegraph* under Carr's premiership is discovered, in a crypt in the recently excavated ancient cemetery near Bondi Beach. Apparently they were buried underneath the grave of a former Telegraph editor. They are now known as the Sydney Sea Scrolls because the front pages are preserved via an ancient technology, a scroll of micro-fiche film. And look!

Every one of these front pages is about sport, sometimes in screaming headlines. New South Wales and Queensland apparently had a brief military conflict over sport, demonstrated in the headline: State of Origin Wars. The interpretation that this was a metaphor for a rugby league game is instantly dismissed. Australians did not live by metaphor. The Sydney Sea Scrolls give great impetus to the emerging consensus that Australians, or at least those in New South Wales under Carr, not only worshipped sport, but that Carr was one of its high priests.

Then we progress to another subtle argument. Carr is described in the single remaining article about him, by someone who claims to have been his friend, a scribbler named Greg Sheridan, as a bookish intellectual with an absence of interest in sport. But did this Sheridan ever exist? If so, he was very obscure. There is no historical record of him. This surely is a later forgery by the anti-sport forces which were a minor movement in Australia at the time. By analysing historical context closely, the scholars conclude that it is completely implausible for an Australian man of his period, much less a popular political leader like Bob Carr, to have no interest in sport. Why, scholars ask, did Carr go by the name of Bob? This is famously the name of countless Australian sporting heroes, whereas Carr's actual first name was Robert. Bob Hawke, who embraced the sport religion, also chose to use the sports devotees' name. It was a convention for intellectuals to call themselves Robert, like Robert Hughes. And look at Bob Bradman (a few records have his first name as Don, but scholars dismiss these as unreliable).

So yes, Australians worshipped sport and Bob Carr was the high priest of the sports cult.

This of course is fanciful. From where we are now, it's absurd. But all the inferences to get to these false conclusions would be reasonable. They would also be wrong. What a pity the quest for the historical Bob Carr didn't have access to four accounts of his life written by his friends, or by people recording his friends' memories.

I'm not suggesting historical research and theorising are worthless. But it is difficult for scholarship of this kind to maintain a becoming sense of its own proper modesty. And naturally it ought to pay the greatest attention to the testimony of eyewitnesses, which is what we have in the Gospels themselves, according to scholars like Richard Bauckham, and according to the Gospels. But if we believe nothing in the Gospels, there is very little real evidence to go on to make up theories about Jesus (therefore, you can make up any theory you like).

There are also non-Christian references to Jesus in the ancient world. By 64 AD the Roman Emperor Nero was blaming Christians as a group for the fire that destroyed much of Rome, according to the Roman historian Tacitus, who also mentions Jesus' execution under Pontius Pilate. Tacitus detests Christians and no one doubts his record of Nero. Think what this means. By 64 AD, barely 30 years after Jesus' death, Christians are a sufficiently sizeable, and in some way troubling, minority in Rome that Nero decides to persecute them. And the Christians maintain their beliefs to their deaths. It suggests a mighty power in the life and death and resurrection of Jesus.

The first-century Jewish historian Flavius Josephus also made two separate references to Jesus in his famous history. It seems very likely that the more important of these was originally fairly neutral and was later added to by a Christian who believed in Jesus. The great Jewish Oxford scholar Geza Vermes wrote definitively about this and concluded that the Josephus reference to Jesus was authentic. Josephus described Jesus as a 'wise man' and 'a performer of paradoxical deeds' who was 'crucified by Pontius Pilate'.

Vermes completely rejects the Christian interpretation of Jesus and sees him as a Jewish teacher who was fitted up with universalist ambitions after his death, by his followers. I think Vermes completely wrong on that, but it's telling that he accepts that Jesus lived, and that he died by crucifixion.

There are a couple of other sources from the ancient world. Another Roman historian, Gaius Suetonius Tranquillus, mentions Jesus. Lucian of Samosata, a second-century Greek writer, recounted the doctrines of Christians as he saw them and their founder.

This is a sketchy little record, if you don't count the New Testament. But that's what you'd expect. When Jesus was crucified, he was an obscure figure in a distant, minor part of the Roman Empire. Only his most faithful followers thought he was going to bend the arc of history.

Finally, as Dickson points out in *Is Jesus History?*, no one in the ancient world who dealt with Christians, whether Nero in Rome or the city authorities in Jerusalem, ever suggested that Jesus was imaginary. It takes many centuries before you can get to an idea as silly as that.

So it is easy enough to establish from non-Christian sources that Jesus lived. Then there is a super-abundance of Christian sources describing what he said and did and the effect he had on people. It is only if every Christian source is rejected out of hand and declared inadmissible that Jesus is poorly documented. Imagine a court case in which the court decided that everyone who ever met the defendant, everyone who ever saw the incidents being investigated, must be forbidden from giving testimony. Imagine, too, ruling out any book on politics that actually interviewed and was informed by the key players, and relying instead only on academic books written by people who had no firsthand sources. You could do it, but it would be eccentric.

The quest for the historical Jesus is also rendered ineffective by the understandable but crippling bias to naturalism of modern scholars. I lunched once with an interesting churchman who was a veteran of the quest for the historical Jesus. He was an agreeable companion, but he began our lunch by saying that Jesus was a devout and observant Jewish man from the Galilee who would have had no thought that he was the Son of God.

Well, yes, I thought, unless of course he was in fact the Son of God. Then he would have had that thought in spades. You can't use context to argue that an individual who radically contradicts the context is implausible. Otherwise there would be no history at all, because people are full of contradictions.

If the figure history is studying is divine, or claims to be divine, and the historian rules out, from the beginning, the merest chance of divinity, then that will skew the research.

The opposite charge is often made against Christian scholars, that they begin by accepting Jesus' divinity. But that is no more an a priori ideological position about history than is ruling out Jesus' divinity.

In theory, it ought to be possible to imagine a scholar with a genuinely open mind on questions of divinity. But a genuinely open mind means being open to the possibility of divinity, which really in effect means believing in divinity. I suspect there are very few scholars who come to Jesus with that kind of open mind.

On reading numerous Christian Bible scholars, I get the impression that they try to pretend that, in effect, as historians they don't believe in the possibility of divinity or at least at one level write as though they don't necessarily believe in the divine, but hope that their historical investigations will finally leave them no choice but to accept divinity as the only explanation that satisfies the facts. Often they try hard to find a double possibility, where there can be both a divine and a naturalistic explanation for something.

Certainly, though, it is a crippling disability for a secular scholar to come to the study of Jesus with the preconceived absolute conviction that there is no divine, there is no miracle. That will distort historical research because it will lead the historian to embrace fanciful and exotic explanations to try to explain something which is inexplicable.

Again, the analogy with the arguments about the existence of God can be helpful. One of the most difficult features of our universe, and especially of life, and even more especially of human life, is its extreme, extreme, extreme improbability. Certain atheists when they come up against this improbability propose the hypothesis that there is actually an infinite number of universes existing simultaneously and we just happen to be living in the one sympathetic to life. The other explanation, which the vast majority of humanity hold today, and the vast majority of human beings who have ever lived held, is that God created the universe with us in mind. Reason alone certainly cannot prove or disprove either hypothesis, but it seems to me that just creating out of whole cloth a notional infinity of universes, without a single speck of evidence, involves much more magical thinking, a much more radical leap of faith, than does believing in God.

Brant Pitre, a famous Scripture scholar, investigates the limits of naturalism in Biblical scholarship in his vigorous and bracing book *The Case for Jesus*. The scholarly consensus on dating the Gospels that we outlined earlier (Mark in the 60s or 70s through to John in the 90s or a fraction later) is, Pitre asserts, by no means established beyond doubt. It's really by no means established at all.

As we saw earlier, the discovery of a fragment of John's Gospel, all the long way away in Egypt, which could be dated to the first or second century, established beyond doubt that John was written in the first century, or at the latest, the beginning of the second century. Without that fragment, who knows when scholars would be dating John's Gospel from, even now?

But most guesstimates about dating the Gospels are based on far less robust considerations than that.

Pitre invites us to consider just one of the key factors in dating the Gospels. The Jewish Temple in Jerusalem was destroyed in 70 AD. The Jewish population of Israel had rebelled against Roman rule in order to establish an independent Jewish state. After some initial military victories they were ultimately crushed by the Romans, who destroyed the temple altogether.

In the Gospels of Matthew, Mark and Luke, Jesus foretells the destruction of the temple. Therefore, many scholars conclude, because Jesus cannot be divine and cannot foretell anything, the Gospels were either all written after 70, or most were written then, with the passage in Mark's Gospel foretelling the destruction of the temple being vague enough to just be let go (or it may have been added later).

Ironically, those scholars who rule out prophecy altogether do so on the basis of faith, their faith that no such thing could happen, whereas those who accept it as a possibility do so on the basis of evidence.

As a matter of fact, the scholarly prejudice against the divine actually forecloses perfectly reasonable naturalistic explanations as well.

Jesus' prophecy does not involve much detail. He warns people to be careful that such an event could happen in winter, whereas the actual destruction of the temple occurred in summer. If you were adding this prophecy into the Gospel after the event to make Jesus look divine, you would at least make it more accurate.

In any event, as every scripturally literate Jew knew, the temple had been destroyed before, in 586 BC, by Nebuchadnezzar, the king of Babylon. So the destruction of the temple, though dreaded, was an easy thing to imagine. Not only that, there was always a seething Jewish discontent with Roman rule. The Jewish people dreamt of their own national home. There were several parties within Jewish life who actively wanted a military campaign to bring this about. A number of those who eagerly awaited a Messiah hoped he would smite the Romans and win back national independence.

Therefore, it would have been quite plausible for Jesus to envisage the destruction of the temple, including the role of foreign armies, without being divine. Josephus reports that another man named Jesus, son of Ananias, in the mid-60s AD, himself prophesied the destruction of the temple.

But if you're open to the possibility that Jesus is divine, then the explanation that he actually prophesied the destruction of the temple is also perfectly acceptable.

So it is mainly prejudice that prevents scholars from considering such a possibility, and the second-order effects of prejudice that prevent them from considering that perhaps Jesus naturalistically forecast the destruction of the temple. This dodgy thinking about the temple prophecy has been a significant factor in earlier scholarly dating of the Gospels. A thousand Biblical studies and a thousand dubious conclusions have been based on assumptions in previous scholarship which were often unproven, and many times just plain wrong.

Then there is this vexed question of Q. For the purposes of convenience I have mostly gone along with the supposed order of the writing of the Gospels: Mark, then Matthew, then Luke, then John. But as Pitre points out, this, too, is far from proven. Modern Biblical scholarship makes much of a notional document conventionally called Q to serve as a source for the Synoptic Gospels. But no manuscript of Q has ever been found. No reference to it in the ancient world has ever been discovered. There may have been a source document for some of the Gospel material. I'm sure Christians were writing things right from the start. Luke, in the foreword to his Gospel, talks of the many other written accounts. Q is a reasonable speculation, it's not a proven fact. Yet it exists in much scholarship as though it were an inscribed stone monument, readily observable by all.

Which brings us to surely the greatest historical claim of all—the resurrection. All four Gospels relate it, so do the letters of Paul. Whatever you conclude about the authorship of the Gospels, there are at least several independently written testimonies of the resurrection. And the historical record establishes that Christians believed in the resurrection from the earliest years after Jesus' death.

This comes again from Paul, the earliest of the Christian Scripture writers. In 1 Corinthians (15:3), written just two decades after Jesus' death, Paul writes: 'I delivered to you as of the first importance what I also received: that Christ died for our sins in accordance with the Scriptures, that he was buried, that he was raised on the third day in accordance with the Scriptures, and that he appeared to Cephas, then to the twelve. Then he appeared to 500 brothers at one time, most of whom are still alive, though some have died. Then he appeared to James, then to all the apostles. Last of all, as to one untimely born, he appeared to me.'

Paul states that he is reinforcing a teaching which he has already taught to the Corinthians. He is strengthening and deepening their faith. Belief in the resurrection is something they already have. From the very start of Paul's ministry he was preaching the resurrection.

In the ancient world, and specifically in the Jewish world of that time, there was no tradition of believing in bodily resurrection of the kind claimed for Jesus. What is so suggestive in the passage from Paul is the specific and incidental nature of the description. Lots of people are named. In the pre-selfie days of 2000 years ago, naming witnesses was the primary method of establishing the authenticity of events. Paul's account is matter-of-fact, almost like a police report. This bloke saw Jesus, then that woman. Lots of the people Paul wrote about were still alive when he wrote.

There is plenty of evidence in the Gospels and the Acts of the Apostles that numerous disciples were initially sceptical of reports of Jesus' resurrection. Some of them needed to see him and interact with him to be convinced. They were not people who hysterically believed in anything, even when it came from their friends.

A couple of other details are suggestive. The first witnesses to the resurrection are women. It is a regrettable fact of the ancient world that the testimony of women was regarded as vastly less reliable than that of men. If later authors really wrote the Gospels, and they were contriving not to give an account of what really happened, but to compose something that would compel belief, they would not have made the first witnesses women.

We also know that Paul and Peter were later executed for their beliefs. They were two of the most important figures—perhaps the two most important figures—in the early Christian movement. If they were knowingly perpetrating a fiction, it is remarkable that they kept up the fiction to death, embracing death rather than abandon the fiction. You tend to trust the sincerity of witnesses who accept death rather than change their story. Many Christians were killed for their beliefs in this period.

John Dickson recounts evidence that the Jerusalem city authorities in the decades following Jesus' death and resurrection argued that Jesus' tomb was empty because the disciples stole the body. Matthew recounts this in his Gospel. And Justin Martyr, a Christian writer, recounts it in the second century. Generally in the ancient world opponents of Christianity disputed the resurrection, but seldom disputed the empty tomb.

History can never prove the resurrection. Nor can it ever disprove the resurrection. Whether you can countenance the resurrection as a possibility depends on whether you can accept the possibility of miracles. I respect, though I disagree with, atheists who do not believe in God and therefore do not believe in miracles. But I find it difficult to understand the position which holds that God exists but cannot do miracles. Why would we think God can do only the things we can do? If God exists he can, not to put too fine a point on it, do whatever he likes. The only thing he can't do is contradict himself. God is always God.

The broad historicity of the New Testament story is further borne out by the testimony of the historical figures known as the Apostolic Fathers. Clement of Rome, Ignatius of Antioch, Polycarp of Smyrna and Papias of Hierapolis are well-established historical figures. They represent the next generation of Christian leaders after the first Apostles. Their lives overlapped with some of the Apostles. They left substantial writings. Some earlier scholarship doubted the authorship of these writings but there is now wide acceptance that most of the writings are authentic.

They wrote about the teachings of Jesus before there was an accepted New Testament. They also wrote about the first Apostles. The most ancient Christian tradition held that they knew some of the Apostles personally: Polycarp and Ignatius knew John, Clement knew Peter. They in part confirm the Apostles, who confirm Jesus. If the whole story of Jesus is somehow a fictional conspiracy, it was a conspiracy involving a huge number of people across many different locations and established very early. Clement, Ignatius, Polycarp and Papias provide exactly the sort of confirming testimony you would expect if the Gospels were true. That is because the Gospels are true.

Finally, we should never ignore the literary and psychological case for the truth of Jesus. At the beginning of this chapter

I cite Pierre Ryckmans' original translation of the *Analects of Confucius*. I knew Pierre modestly well. His was the most supple intellect I have met. He was a profoundly believing Christian, but also one of the most incisive and important interpreters of Chinese culture and civilisation, and for a brief time, politics. His native language was French, he wrote exquisite English and he was a master of Mandarin. His interests were broad. He wrote a masterful novel about Napoleon and was an avid sailor. His *Analects* are a gift to modern readers—they make the great Chinese sage newly available and fresh to a Western audience.

The sayings of Confucius were not formally compiled until a long time after his death, but Ryckmans, like most scholars, has no trouble believing in the historic Confucius, in part because of the unity, strength and distinctiveness of Confucius' voice in the *Analects*.

He compared the Confucius of the *Analects* (who certainly does not claim divinity) with Jesus of the Gospels. While notionally summarising another critic's view, Ryckmans argues of the Gospels that there is a masterly, powerful unity of style 'which derives from one unique and inimitable voice; there is the presence of one singular and exceptional personality'.

Ryckmans finds the Jesus personality in the Gospels absolutely arresting, and comments: 'If you deny the existence of Jesus, you must transfer all these attributes to some obscure, anonymous writer, who should have had the improbable genius of inventing such a character—or, even more implausibly, you must transfer this prodigious capacity for invention to an entire committee of writers.'

The personality of Jesus shone through the Gospels for Ryckmans. The points of detail over which the Gospels have different treatments can theoretically be reconciled. But faith doesn't depend on such reconciliation. For in their slight raggedness you have a further sense of the truth. The neater a document is, the more I'm inclined to think it manufactured later and artificially. The Gospels are consistent on the big things, but at least in presentation a little different on minor things. And of course each of the four Gospels emphasises different, but not contradictory, aspects of Jesus.

Many of the most acute literary minds have responded to the Gospels in something like the manner of Ryckmans. The legendary novelist Graham Greene became sceptical of a lot of Christian doctrines, but he responded to the powerful truth of the Gospel narratives. He remarked: 'I find it very disagreeable when a historical event like the crucifixion is turned into some woolly sort of symbol. The twentieth chapter of St John's Gospel can stand with the best of eyewitness reports.'

And now, with so many copies of the Gospels having been made over the centuries, there is agreement on the text across more than 90 per cent of the New Testament. And slight dis-agreements of a word or a phrase, and very occasionally a small passage, do not affect any central Christian doctrine or belief.

Most Christian traditions regard the Gospels as historically true, not just true in some metaphorical or literary or poetic or even moral fashion. The Catholic Catechism explicitly asserts the historicity of the New Testament. The defence of the physical as well as spiritual truths of the Gospels (which bears no relation to a literalist reading of the Old Testament) is one of the magnificent contributions of the Evangelical Protestant tradition. It's a reason to love the Evangelicals. This is shared by the Pentecostals and all the Eastern Orthodox Christian churches and most other Christian groups.

It is part of the distinctiveness of Christianity that it locates God in history, history 2000 years ago, and history today.

Finally, as a lifelong journalist I have a particular reason for recommending the Gospels. They validate accurate reporting, even if the editing varies from edition to edition (we journalists typically blame a lot on editors). Or, to put it another way, they are true.

CHAPTER 3

The Jesus you meet in John, and the Jesus Kanishka met there

Jesus shifts his cross from his shoulders to ours,
and from ours to his, so that we are forever weeping
either from pain or compassion.

Léon Bloy

No man can live without joy.

Thomas Aquinas

Nowhere in human literature is there a claim as grand, as sweeping, as majestic as that with which the disciple John begins his Gospel. He writes: 'In the beginning was the Word; the Word was with God and the Word was God. He was with God in the beginning, and through him all things came into being. Without him not one thing came into being. What has come into being with him was life. And the life was the light of all people. That light shines in the darkness, and the darkness could not overcome it.'

The Jesus in John is different from the Jesus in Matthew, Mark and Luke. Not contradictory. But different. The Gospels as they are read in the order in which they appear in the Bible involve the characteristic slow but progressive disclosure of the divine. Here in John, the last Gospel, all is plain and splendid.

Tom Holland, in his book *Dominion*, comments of John's Gospel that it 'had no parallel in the utterances of Persian kings, nor of Greek philosophers, nor of Jewish prophets'. Geoffrey Blainey, in *A Short History of Christianity*, singles it out as the most popular of Gospels among Christians. As we saw in the last chapter, the Bible scholar Richard Bauckham takes the striking view that the Gospel of John may be telling the truth not only in matters of Jesus, his divinity and the meaning of life, but also in the matter of its own authorship. For at the end of the Gospel John writes: 'This is the disciple who is testifying to these things and has written them, and we know that his testimony is true.' Bauckham believes that claim of authorship; he argues a minority view among scholars: that the apostle John is indeed the author of this Gospel.

The former Pope Benedict XVI, in his captivating *Jesus of Nazareth*, agrees with Bauckham that the testimony in the Gospel comes from John. The Gospel is not fanciful or a later invention. It is, Benedict says, a 'Jesus memory' not a 'Jesus poem'. He is just a fraction more typically modernist than Bauckham in thinking that there might possibly be one transcriber/arranger between John and the final Gospel text, but the testimony is John's, as the early Church fathers—some of whom knew some of the Apostles and their friends—believed.

So here we have the experience of Jesus, in the eyewitness testimony from his 'beloved disciple', possibly the person, after Mary, who knew Jesus best, coming to us direct, with urgency and power, across 2000 years and just one translation from Greek to English.

That the Gospel was written in Greek, rather than Hebrew or Aramaic, is no argument against John being the author and the Gospel being written early. A number of well-educated Jews in Biblical times, especially if they had roles in the temple, spoke Greek. Indeed some books of the Old Testament were originally written in Greek. And if John was poorly educated, as is sometimes thought, then he could certainly have dictated the Gospel to a follower.

One thing to love in John is his passion, his fiery, urgent determination to shout his message out. Apart from the Gospel that bears his name, John is also named as the author of three letters preserved in the New Testament, two of them very short. The first, the longest, is stylistically closest to John's Gospel. It is as urgent with its message of wonder and praise and astonishment at knowing Jesus and his truth as is the Gospel.

The first letter of John begins: 'We declare to you what was from the beginning, what we have seen with our own eyes, what we have looked at and touched with our hands, concerning the Word of life. This life was revealed, and we have seen it and testify to it, and declare to you the eternal life that was with the Father and was revealed to us—we declare to you what we have seen and heard so that you may also have fellowship with us and truly our fellowship is with the Father and his Son, Jesus Christ.'

Pay attention! John screams at us across 2000 years. Look! Look! He reaches out to us from the very pages of the New Testament. Here is the truth, I've seen it with my own eyes, touched it, heard it. This is the good news. This is for you.

There is no tone quite like John's anywhere else in the Bible. It is a distinctive voice. Without exalting the status of a journalist, any decent reporter knows a tiny fraction of what John feels like—look at this story, I can't wait to get it out of my pocket, out of my head, onto the front page where it belongs. John's prose searches us out in its urgency, its demand to be listened to.

Benedict, like others, marvels at how different John is from the other Gospels. Benedict comments that in the Synoptic Gospels, Matthew, Mark and Luke: 'we have realised that the mystery of Jesus' oneness with the Father is ever present and determines everything, even though it remains hidden beneath his humanity. On one hand it was perceived by his sharpest opponents. On the other hand, the disciples who experienced Jesus at prayer and were privileged to know him intimately from the inside, were beginning—step by step, at key moments with great immediacy, and despite all their misunderstandings—to recognise this new reality.'

In contrast, Benedict comments: 'In John, Jesus' divinity appears unveiled.'

Yet Jesus in John is still a living human being, a vibrant man. The human, gentle, welcoming and forgiving side of Jesus, which is the gentle, welcoming and forgiving side of God, is strongly there in John, as well as the full-throated statements of divinity.

There occurs in John one of the most poignant encounters in all the Bible. Jesus has been speaking and teaching at the temple and this is upsetting the authorities, who can't understand his miracles and don't like the thrust of his teachings. So they bring before Jesus a woman who has been caught in the act of adultery and they say to him: the punishment for this crime is stoning to death, what do you say to this?

It is worth pausing to note that they didn't bring before Jesus the man she was presumably caught in the act of adultery with. The ancient world, before Christianity, was frequently cruel towards women and exhibited fantastic double standards. Sociologists of religion like Rodney Stark in *The Triumph of Christianity* believe one of the reasons early Christianity spread so quickly was that it offered a better deal for women and girls than anything which had ever come before it. Christianity viewed women as equal human beings to men, which was not characteristic of the ancient world. Christianity forbade the killing of girl babies, a practice that was common because they were seen as not as useful to a family as boys. It instituted marriage as a consensual relationship of mutual love. It imposed some limits on sexual behaviour by rapacious men. If you don't like all the toxic behaviours Christianity addressed, you'll be a critic of the ancient world, and glad that Christians, working out the social implications of their religious teachings, reformed these practices.

But all that was not going to help this one woman brought before Jesus. The authorities wanted to trap Jesus into some false statement, or perhaps to have him endorse or order some unpopular action.

Jesus' response on this occasion was unexpected, surprising, something which put everyone off balance. Jesus could at times be angry. He could certainly rebuke the powerful. He most often taught in parables. He was a literary artist of the highest order in the way he drew endless images, most of them rural, reflecting his own upbringing in the small village of Nazareth—the good shepherd, the prodigal son, the parable of the talents.

But there were also times when his silence was itself fiercely powerful. It was not the silence of emptiness or rejection or despair, but the silence of great moral power. Instead of answering the scribes and Pharisees in their accusations against the woman, Jesus bent down and began writing in the ground with his finger. The Gospel doesn't say what he was writing. Ancient Christian tradition has it that Jesus was writing references to the sins of some of the people in the crowd. But we don't know that. It's not in the Gospel.

What we do know is that as he wrote on the ground, Jesus remained silent. There might indeed have been a righteous, unspoken contempt in this silence, for Jesus never saw a mob arrayed against an individual and sided with the mob. He never saw the powerful lined up to punish the weak and favoured the powerful.

But the mob, or some of them anyway, kept on at Jesus about the woman. You can tremble with her in terror even now, two millennia later. Mobs are unpredictable. They develop a corporate emotion like an individual working up his anger. They are organically prone to violence. The prospect of the accused woman losing her life then and there, in terrible bloody violence, was real.

Finally Jesus looked up at the crowd and uttered the words that have lived as a rebuke to hypocrisy and harshness ever since: 'Let anyone among you who is without sin be the first to throw a stone at her.' Having said this, Jesus resumed his writing on the ground. And the crowd, abashed and perhaps for a moment ashamed of itself, melted away. The woman stayed there with Jesus, and when he realised they had all gone, he asked her: has no one condemned you?

No, she said, no one. Then neither do I condemn you. Go on your way and do not sin again.

Jesus has perhaps saved the woman's life. They, the crowd, have no right to condemn you and I do not condemn you either. In time he would supplant the old customs, like stonings for adultery, and replace them with the new imperatives of eternal life, of the kingdom of heaven.

At the same time, and this is part of this most beloved story which yet not everyone is comfortable with, Jesus also told the woman not to sin again. He didn't say your private marital arrangements are a valid lifestyle choice that should suit your own needs and preferences, none of my business, just something you should think over seriously. Instead he said: go on your way, and do not sin again.

Protection. Repentance. Forgiveness. New resolution.

Jesus' message was certainly one of selfless and universal love. But he still insisted on the moral life, at least aspiring to the moral life. He understood that people were wounded and would fall over, and he helped them back up, he offered them forgiveness. But the principle of the moral life, found in the Ten Commandments, was still essential, still central in fact. He also insisted on the love of God and the love of neighbour. Distinctively, Jesus also taught the radical love of enemy. (G.K. Chesterton once drolly remarked that Jesus taught we should love our neighbours and our enemies because so often they were the same people.)

He powerfully taught that the two kinds of love (of God and of neighbour) are connected. If you love God you will surely love your neighbour. But he didn't collapse them into the same thing. This is a modern conceit that has become all but universal in Western culture. It's part of what some Christian writers call moralistic therapeutic deism. The idea is that if you're nice to other people, that is sufficient for God. One reason this doesn't work is that your feelings will only occasionally impel you to love and human solidarity. If your love of others is based on your feelings, it will have little defence when your feelings are sour. Human feelings are all too often vindictive, vengeful, even sadistic. If God is not in the equation, there is no more reason not to honour those feelings than there is to honour the periodic feelings of kindness which are also part of human nature.

In any event, Jesus is clear. The love of God requires love of neighbour, but God has a direct relationship with every human being. People need to attend to that relationship—to love God—directly. Here one other point of Christian belief is important. God is not just good. God is goodness itself. Every emanation of goodness in the universe reflects God and in some way is sustained by God. Therefore, to love God is to love goodness. Throughout the Gospels Jesus identifies God with goodness.

In John, Jesus makes this very clear in his dialogue with Nicodemus. Socially and financially, Nicodemus was at the opposite end of the scale from the people Jesus often surrounded himself with. Jesus always loved the poor, but he didn't despise the rich. He was not an avatar of class hatred and he was not a proletarian revolutionary. He certainly disliked hypocrisy from the privileged. But his preferred response, in his encounters with people, was simply to abolish all social hierarchies. Some of his teaching about becoming like little children not only involved being like them in innocence and trust, but having, like children in the ancient world, no social status. But if the rich, the powerful and the respectable came to Jesus with good hearts and honest intentions, they were welcome like anyone else.

Indeed the Acts of the Apostles, and some of the letters of Paul, display a sharp awareness of the need for fundraising. The early Christians shared their property but soon enough had to work out ways of sustaining livelihoods, of requiring people to work and contribute. Wealthy benefactors at times supported the community with money and property.

This would all come after Nicodemus. He was a Pharisee, a high official of the temple, a leader of the Jewish community in good standing. He visited Jesus (John 3:1) more or less secretly one night. He recognised Jesus' holiness and sought from him wisdom and explanation. Nicodemus was perplexed. He wanted to know what was going on. Who was Jesus exactly, what did his miracles and teaching really mean?

Jesus answered Nicodemus with one of the great spiritual teachings of his ministry: 'No one can see the kingdom of God, without being born from above.' What does that mean? Nicodemus persists. Jesus replies: 'No one can enter the kingdom of God without being born of water and Spirit. What is born of the flesh is flesh, and what is born of the Spirit is Spirit.'

In his dialogue with Nicodemus, Jesus is explicit about his own identity: 'No one has ascended to heaven except the one who has descended from heaven, the Son of Man . . . so that the Son of Man must be lifted up, that whoever believes in him may have eternal life.'

Throughout the Gospels, Jesus refers to himself as the Son of Man, so there is no ambiguity in what he is saying. He goes on to give Nicodemus the eternal answer about who he is and what he is doing: 'For God so loved the world that he sent his only Son, so that everyone who believes in him may not perish but may have eternal life. Indeed, God did not send the Son into the world to condemn the world, but in order that the world might be saved through him.'

Nicodemus doesn't at first seem to react, or at least his reaction is not recorded. Later, when the priests of the Sanhedrin are discussing how to move against Jesus, Nicodemus says to them that they cannot condemn a man without giving him the chance to be heard. At this stage Nicodemus is probably acting against his own cowardice. He's not quite ready to announce that he believes in Jesus, but it hurts him to hear Jesus defamed, treated unfairly and abused. Many people have felt that way in history. They don't want their beliefs to force them into public choices, yet nor will they leave the truth naked and undefended, nor will they see their friends mocked without some effort to come to their defence, even if the effort in the end is feeble.

After the death of Jesus, Nicodemus comes forward. It is a long and basic truth of humanity, that you should be loyal to your friends, especially when they are dead and the whole world is against them. Jesus was a friend of Nicodemus. He was also the Son of the living God, the bringer of light and the bearer of truth. But he was also a friend.

Joseph of Arimathea, a man of wealth and position, was, like Nicodemus, a follower of Jesus, but in secret, because he feared what consequences his public espousal of Jesus might bring. But Joseph comes forward and asks Pontius Pilate for Jesus' body so that it might be buried properly. This was uncommon for victims of crucifixion, whose bodies were often thrown into mass graves. Nicodemus went with Joseph of Arimathea and brought with him a huge quantity of myrrh and aloes. The two men took the body of Jesus and wrapped it with the spices in linen.

We can spare some sympathy, and even some admiration, for Nicodemus here. He understands early on that Jesus is immensely significant. He hears directly from Jesus why this is so. He apparently believes this but is not quite brave enough to come out of the closet as a Jesus supporter. That is the sort of thing that could shorten your life span. Yet he is unwilling to condemn Jesus either, and makes some feeble effort on his behalf. But then, in Jesus' death, Nicodemus is probably ashamed of himself. Mere fidelity to truth, mere self-respect at the most basic level, compassion for Jesus, a desire to make amends for his own weakness, a continuing faith in Jesus—some mixture of these emotions moves Nicodemus. So he then makes his sentiment public enough by honouring Jesus in death. Those who in their lives or words or actions proclaimed Jesus after his death, but before his resurrection, it seems to me deserve a special place in remembrance. They didn't lose faith in Jesus, despite the shock and terror of his death, even before the inspiration of his resurrection. Not only that, they still honoured him publicly.

As I say, you should be loyal to your friends, especially when they are dead, and the whole world is against them.

It is not only Nicodemus to whom Jesus reveals his true identity in the Gospel of John. In John 4, he somewhat surprises, if not scandalises, his followers by talking to a Samaritan woman at the well and asking her for a drink of water. The Jews and the Samaritans were famously at loggerheads (though sharing common Jewish heritage) and didn't normally mix with each other. In her conversation with Jesus, the Samaritan woman says to him: 'I know the Messiah is coming (who is called Christ).' Jesus replies: 'I am he.'

The single most explicit claim Jesus makes to be one with God, to be eternal and part of the godhead, comes in a dialogue where Jesus is being challenged in the temple. He seems to be claiming a status greater than Abraham. But Jesus is not yet 50—can he really claim to know Abraham? Jesus replies: 'Very truly I tell you, before Abraham was, I am' (John 8:58).

This is immensely significant because in the Old Testament when God declares himself to man he says: 'I am.' To deny the divinity of Jesus it is necessary to deny the entirety of John's Gospel.

Occasionally those who dispute the divinity of Jesus argue that John's Gospel is a late invention by the Church designed to exaggerate the claims of Jesus. As we have seen, the claims of Jesus' divinity are more guarded but unmistakably present in the other Gospels. They are also present in the letters of Paul. And the dating of John is getting earlier and earlier. Richard Bauckham in his study of John, *Gospel of Glory*, makes the persuasive case that the understanding of Jesus, what scholars call the Christology, in John, though fuller and grander and more explicit than is evident in the other Gospels, is entirely consistent with them.

Thus in John the term 'eternal life' mostly replaces 'kingdom of God', but John nonetheless uses the term Kingdom of God a couple of times. Jesus' acknowledgement that he is the Messiah, but his general reluctance to use the specific term himself, are the same in John as in the Synoptic Gospels. In John, Jesus seldom uses the term 'Son of God' about himself, but frequently refers to himself as 'the Son' in relation to the Father. That, too, occurs in the Synoptic Gospels, though infrequently. Some elements that are present in the Synoptic Gospels, such as the Holy Spirit, are more fully developed in John. The idea that Jesus has been sent by the Father is present in the Synoptic Gospels but much more fully developed in John.

The Gospel of John contains fewer incidents from Jesus' life but more extended dialogues. Nonetheless there are in John numerous incidents and miracles from Jesus' life.

The presentation of the crucifixion is fractionally less graphic in John than in the other Gospels, Mark particularly, but it is graphic enough. Everyone in the ancient world knew how gruesome and ghastly crucifixion was. Although John maintains his tone of wonder and even happiness throughout most of the Gospel, he doesn't shirk the passion of Jesus in his account. Nor, with Jesus foretelling Peter's own martyrdom, does he avoid the difficulties Christians will face. And there are other passages in John where Jesus talks of the persecution his followers will face in the future.

It is wrong to suggest that John contradicts the other Gospels. I think it is a sign of positive genius in Christianity to have four separate accounts of the life of Jesus, agreed on all the big things, but bearing the distinctiveness of their author's purposes and circumstances. As John himself points out at the end of his Gospel, only a tiny fraction of Jesus' life is there. Jesus is everything in the Gospel, and all that you need to know of Jesus historically is in the Gospels. Yet Jesus is much more than just the episodes and words contained in the Gospels.

It is the old combination of a simple doctrine and a giant mystery. The simple truth is that Gospels are themselves the truth and contain everything we need to know about Jesus. Yet Jesus, the centre of Christianity, is infinitely more than the Gospels contain.

There is a moment in John when Jesus asks his apostles if they want to leave him. Peter says: 'Lord, to whom can we go? You have the words of eternal life. We have come to believe and know that you are the Holy One of God.'

Peter is an intensely appealing figure throughout the Gospels. He has all the feel of a flesh-and-blood man frequently caught in circumstances he struggles to comprehend. He receives flashes of startling insight and faith. He wants to be faithful, he wants to respond to his own faith and to the overwhelming personality of Jesus. But his flesh is weak. He falls asleep in Gethsemane. He three times publicly denies knowing Jesus after Jesus is taken into custody.

Peter is not an intellectual like Paul. Yet Jesus picks Peter to lead his church, to be the rock upon which all his church will stand. Jesus trusts Peter far more than Peter can trust himself.

It is worth considering an episode in Matthew (16:15). Jesus asks his disciples who they think he is and Peter answers: 'You are the Messiah, the Son of the living God.'

Jesus then says: 'Blessed are you, Simon son of Jonah. For flesh and blood have not revealed this to you but my Father in heaven. And I tell you, you are Peter and on this rock I will build my church, and the gates of Hades will not prevail against it.'

Peter would have felt overcome here, perhaps a little bewildered. Peter had confidence in Jesus, but he had no confidence in himself. Throughout the Gospels Jesus has a running dialogue with Peter: do you love me, who do you say that I am, stay awake, feed my sheep. These are all moments when Peter is flustered and unsure of himself. But when Peter is in control of himself, he is always trying to serve Jesus as well as he can.

It's telling that Jesus didn't choose the most brilliant, the best educated or even the most charismatic, nor even necessarily the bravest, of the apostles to lead the church. He didn't choose his relative, James. He didn't choose his best friend, John. Though Peter could be uncertain, at other times he was overconfident, telling Jesus that he would never deny him. That Peter, after Jesus had made this great pronouncement and called him blessed, should still be unable to stay awake in the Garden of Gethsemane, and then later should deny Jesus publicly after Jesus is arrested, were bitter signs to Peter of his own weakness and fallibility. He wept savage tears at the shame of his own denial of Jesus. Whatever you say about the apostles in the Gospels, they are not supermen. They make their mistakes.

But ultimately, throughout his derelictions and his heroism, Peter never loses faith in Jesus. And more important, Jesus never loses faith in Peter. Towards the end of John, Jesus foretells the death and martyrdom that Peter will endure.

In John, Jesus has a long, intimate dialogue with his disciples before the Passover, not long before he is to be crucified. At the start of this long dialogue, Jesus washes and wipes the feet of all his disciples. This is classically the act of a slave. It is Jesus pouring out his power so as to take for himself the lowest status, in order to serve the disciples. This example has been the inspiration for Christian charity for 2000 years.

Jesus' dialogue that night with his disciples is sustained and rich. He no longer calls them servants, he says, but friends. He tells them of his new commandment: 'That you love one another as I have loved you.' He also tells them there will be hard times ahead, but they should take heart: 'In the world you face persecution. But take courage; I have conquered the world!'

John's overriding theme is the staggering reality that God has become man, that Jesus is the son of the living God. This is revolutionary, it sets the world alight. Also that Jesus promises eternal life, that Jesus is the path to the Father, that the kingdom of God, eternal life, has begun on earth with Jesus' coming and that it lives already in the heart of every believer.

Afficionados say that John's Gospel is written in simple Greek, with a spare and limited vocabulary, but that it is intense, creating a depth of feeling and meaning. It is surely one of the most astonishing and consequential pieces of writing in the history of the human race.

It has changed multitudes of lives. Let me introduce you to one life transformed directly by the Gospel of John. When I speak to Kanishka Raffel for this book, he is Dean of St Andrew's Anglican Cathedral in Sydney. I first heard of him several years before this from the Liberal MP Andrew Hastie. When Hastie was sent as a soldier to Afghanistan, he did three things. He wrote a letter to his wife, Ruth, to be opened in the event of his death. He chose a friend to deliver the letter, to be part of the notification party to go and see Ruth, should the worst happen. And he asked the Reverend Kanishka Raffel to take the funeral, in such an event, and preach on Lazarus, whom Jesus raised from the dead, according to John's Gospel.

Hearing this made me curious to meet Kanishka Raffel. Now let me tell you that one of the secret, eccentric, slightly guilty pleasures of journalism is that it gives you licence to ring innocent people out of the blue and say you'd like to come and meet them, theoretically for information about some possible article or other, as often as not simply to satisfy your curiosity.

Maybe I got Kanishka's phone number from Hastie. Maybe I just rang him at St Andrew's Cathedral. In any event, we caught up for a meal and have stayed in touch since. He has a well-earned reputation as a good preacher—strong voice, clear mind, lots of conviction. These qualities led, unsurprisingly, to his election a little later as Anglican Archbishop of Sydney, the first of Asian background, not to mention the first former Buddhist.

But the thing I find most notable about Kanishka is the sense of sheer joy that he has in his Christian belief. It's as though he gets an extra shot of life from his faith. He's invigorating to be around. He spreads good cheer. You feel somehow better just being in his company. He's upbeat in his confidence in the faith. You get the idea that Christianity is still a happy surprise for Kanishka.

I wonder if a little bit of John hasn't rubbed off on him. Perhaps it's something else. Like many people who come to Christianity in adulthood, he has retained the sense of wonder at the Christian story.

Kanishka's Sri Lankan parents formed a mixed couple, his mother Buddhist, his father of Christian background, an unconventional match for Sri Lanka in the 1950s. Kanishka was born in London and moved to Australia as a child. The predominant religious influence on him was his mother's Buddhism. She was a doctor and the family lived in Canada for a while but found it very cold. So they settled in Sydney. When Kanishka was just a young child his father died suddenly of a heart attack. With his mother having no family in Sydney and being a migrant woman and suddenly a single mother, circumstances were daunting, so for a while the family returned to Sri Lanka.

In bringing the family back to Sydney, Kanishka recalls: 'My mother made quite a brave decision with our interests at heart.' He was a bright kid, and from Carlingford High he went to Sydney University and studied honours English and Law.

Kanishka's journey in faith is singular, pivots entirely on John's Gospel, and is worth recounting: 'We were raised as Buddhists. As small children we would chant Buddhist prayers at home. In 1975 a Buddhist temple opened in Stanmore and we attended it sometimes, especially on the anniversary of my father's death. In my third year at uni I decided to get more serious in my Buddhism. I read some books. I practised meditation at home pretty seriously. The Buddhist discipline is more private and interior, the temple wasn't prominent in it. At the end of 12 months I was happy and comfortable with the ethics of Buddhism and the practice of meditation. I was agnostic about Buddhist metaphysics. If karma and reincarnation are right you can't do anything about it anyway, it doesn't matter what you believe.'

The change to come in his life was completely unexpected, like one of those howling Sydney thunderstorms that comes from nowhere and rises up seemingly in a few minutes on a hot summer's afternoon.

'In 1985/86 I went on holidays with some friends. We picked up one of our group from a [church] beach mission. He was studying medicine. We'd been friends since about the age of 15.'

The group stopped at the beach mission for lunch: 'They had a prayer session.'

His friends invited him to stay for the session, or he could have read a book or done anything else he liked during the prayers. He stayed: 'They were all sitting around in beach gear, bowing their heads and talking to God about real things. Buddhist prayers on the other hand are not really intercessionary because you're not really talking to anyone. So for the first time I witnessed that.

'That night I asked my friend what does it mean to be a Christian. He said it means he's lost control of his life to Jesus Christ. This concept was like a pebble in my shoe. It was a challenge to me because Buddhism is all about taking control of your life, especially your desires and passions, because uncontrolled desires and passion are the root of all evil.'

His friend asked Kanishka whether he would read one thing about Christianity. Kanishka agreed and was expecting, indeed a little hoping, that it would be a book by C.S. Lewis or some such. Instead his friend gave Kanishka the Gospel of Mark and the Gospel of John.

It was a hot January night and hard to get to sleep. Kanishka read Mark's Gospel without incident. Then he read John's Gospel.

It was the year at university that he devoted to the study of literature: 'I read the opening of John's Gospel and thought at first that sounds like a fairy tale. Later I realised it's one of the great literary masterpieces. I was struck at first by its historicity. It's located in a specific time and place. Buddhist scripture isn't really like that, it doesn't give you any idea of where or when.

'John's Gospel has a sort of historic immediacy. It reflects its being written so near to the time of the events it's describing. John asserts it is an eyewitness account. More significant, the person of Jesus is just so much more three-dimensional. Some of the teachings of Jesus have the same sort of cadence as the teachings of Buddha, but it was set in a specific time and place.'

Particular incidents in the Gospel stood out for Kanishka—Jesus' meeting with Nicodemus, then with the Samaritan woman. He found these incidents had the ring of truth about them: 'The authenticity of the person of Jesus comes through. The Buddhist scriptures didn't give me a sense of Buddha as a human being. But Jesus emerges as an authentic human being, intriguing, compelling, provocative and challenging.

'I felt challenged personally. At times Jesus says things and the people he's talking to are divided. And I found myself challenged by this—what side of this divide am I on? I thought at first, I'm against Jesus, I'm a Buddhist, I don't believe in God.'

That night, John's Gospel robbed Kanishka of sleep. He read the Gospel through two and a half times. He was reading it for the third time and was struck in Chapter 6: 'Jesus says no one can come to the Father unless the Father sends them to me and on the last day my Father will raise them up. That was a direct challenge to Buddhism, which believes in an endless cycle [of life] and perhaps you can escape from it.

'I was a law student as well. Chapter 6:45 says if you've learnt from the Father you're drawn to Jesus. I'm thinking: how do you learn from the Father? Maybe it's by reading this. Maybe it's happening now. No, I thought, this can't be happening now. But I was utterly convicted that this was indeed what was happening now. I recalled that I had a Gideon's Bible. It had a prayer at the back that I didn't understand most of the words of, but that's the prayer I prayed. The next morning I knew I was a Christian.'

That was a radical and ultimately life-defining transformation for Kanishka. I ask the Oprah Winfrey question: how did that make him feel?

'I hadn't read it to relieve myself of a burden, but subjectively I did have the feeling of being unburdened. For a time, for some weeks, I was just floating. I began to tell people this had happened. When I told my friends they said, well, we've been praying for you for years. Praying for their friend, Kanishka. That was very humbling. When I summoned up the courage to tell my mother, the first thing she said was "That would please your grandmother" [Kanishka's father's mother]. My wife said to me later that your grandmother would have been praying for you all your life.'

Kanishka's mother at first found her son's conversion troubling and difficult. She was worried that it meant Kanishka was moving to reject his Sri Lankan cultural heritage, which he wasn't. But more than that, she worried that it meant perhaps some estrangement of son from mother, which it absolutely did not, or was in some way a critique of the way she had raised Kanishka, and it certainly wasn't that either. She was a scientist, but believed in reincarnation and had a view that Kanishka was perhaps the reincarnation of her first son, from her first marriage, who had died.

Kanishka was 21 at this stage. He joined the Christian group on campus and went to church there, but he didn't go to his local church too often on a weekend because it was upsetting to his mother.

In moving away from Buddhism, Kanishka has not become an enemy of Buddhism: 'Conscientious Buddhists practising the Eightfold Path of Buddhism, among whom are members of my own family, are admirable people. I was drawn out of myself to the love of God and the love of neighbour. I stopped being the centre of my universe; God became the centre of my universe.

'I didn't become a saint. No one becomes a Christian without being humbled. I cannot save myself and I am loved in a way I cannot deserve and don't necessarily even desire. I found the love of Jesus so wonderful, I wanted other people to experience it. I didn't know words like mission. I would look at people in the street and want to say: do you know this?'

There were three psychological stages to Kanishka's early Christian experience: the feeling of unburdening, the reorientation of his motivation and the realisation that the Church was his family: 'I could go into any Christian community and be treated like a brother by people who had loving, serving relationships with each other.'

The idea of ministry arose more or less spontaneously. Kanishka had discovered the keys to life. He wanted to help. He went to the pastor at his local church and said he thought he would finish his arts degree and then just come along to the church and be a full-time volunteer. The wise pastor counselled, no, don't do that. God has put you in the law degree. So finish that, but we'll get you serving in the church anyway.

About this time Kanishka and his wife-to-be, Caleigh, began courting. She too had thought of working full-time for the Lord, perhaps in missionary activity. They knew that whatever they did, they wanted to do it together. At a Christian conference in the Blue Mountains in 1990 the conference leader challenged the people there to 'lead the best life you can for Jesus'.

Kanishka recalls: 'Soon after that we decided to do that full-time if God allowed it.' He had two years' practise in the law and then went to Moore College to study to become an Anglican minister. This in due course led to a brief stint as a curate (a minister subordinate to the rector) in a parish in Canberra, at Wanniassa, where he met the former deputy prime minister, John Anderson, who became a friend and admirer.

Then, remarkably, Shenton Park parish in Perth needed a rector. Kanishka applied, and he and his wife and daughters lived there for 15 years, until he came back to Sydney, to the Anglican Cathedral, in 2016. Andrew Hastie was one of his parishioners at Shenton Park.

The Sydney Anglican diocese is an Evangelical diocese. Kanishka embodies in his life and ministry the characteristic features of the Evangelicals. This is a Bible-centric tradition, which gives primacy in all its teaching and activities to the Bible as God's word. It concentrates on the proclamation of Jesus as Lord. It is activist and interested in making converts. It wants to spread the word. It also believes in living according to the values of the Gospels and this includes charity and justice. It regards the Bible as completely trustworthy and sees the cross as the engine of history. Evangelicals want to be New Testament Christians.

Kanishka prays frequently with others, in pastoral contexts or in church. He and Caleigh pray together. He prays alone every morning. He takes a small portion of Scripture, prays it and ponders it, and, he says, 'I lay the day before God, asking for his help and forgiveness.'

Scripture itself is a central part of his prayer: 'To voice in prayer what God has said of himself, that grounds me. To say back to God the things he has said of himself, he's worthy of that. And it strengthens you. The worse the day is, the more you need to cling to the truth of who God is.'

Kanishka still finds magnificent inspiration in both the beginning and the end of John's Gospel: 'The prologue of the Gospel is strong in so many ways, theologically, and in a literary way. Life, belief, the Word, truth and grace are all in the prologue. It's a hymn of praise.'

He appreciates the distinctive character of each Gospel: 'Matthew begins with a genealogy, Mark begins with an Old Testament quote, Luke begins with the wonderful Christian nativity story. John has that hymn of praise to the Word made flesh.

'The restoration of Peter in John really means the restoration of all of them [the disciples]. Peter was representative of all of them. The apostles are back fishing, whereas Jesus had called them out of fishing to be fishers of souls. While they're fishing, he's already making the breakfast. Jesus has just encountered the world, the flesh and the glory—and he's making breakfast. The great statement of glory—then he's making breakfast. They're so beautiful, the domestic scenes.

'In John's Gospel you get the interaction of Jesus with Pontius Pilate. Pilate says: What is truth?'

On a hot January night, a long time ago, John's Gospel revealed to Kanishka the answer to that question.

CHAPTER 4

Mary

The nursery tale could not vie with her in simplicity,
the wisest theologians could not match her
in profundity.

Willa Cather, *Death Comes for the Archbishop*

Only a woman, divine, could know all
that a woman can suffer.

Willa Cather

The first person in the Gospels to proclaim Jesus was Mary, his mother. And she remains today, more than 2000 years later, the most popular Christian saint. She is the most influential woman in human history, and the most loved.

Take just one example of her enduring presence from popular culture. One of the Beatles' greatest, most popular songs was Paul McCartney's 'Let It Be', their last single and also the title of their last album together in 1970. McCartney wrote this song about his own mother Mary, who came to him, rather Biblically, in a dream to offer him hope and consolation at a tough time in his life. She had died of cancer when he was 14.

The title of the song, 'Let It Be, are the first words that Mary says to the Archangel Gabriel after he announces to her that she is to be the mother of Jesus. Another line in the song, about a light that shines, is strikingly reminiscent of the passage near the beginning of John's Gospel: 'The light shines in the darkness'.

Tens, perhaps hundreds, of millions of people around the world heard this song, and either thought it was about Mary from the Gospels or took comfort from that image anyway. Certainly I was one of those people. I can still remember when I first heard the song on the radio, more than 50 years ago, as a young teenager myself, smiling at the vision of Mary and thrilled that she was the subject of such a popular piece of mainstream culture.

McCartney has been very clear. The song is about his own mother. But he has also been happy, you might say morally generous, in welcoming the religious interpretation. If people hear it that way, as though it's about Mary of the Gospel, he's happy about that. He once said in an interview: 'I think it's a great thing to have faith of any sort, particularly in the world we live in.'

And was all that use in the song of Biblical language unconscious, unintended, just an accident? McCartney came from a Liverpool Catholic background, though his family was not especially religious, and he sang for a while in an Anglican church choir. A man of his generation would have had the Bible verses rattling around at least in the back of his mind, more perhaps than later generations. It's no less an act of creative genius to press the words of the Bible into the service of good art or a good cause than it is to make up new words altogether. The highest literature, as well as popular culture, often builds on a classical reference.

Martin Luther King's epic 'I Have a Dream' speech, decrying racial discrimination and calling for Americans to come together across the racial divide and live out the universalist promise of their founding documents, was full of Biblical phrases and Biblical cadences. That is part of what made it one of the greatest political speeches of the twentieth century.

I didn't think our culture could do that anymore, now that the Bible is much less read and known in popular culture. And it's true that 'Let It Be' was released in 1970, only seven years after King made his famous speech. Nonetheless, it's a perennially fresh song.

The enduring popularity of 'Let It Be', and the continued religious associations so many people give it, are encouraging in their way. They are one piece of evidence—as though we really needed it—that Mary retains a hold on the popular imagination, an honoured place in the popular mind. This is rare now in the Western mind for the Christian saints. But more than 2000 years after Mary entered history, she is still offering balm and comfort to a troubled world.

It's worth sometimes looking at the place of Christians in popular culture, because most people live in the popular culture. But of course, Mary doesn't depend on the Beatles.

It is also true that it is too easy to miss the vibrant humanity and historic agency of Mary, her leadership in some respects in the Gospels. The culture still treats Mary with respect, and that's a good thing. We should respect her in her own right, and we should respect the mother of Jesus.

But the long history of devotion to Mary in a number of big Christian communities, especially Catholics but others too, has perhaps in its own way slightly obscured just how active and decisive a figure Mary is in the Gospels.

The best place to meet Mary in the New Testament is in the Gospel of Luke. You meet her elsewhere in the New Testament, too, in the Gospel of Matthew, which has a Christmas story with different details from Luke's, in a perplexing episode in Mark, and in the account of the wedding feast of Cana in John's Gospel, as well as John's account of the crucifixion of Jesus, and then a little in the Acts of the Apostles. There is really a lot of Mary there.

Luke is in many ways the sweetest of the Gospels. There are more women in his Gospel than in the others and there is an ancient tradition that Mary was Luke's chief source, just as there is a long tradition that Peter was the chief source for Mark. According to tradition, Luke was a physician, and the Greek of his Gospel is said to be the finest Greek in the New Testament. He was also a friend and follower of Paul.

All historical writing, political writing, biography, certainly all journalism, is influenced by its sources. John and Matthew are Gospels whose traditionally accepted authors were eyewitnesses to Jesus. Luke and Mark were reporting the eyewitnesses. It's not inconsistent with believing that the Gospels are true to recognise that they have different emphases, and this is partly influenced by their different sources.

Only Mary, directly or indirectly, could have provided to Luke the account of her learning of her miraculous pregnancy. That in a sense ought to be the first clue to Mary's agency, in a sense the first clue to her dynamism and activism. She knew part of the story that no one else could know. She gave that to us through Luke. By briefing Luke, she controlled how the story was told.

The best books on US presidents over recent decades, apart from a very few memoirs, have been those by *The Washington Post* journalist, Bob Woodward. People criticise Woodward's books because they are so dependent on, and generally favourable to, their chief sources. I have the reverse reaction: that Woodward's relative transparency about his sources is a strength of his books. Often you don't have to do much detective work to determine the identity of Woodward's sources. If he tells you what someone thought first thing when they woke up, what they had for breakfast, what they said in private conversation to their spouse, you know that Woodward is never making this up. You also know he got the information from the person concerned. And you can confidently bet that this person gave him lots of other information as well.

I believe the Gospels are true and I believe they are inspired. But they did not float down from heaven in completed form. The work of God in the world has to be carried out by flesh-and-blood men and women, even the best of them, like the apostles, fallible and uncertain. In the case of the Gospel writers, they were living through extraordinary and dynamic times, times that were acutely dangerous for Christians. The evangelists who were themselves witnesses needed to order their memories and work out what to write and what to leave out, no doubt supplementing those memories by talking to contemporaries. Those Gospel writers who were not eyewitnesses themselves had to get the story from their sources, in this case primary sources.

The first thing a journalist sees in Luke's Gospel is a scoop, an exclusive, which must have had a great source for the Christmas story, for Mary's story, or to be more theologically correct, Mary's part in Jesus' story. Matthew has the same story in broad outline, but Luke has the detail. Luke himself tells us of his journalistic methodology at the start of the Gospel. Lots of people have written about these subjects, Luke says, and he too, 'after investigating everything carefully from the very first' is going to provide an orderly account of the whole story. In the early parts of the Gospel, Luke frequently tells us that Mary thought things through, pondered them deeply and held them in her heart. As the Bible scholar Richard Bauckham points out, in the ancient world this generally means committing something firmly to memory. Mary's shaping of her own narrative, and the world's appreciation of it, through Luke's Gospel is our first sign of her activism. Mary's story is important because it sheds light on Jesus, but Mary herself, like Peter, John, Paul and the others, is an arresting human figure.

The dates mean that Mary would have had to live to a reasonably old age by the standards of the time to have briefed Luke directly. If Mary was 15 when Jesus was born, and if he died 33 years later, she would have been 48 at the time of his death. These figures are a bit vague and subject to scholarly debate. We know, because Luke tells us, that Luke did not know Jesus directly. He was in the next generation of followers. But if Luke came on the Jerusalem scene, say, ten years or so after Jesus' death, that still makes Mary only 60 or so by the time Luke was around. Luke was a physician who wrote beautiful Greek. Both of these factors would have attracted Mary. He may not have written the Gospel immediately Mary gave him the scoop. Writers and journalists of all kinds make notes, which they later use at the right time, so Mary does not necessarily have to have been around when Luke actually wrote the Gospel, the conventional dating for which is 70 AD, which would make Mary very old. She could have briefed him long before that.

I like the idea that Mary briefed Luke directly, choosing him as the right reporter to carry her story. Of course, it reflects no less on her agency if she gave her story to another trusted confidante who passed it on to Luke. And possibly she had made the story of the Angel Gabriel visiting her, and her response, generally known, although that part of the story does not appear in Matthew. It looks like a real scoop for Luke.

In truth the agency of Mary, her dynamism, is evident throughout her personality. First of all, it is there in her accepting the gift of the Holy Spirit. As Michael Lloyd points out in his entertaining book *Café Theology*, Mary had to say yes to the Holy Spirit for the rest of the story to proceed. She had to say: let it be. The Holy Spirit does not conscript people. Human beings are not shanghaied against their will into the divine plan. It may be against their inclinations, but they always have to say yes to God for it to proceed, they always have the choice to say no. Lloyd quotes W.H. Auden to the effect that: 'on God's side it's not an exercise of force'. And St Augustine: 'He who made us without our help will not save us without our consent.' Jesus himself says that many are called, but few are chosen.

Consider the unique, and uniquely vulnerable, position Mary was in when the Archangel Gabriel came to visit her. Mary is a teenage girl betrothed to Joseph, a carpenter. We know Joseph is a good man. Under the customs of the time Mary's betrothal to Joseph means much more than it does to be engaged today. Betrothal was an exclusive, locked-in deal which went on for a few months before actual marriage. Mary and Joseph both live in Nazareth. Joseph is descended from King David and the position of carpenter is neither exalted nor too humble. In so far as Jewish society of that time had anything resembling a modest middle class, or perhaps secure working class, Joseph was it. Joseph and Mary were certainly poor by modern standards, but they had extensive family. Joseph was industrious.

Both Mary and Joseph knew their scriptures and were faithful Jews. But they didn't expect an irruption of the miraculous into their lives. The angel Gabriel arrives to talk to Mary. Jews of the ancient world were more accustomed to angels than we are and we are the losers by comparison. But still, when an angel had appeared with good news to Zechariah, a priest at the temple and the husband of Mary's cousin, Elizabeth, he was terrified and completely overcome by fear. The angel's news to Zechariah was that Elizabeth would bear a child, though she and her husband assumed she was too old. But despite Zechariah's long religious faith, he couldn't cope with the angel's visit.

Mary was different. Though a teenage girl and without the standing of a temple leader like Zechariah, she was much calmer in her reaction to much greater news. Nonetheless she was confused and worried about the sudden appearance of the angel. He reassures her that she is blessed, she enjoys the love of God. But Gabriel's message to her is revolutionary. She will bear a child to be named Jesus, he will be called the Son of the Most High and his kingdom will have no end.

Mary replies that this cannot be, since she is a virgin. The angel tells her that the power of the Holy Spirit will come upon her and Jesus will be called the Son of God.

Here is Mary's decisive reply, critical for her own destiny and for all of human history: 'I am the servant of the Lord. Let it be with me according to your word.'

I am the servant of the Lord. Mary's radical obedience to God, her openness to God's plan for her, is combined with a radical activism.

Gabriel also tells Mary that her cousin Elizabeth, has also become pregnant, though Elizabeth is beyond child-bearing years. The first thing Mary does, after she gets the angel's news, is to go alone and visit Elizabeth and to stay with her for three months. Travelling alone in the ancient world for women and girls was not so easy. Mary has, as the military instructors put it about promising young officers, 'a bias for action'.

In the Gospel of Matthew, we see Joseph's reaction to Mary's news that she is pregnant. We don't know exactly what happened between Mary and Joseph. But we know a few things. For Mary to be unfaithful to Joseph before marriage would be adultery. And the punishment for adultery was for a woman to be stoned to death. Matthew tells us that Joseph was a good man and did not want to expose Mary to public humiliation. He obviously cared for her deeply and thought the world of her. Imagine his distress and confusion at finding that she was pregnant. So he planned to 'dismiss her quietly'. We don't know whether Mary told Joseph of the visit from the angel Gabriel and he didn't believe her, or whether she hadn't told him and was waiting for him to understand anyway, to intuit the truth, to grasp it by faith.

But here is one lesson out of this episode. Even the most magnificent faith, the deepest union with God, the most robust and deep-seated and genuine virtue, provides no magic pathway out of the intractable messiness of life. Indeed being faithful to the truth can sometimes make life much messier than it would be otherwise. No one in the New Testament, and no Christian any time that I've ever heard of, has a magic life free of pain and difficulty, confusion and heartache. The message of the cross is not that Jesus abolishes all pain for us, but that he stays in solidarity with us in pain, that he takes our pain on himself, and that finally he redeems pain and conquers suffering and death. He gives us a way of dealing with the pain that is an inevitable part of life. But that doesn't mean Christians avoid the difficulties, the messy stuff, the awkwardness, sometimes the humiliations of all that life can bring. Although of course life also brings fun and joy.

But just try to imagine Mary's courage in this circumstance. She has faith in God. But she has also relied on Joseph, as each of us needs to rely on other people. Who will she rely on if he abandons her? We have no reason to think Mary knew how it would all develop. Proceeding purposefully in the middle of uncertainty and confusion is sometimes the hardest thing. It's a character trait Mary consistently displays.

An angel visits Joseph in a dream—which would be less disturbing than the angel visiting in the middle of the day—and tells him the truth of Mary's pregnancy, and that Joseph should go ahead and marry her. This Joseph does. Does Joseph himself feel guilty for having doubted Mary? Joseph becomes a fine husband and father, protecting his family, steady and reliable. He is the quiet man of Christian saints. St Joseph the Worker. He is not biologically related to Jesus, but he is in every way a loving earthly father. He is an inspiration for all fathers, especially foster fathers and stepfathers.

The outsiderness of Christianity is all through the New Testament. Jesus, Mary and Joseph, the holy family, tell the story, at different stages, from a purely human standpoint, of an unmarried pregnant teenage girl; a foster father; an improvised birth away from home; refugees fleeing persecution across borders; and ultimately a mother who has to endure her worst nightmare in the arrest, public vilification, torture and death of her son.

But back to Mary. When she reaches the home of her cousin, Elizabeth greets her with delight. Elizabeth, herself carrying a son who would become John the Baptist, knows already that Mary's son will be 'the Lord'.

Mary then speaks to Elizabeth, and the speech she makes, known as the Magnificat, is one of the most memorable and powerful made by any disciple anywhere in the New Testament. It is indeed one of the great speeches in human history.

Mary says: 'My soul magnifies the Lord, and my spirit rejoices in God my saviour, for he has looked with favour on the lowliness of his servant. Surely, from now on all generations will call me blessed. For the Mighty One has done great things for me, and holy is his name. His mercy is for those who fear him from generation to generation. He has shown strength from his arm; he has scattered the proud in the thoughts of their hearts. He has brought down the powerful from their thrones, and lifted up the lowly; he has filled the hungry with good things, and sent the rich away empty. He has helped his servant Israel, in remembrance of his mercy, according to the promise he made to our ancestors, to Abraham and to his descendants forever.'

Mary's personality is unmistakable here. Four things strike us about this magnificent speech.

First, Mary is grateful—grateful for life and grateful for the special role she will play and grateful for her unique closeness to Jesus. Despite what we said earlier about life's messiness, the first response of anyone to life is surely gratitude. The American Christian TV personality Fred Rogers had a prayer he recommended to everyone: 'Thank you, God'. Mary's phrase that from now on all generations will call her blessed is not a boast but an exaltation at the extent of her good fortune.

Second, God is at the centre of this event and of this prayer. God is at Mary's centre. Throughout the prayer, she declares that God has done this, God has done that, he is merciful, faithful, gracious.

Third, there is the ubiquitous Christian inversion of power. God has 'filled the hungry with good things and sent the rich away empty'. Scot McKnight, in his wise, graceful little book *The Real Mary*, records that for a time in the 1980s the Guatemalan Government banned any public recitation of the Magnificat. You can see why Herod didn't like it. The New Testament, and Jesus himself, at no point propose a political program for a government to follow. But the New Testament always favours the poor and the powerless. Mary in this prayer favours the weak and the poor, a presentiment of the attitude Jesus will take.

And fourth, the Magnificat is bold, forthright, emphatic, confident. The sheer self-confidence of Mary is inspiring. She is a happy person, though facing all manner of uncertainty, and probably shrewdly understanding that her life will have its share of troubles and more, but she is filled with happiness, and more than just happiness, with energy. My soul magnifies the Lord, my spirit rejoices! This is a woman of courage and conviction.

Sometimes Mary's words are discounted because they bear some resemblance to various prayers in the Old Testament, especially Hannah's prayer in Samuel, although also elements of other Old Testament prayers as well. But this objection to their authenticity is absurd. It is extremely common for religious people to pray some part of their scriptures. For observant Jews in Nazareth 2000 years ago the words of the Old Testament would have been more prominent in their minds than scriptures are for any but the most devotedly religious people today. There was no Kardashian reality TV show to compete for space in their minds. The Jewish scriptures were a central part of their lives. We know that Jesus prayed the Psalms all his life, even on the cross. We also know that Jesus had a deep and wide knowledge of the Old Testament scriptures and this surely came from Mary and Joseph.

Many people I know, including me as it happens, have a prayer they say routinely when taking off in an aeroplane. Almost all Christian prayers come from the Bible. So imagine someone is sitting next to a modestly religious Christian as the plane takes off and then the plane suddenly goes into a dive and crashes. The passenger next to the modestly observant Christian survives, the Christian dies. The survivor might easily testify they heard the words of Scripture from their neighbour just before his death. There would be nothing strange about this. This is what happened in fact in the case of some of the 9/11 terror victims in the US. Flight 93 was the famous flight that took off late, which meant that passengers knew from news alerts on their mobile phones what had happened to the other jets. As a result they fought the hijackers, and, although the plane crashed and all on board were killed, the brave passengers saved the lives of those who were at the plane's intended target, perhaps the White House, or Congress, or even a nuclear power plant.

Because of the delay some of the passengers had time to make phone calls while they were in the air. According to one of the films based on the events, one passenger rang the airline for help, and when he realised there was nothing the airline could do, he just asked the phone operator to recite the Lord's Prayer with him, which she did. No one finds this remarkable. The Lord's Prayer is in its totality a quote from Scripture. So why would we think it strange or unbelievable that Mary, who knew her Jewish scriptures much better than modern Christians would know the Christian scriptures, would respond to the advent of Jesus with words that echo the Old Testament? The idea of some critics that Mary, Jesus and the other figures of the New Testament lack believability because they often speak in tones familiar from the Old Testament is the very silliest modern prejudice. It represents a comprehensive failure of historical imagination.

Before she met Elizabeth, Mary had had a couple of days to think about the news she received from the angel Gabriel. She was carrying the Messiah the Jewish people had been expecting and praying for over hundreds of years. It's not the least surprising that her reaction to her cousin took forms from the Jewish scriptures, which would already have been long engraved on her heart.

This is especially so if she was recounting this episode to Luke years later. The essence of the episode, the headline speech so to speak, would certainly have stayed with her all those years. As Luke frequently comments, Mary would ponder things and hold them in her heart. But if she didn't choose to tell Luke all the small talk, or he didn't choose to write it down, that doesn't mean that the interaction of the two cousins, Mary and Elizabeth, was too formal to be realistic. It just means that, like a good journalist, Luke got right to the heart of the story.

The circumstances of the birth of Jesus were humble as could be, as we considered in Chapter 1. But there was immense joy. Mary was surely reassured by Joseph. She also had confirmed to her the singular nature of her son by the Magi, the wise men, who came bearing gifts, by the shepherds who had heard the news from the angels, and then of course from Herod's later, monstrous decision to kill all the baby boys, two years or younger, in Bethlehem and surrounding areas.

But a different episode is the first to cast a dreadful shadow across Mary's life. When Joseph and Mary take Jesus to the temple in accordance with Jewish custom, there is a man there named Simeon, who, in another gift of the Holy Spirit, recognises that Jesus is the saviour. Simeon says explicitly that Jesus is to be 'a light for revelation to the Gentiles and for glory to your people Israel'.

This makes it clear, by the way, that the mission of Jesus is to spread the good news to all humanity, not just the Jewish community of which he was part.

But it is the next thing Simeon says which must have upset Mary. Simeon turns directly to Mary and tells her that her son will be a sign that will be opposed, and that in connection with her son: 'a sword will pierce your own soul too'.

Most Jews were expecting a Messiah who would lead Israel to national independence. They also understood that he would play both a political and a moral role, but these would be fused in the Messiah winning for Israel a military victory over Rome and establishing a national, independent Jewish state, which could then live morally according to God's law. Several other figures from time to time claimed to be just that Messiah and sought to gain political and ultimately military support on that basis. As devout Jews, Mary and Joseph presumably had some expectation like that as well. In fact, Jesus was to be a spiritual Messiah. That word 'spiritual' is inadequate to describe the full transcendence of Jesus' life, death and resurrection and the message it carried. And there were certainly political consequences of Christianity. But Jesus' Messiahship was for the whole world and meant entry into eternal life. It didn't mean political liberation for Israel from Rome.

There is nothing in Luke or the other Gospels to suggest that Mary knew what the human fate of Jesus was to be. She didn't necessarily believe Simeon's powers of prophecy altogether. But Simeon certainly knew that Jesus was no ordinary baby, was in fact the saviour. Some of what Simeon knew would have impressed Mary. So this idea that a sword would pierce her soul in connection with Jesus must have been deeply disquieting, perhaps terrifying, for it could mean only one thing. How would a mother most suffer for her son? The worst way would be to see her son humiliated, publicly abused, tortured and killed. This sort of brutality was common enough in the world in which Mary lived.

This is the passage, too, which gives us a sense of what Mary suffered at the foot of the cross—a sword pierced her soul. If Jesus himself could later pray to his Father—all things are possible to you, let this bitter cup pass from me, but your will be done not mine—then how much more can we assume that Mary prayed that her son would not suffer the worst. She would have prayed not just for herself, but for the sake of Jesus, her son.

That Mary and Joseph were good parents is evident in Luke telling us that when they went home Jesus grew in wisdom, age and grace under their care. As we have seen, Mary and Joseph were devout and observant Jews. Every year, like so many Jews around them, they came to Jerusalem for the Passover. When Jesus was twelve, the family travelled to Jerusalem in a big group of friends and relatives. The trust that parents had in close relatives and neighbours is evident in that Mary and Joseph began the journey home assuming that Jesus was part of the travelling party. He would have been with other kids his age and everyone in the travelling party would be keeping a general eye on each other and the accompanying children. In fact, Jesus had stayed behind in Jerusalem and it was not until a day's travelling was complete that Mary and Joseph realised he was not one of the group. It is also important to realise that at the time, twelve years old was considered the very cusp of manhood, as we might consider a seventeen-year-old today. That Jesus had a little independence of movement is not so surprising, but naturally his parents were aghast when they found he was not in the travelling party.

Mary and Joseph rush back to Jerusalem but take three days to find him. Could Simeon's words of prophecy, even then, be hurtling through Mary's mind? It turns out all this time Jesus has been in the temple, asking, and answering, questions of the most learned rabbis and teachers, who were astonished at his knowledge. This is the only time in the entire New Testament where anyone in some measure rebukes Jesus, and you can kind of sympathise with the rebuker. Mary says to Jesus: 'Child, why have you treated us like this? Look, your father and I have been searching for you with great anxiety.'

There is so much to like in this statement of Mary's. First, she refers to the unity between herself and Joseph—like any good parents. Second, she refers to Joseph as 'your father'. Jesus is indeed the Son of God, but in earthly matters, at the age of twelve, his effective father is Joseph. Joseph is surely a towering example for stepfathers and foster fathers. It's not blood that matters. It's the love you have for your children. Jesus answers Mary by saying didn't she and Joseph expect him to be in the temple? But, Luke says, they didn't understand what he meant.

The next statement from Luke is fascinating: 'Then he [Jesus] went down with them and came to Nazareth and was obedient to them. His mother treasured all these things in her heart.'

The mystery of Jesus as a human being, as the early Church understood, fully human and fully divine, is never more deeply and fully mysterious than in Jesus' childhood. What did he know at two, at six, indeed at twelve? He had a fully human mind and it developed and learnt. Luke ends this episode by telling us again that, living with Mary and Joseph, Jesus grew in wisdom, age and grace. He grew in wisdom. And he grew in grace. And he was obedient to Mary and Joseph. And he was God.

This is part of the mystery, too, of Mary. When Jesus was very small, she was explaining the world to him. The love of a mother for a child is one of the most powerful forces we know in life. Friends in welfare and law enforcement tell me that among the most tragic things they see are men who have gone badly off the road, become drug addicted or addicted to crime, or vice or evil sensation, and come back home, not to find their mother's love, but to get money from mum, or sometimes to abuse and harm her because they feel the compulsion to dominate someone and she is more likely to take it than anyone else. And so inexhaustible is a mother's love that so often she does indeed open the door in the hope that this time she might be able to help, in her refusal ever to abandon even the most wayward child.

For some period, in the early life of Jesus, Mary was his whole universe. You cannot really approach an infant, except through the mother. Infants themselves remain enigmatic creatures. I have been astonished with my own grandchildren, all of whom have recently passed through infancy, at how much was going on in their brains at so young an age, how they always knew and understood more than I thought they did. Although innocent and indeed vulnerable, they also always had a good idea of who loved them the most, and where refuge lay. I have always thought it a failure of imagination that novelists and poets have so seldom tried to create fictionally the point of view of the infant.

The other incident before Jesus' public ministry that involves Mary is the wedding feast at Cana. This is recounted only in John. There is so much eating and feasting and celebrating in the Gospels. And that's a feature of Jewish culture which has continued. As a Jewish friend tells me: 'Our festivals have three stages—they tried to kill us, we survived, let's eat!' Similarly, the 'crisis' at the feast of Cana is completely domestic. You might say it was trivial, unless you were the host of the wedding and your party ran out of wine.

By the time of the wedding feast at Cana Jesus had just begun to attract a few disciples, although he had not yet embarked on his public ministry. Jesus and his disciples were invited to the wedding—were all the disciples friends of the family or were they invited, as still happens frequently in the Middle East, because they were in the company of someone else who had been invited, in this case Jesus? In the Middle East, and even more often in India, and even in Indonesia, I have been to large and elaborately catered functions to which I was asked at the last moment by a host overflowing with hospitality, more or less on the grounds that I just happened to be around at the moment and it would seem to the host unfriendly to exclude me from the festivities.

At the feast, the hosts run out of wine. Mary approaches Jesus and simply tells him that they have run out. Jesus' response is: OK, so what's that got to do with me? Or with you for that matter? As he says: 'My hour has not yet come.' Mary makes no further direct appeal to Jesus but just says to the servants: 'Do whatever he tells you.'

Jesus then tells the servants to fill six stone water-jars, kept for Jewish ceremonies of purification, with water. When they taste this it turns out to be the most exquisite wine.

This miracle is in some ways unusual for Jesus in the New Testament. Some of the fake Gospels written in the second century have Jesus performing all kinds of miracle tricks, domestic play and the like. Jesus doesn't do that in the New Testament. His miracles normally serve four purposes.

They answer a serious need—to cure the sick or feed the hungry. And they serve as signs of his grace and authority from God. They are very often in response to a heartfelt and faithful request. And finally, miracles are a sign of the kingdom of heaven to come, that it has begun in this world, that it has broken through to our time.

Turning water into wine is the most domestic of the miracles.

In one very limited respect it resembles Jesus' interaction with the Syrophoenician woman (Mark 7:24–30). She asks that a demon be cast out of her daughter and at first Jesus refuses. But she counters his refusal with the words: 'Sir, even the dogs eat the children's crumbs.' And so Jesus replies: 'Because you have said this, the demon has gone out of your daughter.'

Jesus is not rewarding her clever word play, but her persistence and her faith (though she is not Jewish). The mechanics of the miracle are interesting because, as at Cana, Jesus seems initially unwilling to intervene. Several times in the Gospels Jesus advises being persistent in prayer.

It is easy enough to harmonise the theology of all these miracles. God knows in advance what we are going to ask and how often, so rewarding our persistent prayers does not mean in some profound, transcendent, metaphysical way that God is surprised by us. If that were the case, he would not be God. But still, we can make the choice to pray or not.

The theology of the miracle at Cana is also perfectly clear. Mary does not perform the miracle. She has no power of her own. When Jesus seems very slightly to admonish her by saying his hour has not yet come, she makes no further appeal to him. All the power and all the decision lie with Jesus. She puts herself entirely in his hands.

Mary's instructions to the servants constitute her advice to the whole world: 'Do whatever he tells you.' It's good advice.

Yet there is a case, too, for not over-theologising the miracle, as there is for not over-theologising Mary herself. Brant Pitre, in his fascinating book *Jesus and the Jewish Roots of Mary*, makes the case that there are numerous prefigurements of Mary in the Old Testament, just as there are of John the Baptist. Of course, Jesus as the Messiah is anticipated many times in the Old Testament. But in a sense the very fact that there has been so much theology about Mary has to some extent got in the way of just how humanly rich the story of her life in the New Testament is.

If, without ignoring the theology, we first read the episodes involving Mary as human encounters, they have their own deep poetry and resonance. The miracle at the wedding at Cana looks very much like the encounters Jewish mothers have with their sons, or all mothers have with their sons. Which of us who has been a son has not had a conversation with his mother that goes something like this?

Mother to son: You know your Aunt Jean, Cousin Fred, friend of the family Bill etc. was saying how long it is since they've seen you. They're coming over next Saturday. It would be nice if you were here.

Son: Mum, you know I have nothing in common with Aunt Jean, Cousin Fred, friend of the family Bill etc., and I've got a lot of extra work next weekend and I'm committed to a dinner, etc., etc.

Mother: I'll say nothing more about it.

And then as the week goes by, for reasons that you cannot even fully explain, your mother's words echo around your head and finally, notwithstanding everything, you find yourself turning up next Saturday, doing what your mother wants. Of course, most sons, unlike Jesus, often disappoint their mothers. But still, if your mother just tells you she hopes for something, it sets up a powerful force within you that it ought to occur. The sheer universal humanity of the interaction between Mary and Jesus at the wedding feast of Cana is irresistible.

After the feast Mary travels with Jesus and the early disciples to Capernaum to spend a few days. It is evident in Luke that as Jesus' disciples grow in number there are plenty of women among them. The former Pope Benedict XVI draws attention to this in his biography of Jesus: 'Luke makes clear, and the other Gospels also show this in all sorts of ways—that many women belonged to the more intimate community of believers and that their faith-filled following of Jesus was an essential element of that community, as would be vividly illustrated at the foot of the Cross and at the Resurrection.'

If Mary went with Jesus and his earliest disciples to Capernaum for a few days it is surely likely that she was there with the group on other occasions throughout Jesus' public ministry. There is no mention of Joseph and it is likely that he has died by this time. However, just as Jesus asks his disciples to place the love of God even above the love of family, there is an incident where he indicates this is true for himself as well.

Before recounting this, let me offer a word on the question of Jesus' 'brothers' as they appear in the Gospels. The different Christian denominations have different views on whether

Mary remained a virgin for the whole of her life. Catholics, Eastern Orthodox and Coptic Christians assert her perpetual virginity. Catholics explain the passages mentioning Jesus' 'brothers' by arguing that this word is used at other times for cousins or other close relatives, and that Jesus' brothers therefore are close relatives but not biological brothers. The Eastern Orthodox Church often favours the idea that Joseph had been widowed before he married Mary and had children from an earlier marriage. The mainstream Protestant view is that Joseph and Mary had other children after Jesus. The Catholic view is explained vigorously *in Jesus and the Jewish Roots of Mary* by Brant Pitre and the Protestant view is explained equally lucidly in *The Real Mary* by Scot McKnight. In this book I do not seek to adjudicate on matters like this. (This reticence is a kind of miracle in itself. I have my own opinions, but I am not expressing them in this book, which aims to look at the core of Christianity that all Christians who can recite and believe in the Apostles Creed might hold.)

Whole libraries of theological scholarship and argument have been written on this issue and it is indeed fascinating. However, no central doctrine of Christianity rests on the question and I think Christians of all backgrounds can accept that each other's positions arise from honest interpretation and are held with goodwill. I mention it only because this next incident involves those called Jesus' brothers. But I am interested here only in Jesus' relationship with Mary.

At one point in his ministry, the extraordinary nature of so much that Jesus said and did, especially his power to cast out demons, was causing great controversy and excited talk everywhere. In Mark (3:21) Jesus' family is perplexed by this, and are concerned among other things about reports that Jesus and his disciples are so agitated that they could not eat. Hysterical reports came back to them from learned scribes that Jesus had lost his mind.

On one occasion, Jesus was instructing a large group sitting around him. Mary and the family went to see if he was really alright. They called out to Jesus and sent word to him to come outside so they could see how he was. Jesus replied to the messenger by asking rhetorically, who are his mother and brothers? He answered his own question by looking at those around him and saying: 'Here are my mother and my brothers! Whoever does the will of God is my brother and sister and mother.'

I don't see this as in any way demeaning to Jesus' family, much less to Mary, who more than anyone did the will of God. But Jesus is stating some important truths. His work—his ministry—and his message are universal. Whoever loves God is as family to him. And there are circumstances in which the love of God may well take you away from family. Finally, the claims of his ministry exceed even the claims that his family may have, including the claims born out of love for him. That is an important way of understanding an aspect of the crucifixion itself. Jesus knew the pain his death would cause to his mother. And he was not indifferent to that. But this consideration was not enough to disturb the divine plan.

The episode also shows Mary deeply concerned for Jesus and his welfare. She was both his mother and his follower. Later, too, it is reasonable to assume that Mary heard of Jesus' prophecy of his own death and resurrection. The prophecy of resurrection, however much she understood it, would have given her hope and renewed faith in her son's mission, and yet as a mother the prophecy of betrayal and death would have grieved her, as it grieved Jesus himself, as she imagined what it might mean.

Did the knowledge that Jesus would suffer prepare Mary, or did it distress her, or did it just trouble her even as she enjoyed the time she had with Jesus directly, as all human enjoyment is cast over with the shadow of human death?

The final recorded involvement of Mary in the life of Jesus before his resurrection comes at the foot of the cross. We considered this scene in Chapter 1. Mary's faithfulness to her son would not allow her to be anywhere else. It would seem Jesus had only four supporters willing to stand with him at the cross and three of these were women. At the moment of his crucifixion Jesus was so reviled, so despised and humiliated, that just being at the cross with him was an act of real courage.

Jesus looks down from the cross to where Mary and Jesus' disciple John are standing, and, in the depths of his own exhaustion and very near to death, says: 'Woman, this is your son' and to John, 'This is your mother.' The Gospel tells us that from that hour John took Mary into his own home.

Jesus is asking the two people he is humanly closest to on earth, his mother and his best friend, to look after each other. But look again at the depth and power of Jesus' concern for his mother. It's practical and human and straightforward. Treat my mother as your mother, look after my mother.

Simeon's prophecy—a sword would pierce her soul—gives us some idea of how it affected Mary, to stand there and watch every calumny and lie and humiliation and suffering heaped on her beloved son. I have always found this scene the most directly affecting in all the Gospels. The slow death of Jesus, his deep concern for his mother, her agony and her loyalty and that of John and the couple of women besides Mary who are, at that moment, Jesus' only visible supporters.

How can a mother bear that?

Mary is mentioned by name in the New Testament once more, in the Acts of the Apostles. In a section where the only others named are the apostles, she is also named. All the apostles, Luke tells us, plus Mary and some other women, are constantly devoting themselves to prayer.

Mary was the first human being in the Gospel to proclaim Jesus, which she did to her cousin Elizabeth. After Jesus rose from the dead, the first person to see him and to tell the apostles, the first person to bear witness to his resurrection, was also a woman, Mary Magdalene. She was the apostle to the apostles. Jesus had expelled seven demons from Mary Magdalene, and she travelled with him and other disciples. Luke's Gospel says she supported Jesus and his disciples out of her resources. A number of early Christians with money did that.

It's worth pausing for a second to note this strange rhyme in the Gospels. The first person in the Gospels to know of Jesus, then to know Jesus, and to proclaim him, was a woman. The first person to see the risen Jesus, and to tell of his resurrection, was a woman. The majority of those who stood dangerously with Jesus at the cross, in solidarity with him in his worst moments, were women. Something, surely, to remark.

All mainstream Christians regard Mary as a saint and a pivotal figure in human history.

Her popularity has never waned, and surely this is because of the irresistible human drama and tragedy and triumph involved in her life, even though I think we have neglected her agency and strength, her spark and chutzpah. She was not God, she was a flesh-and blood-person, the mother of God, as the early Church determined when it decided that, right from his birth, indeed even within the womb, Jesus was always fully human and fully divine.

I would think that just about every day of my life since my early childhood, with only a few exceptions, I have asked for her intercession with her son. Although this is the most intensely personal and private of matters, I reflect that in that condition I am probably among hundreds of millions of people, and an even vaster society historically. But let no one be scandalised by this. Whenever I seek Mary's intervention, I do not imagine I am praying directly to God, but simply asking a saint to pray to God for me.

In *Dominion*, Tom Holland's insightful interpretation of the influence of Christianity on Western history, he writes: 'Mary could embody for even the humblest and most unlettered peasant all the numerous paradoxes that lay at the heart of the Christian faith. It needed no years of study in a university, no familiarity with the works of Aristotle, to comprehend the devotion that a mother might feel to her son.'

I am wholeheartedly with the unlettered peasants here.

When Gabriel announced to Mary the role she would play, she replied, first, 'Here am I, the servant of the Lord; let it be with me according to your word.'

In the most characteristically Christian fashion, Mary first emptied herself of personal, self-directed power, and opened herself to a future of sacrifice and devotion and uncertainty, as well as great blessing, in order to conform absolutely with God's will.

And then a few days later, words we might all wish we could say and mean: 'My soul magnifies the Lord, and my spirit rejoices in God my Saviour.'

CHAPTER 5

Angels at my shoulder

For he will command his angels concerning you, to guard you
in all your ways. On their hands they will bear you up.

Psalm 91:11–12

Never travel faster than your guardian angel can fly.

Mother Teresa

Angels can fly because they can take themselves lightly.

G.K. Chesterton

Where are the angels now?
The answer is, they are all around. They are part of
Christian belief, and they are with us always. They are also
one part of Christianity that has never departed the popular
imagination. According to an Associated Press survey in 2011,
some 77 per cent of Americans believe in angels. According
to an Essential Research poll in 2017, about 40 per cent of
Australians believe in angels, which sounds about right. We're
a bit less religious than Americans. And according to a YouGov
poll in the UK in 2016, about 35 per cent of Brits believe in
angels.

In this, the age of unbelief, that's a big constituency for
angels. Because beyond the West, which is a culture now of
declining religious belief, many more people believe in angels.

Angels had a golden period in Hollywood in the 1940s. The 1946 film *It's a Wonderful Life* became a Christmas classic and is still watched by millions of people year after year. It concerns an angel, Clarence, a bit of a bumbler but, like all angels, good-hearted, who is sent to earth to rescue a bitterly disappointed man, played by Jimmy Stewart. On Christmas Eve the Jimmy Stewart character is about to commit suicide because he thinks his life has been worthless and his family might be better off without him. Clarence shows him all that he has achieved, how wretched his wife, and his town, would be without him. The film was nominated for best picture (and a slew of other categories) at the Academy Awards of 1946, though it didn't win.

The very next year, *The Bishop's Wife* was also nominated for the Academy Award for best picture (it also didn't win). It was all about another angel, played by Cary Grant, the most charming man on the planet, sent to straighten out a bishop in his confused spiritual priorities, and finding himself falling a little in love with the bishop's wife.

Angels never did quite as well as that again in Hollywood. They went a little downmarket to find sustained success on television. Michael Landon, no Cary Grant but a legitimate heart-throb nonetheless, played an angel for the five years of the TV series *Highway to Heaven* in the 1980s. Then *Touched by an Angel* ran successfully on TV for ten years from 1994. Both the TV series, like the Hollywood movies, showed angels helping people through their various troubles. Lately the heavenly creatures have moved into the bestselling book domain with titles such as *How to Talk with Your Angels*, and a host of other books.

All this is a long way away perhaps from the Christian understanding of angels. But it is important for several reasons. First, it indicates that angels have a secure place in the popular mind. Second, it is a rare example where modern Western entertainment actually agrees with pretty much all pre-modern societies, which understand that there is something like angels in God's creation.

And third, the angels in Western popular culture do derive directly from the Christian understanding of angels. All three Abrahamic faiths—Judaism, Christianity and Islam—feature angels heavily. In the Christian Bible the angels are there from Genesis at the start of the Old Testament all the way through to the Book of Revelation at the end of the New Testament. There are nearly 300 angelic episodes and explanations across the Bible. If you are a Christian and you don't believe in angels, you must have a very selective view of the Bible. (If you don't believe in angels or miracles, your Bible would be a pretty thin volume indeed.) The presence of angels is a strong theme of the Bible.

So who and what are angels, and why do Christians believe in them? Let me not hide in the bushes here myself. I certainly believe in angels. We Catholics have a sacrament called Confirmation, which confers on the recipient the gifts of the Holy Spirit. We get to choose a Confirmation name, an extra Christian name. I chose Raphael, the third of the archangels, along with Michael and Gabriel, mentioned by name in the Bible. Raphael is the angel charged with the task of healing.

Angels are a pretty unavoidable part of almost all mainstream Christian belief. John Calvin, in *The Institutes of the Christian Religion*, wrote: 'Angels are the dispensers and administrators of the divine beneficence towards us. They regard our safety, undertake our defence, direct our ways, and exercise a constant solicitude that no evil befall us.'

Martin Luther, in his *Table Talk*, said: 'An angel is a spiritual creature without a body created by God for the service of Christendom and the Church.'

Thomas Aquinas, the greatest of the medieval theologians and still a decisive influence on Catholic theology, in his *Summa Theologiae*, wrote at great length about angels. He understood something of them primarily because they figured in the Bible, but he also tried to understand them in terms of philosophy, and the philosophy of God: 'There must be incorporeal creatures because what God chiefly intended in creation is to produce a goodness consisting in a likeness to himself.'

Pope Francis once addressed scepticism about angels directly. In a 2014 homily on the Feast of Guardian Angels, he said he certainly believed in angels: 'The doctrine on angels is not fantasist. No, it's reality. According to church tradition we all have an angel with us, who protects us and helps us understand things. How often have we heard "I should do this, I should not do this, that's not right, be careful . . ." So often! It is the voice of our travelling companion.'

Francis was also making a point about the real work of the devil and the real work of angels. The devil's work is not primarily, as it sometimes seems, walk-on parts in Hollywood movies, but to tempt us to embrace evil. The angel's work is primarily to help us resist evil, and embrace instead the good and the true. Abraham Lincoln understood the same theology when he appealed to his fellow citizens to listen 'to the better angels of our nature'.

The angels' vocation to help men and women is evident in the times they come to help Jesus in the Gospels. In the account of the devil tempting Jesus in Matthew (4:11), Jesus finally dismisses the devil, having three times rejected his lies and false promises and his attempted corruption. But this effort has drained Jesus, for as soon as he does this, angels come and minister to him. One of the most agonising scenes in the Gospels is Jesus' passion and prayer in the Garden of Gethsemane, before his crucifixion. His trials there are so great that, as Luke tells us, his sweat became like drops of blood falling on the ground. In the midst of this trial, Luke (22:43) also records: 'Then an angel of heaven appeared to him and gave him strength.' Jesus is a man, and God has provided, in his abundance, that all men and women have the help of angels. Which is no bad thing. Angels also help the early Christians a good deal in the Acts of the Apostles.

Human beings know, almost instinctively it seems, that there are angels about. Angels have a very widespread support base across the planet. Hinduism has traditions that involve close cousins of guardian angels. Virtually all spiritual traditions have a sense of purely spiritual beings who exist beyond the material and are often more powerful than people. You can dismiss this entirely as superstition, if you wish. On the other hand, one of the benefits of Christianity is that it brings an order to the spiritual world. Christianity frees people from superstition, not by teaching them that there is no such thing as the spirit world, but rather by teaching them that the spirit world, like the physical world, is under the dominion of God.

Where there are echoes of Christianity in folk traditions, or even in sophisticated non-Christian religions, and particularly non-Abrahamic religions, they are not contradictions of Christianity's distinctiveness. Nor do they suggest that Christianity is just another superstition. Rather they are a sign of the instinctive sense in humanity of the deeper realities. Christians believe that Jesus becoming man expressed a divine revelation of God. The idea that humanity, even beyond Judaism, was in some measure always expecting this revelation, and sensed already the larger spiritual universe that humanity inhabits, is not an argument against Christianity but a confirmation of Christianity's deep fulfillment of human reality. Angels are everywhere, and always have been. Lots of folks have been aware of that, intuitively.

In certain respects Hollywood, in the midst of all its natural, and sometimes unnatural, madness, has mostly got two things right about angels. First, one of their biggest jobs is to help human beings. Second, they are very often messengers.

The New Testament itself tells us that angels, like us, are created by God, but that they are above us in their natures, yet exist partly to help us. They are in no sense God, or gods, themselves. They are created by God and worship God. Angels offer a symmetrical completion to the order of creation. Consider the spectrum, as it were, of creation. There are inanimate objects like stone, or the dust of galaxies. There are organisms which are living but have no self-awareness or conscious intelligence, from amoeba to plants, and which therefore combine matter and life. Above this, there are animals that are matter combined with some form of intelligence, some animating spirit. There are human beings, which are both matter and spirit, and the human spirit involves free will and intelligence. The great philosopher Jacques Maritain argued that there are two mistakes commonly made in understanding human beings. One is to see them as just beasts with no spirit; the other is to see them as entirely rational and spiritual, without all the physical needs and capabilities and perplexities of human bodies.

So human nature, combining spirit and flesh, spirit and matter, is a very high order of creation. And then above human beings are angels, who are pure spirit. Thus the created order runs from matter, through matter and spirit, to pure spirit. There would be a strange gap if there were no angels.

The New Testament, as I say, tells us that angels are above human beings. Paul says that when God chose to become human, in the person of Jesus, he became, temporarily, inferior to angels in nature. In Hebrews (2:9) Paul, or the disciple of Paul some scholars think wrote Hebrews, says: '. . . we do see Jesus, who for a little while was made lower than the angels'.

Paul has quite a lot to say about angels. There must have been a problem of some early Christians actually worshipping angels, because Paul several times warns against this practice. This is quite different from asking angels to help us, which is not worshipping angels, because it is not in any way giving them the status of God. It is also the case that although humans are of a lower nature than angels, there are aspects of the human relationship to God that are beyond even the angels. Again in Hebrews 2:16, Paul teaches: 'For it is clear that he [Jesus] did not come to help angels, but the descendants of Abraham.' In other words, Jesus did not suffer and die on the cross to redeem angels, but to redeem human beings.

There is a tradition, or if you like a speculation, that the fallen angels, who became devils, rebelled over the idea that they would have to serve human beings, or perhaps over the idea that they would have to worship a man, Jesus Christ, when men are below angels in status. According to this tradition, the pride of the fallen angels meant they could not bear to serve a being of a lower nature than theirs.

The matter of the fallen angels is referred to directly in the New Testament. Jesus himself, who several times talks of angels, also declares (Luke 10:18) 'I saw Satan fall like lightning from heaven.' Then Jude, in the epistle that bears his name, writes: 'And the angels who did not keep their own position, but left their proper dwelling, he [God] has kept in eternal chains.' Jude also refers to the Archangel Michael contending with the devil. Similarly, in the second letter of Peter, there is a reference to God not sparing the angels who sinned.

So in the way of things, from the Bible we know a lot about angels. But there is of course vastly more that we don't know. There are some intriguing ideas.

J.R.R. Tolkien, author of *The Lord of the Rings*, thought a good deal about angels. In his correspondence with his sons in the armed services during World War II, he reminded them never to be slow to seek the assistance of their guardian angel. And, as I recount elsewhere in this book, his wizards, especially Gandalf, were a kind of angel, superior beings whose main job was to help inferior beings, especially hobbits. In some measure, Gandalf was Frodo's guardian angel. We shouldn't treat Tolkien's writing crudely here. He did not write a direct allegory, but Christian belief inspired and infused his work, and was absorbed into its symbolism.

In his correspondence, Tolkien recounts a diaphanous vision of his own regarding angels. Christians believe God is a single nature and is yet a community of love, three persons within that single nature. The Holy Trinity consists of Father, Son and Holy Spirit. The love of the Father and of the Son is the Holy Spirit. This of course is a mystery, but it is a mystery that coheres with all Christian belief. For God is not just good, God is goodness. God is not just loving, God is love.

Tolkien speculates whether God's love for human beings may not have been so great and so intense that it is personalised in the angels. He described this in a letter written in 1944 to his son Christopher, who was in the air force. Christopher had written to his father about, among other things, seeking the help of his guardian angel. Tolkien wrote to his son of an experience he had, when praying in church, of seeing a shaft of light pick out particular motes of dust. One mote was 'glittering white because of the individual ray from the light which both held and lit it'. The ray of light, Tolkien thought, was like the guardian angel of the mote of dust, 'not a thing interposed between God and the creature but God's very attention itself, personalised.'

Tolkien writes to his son: 'As the love of the Father and Son (who are infinite and equal) is a Person, so the love and attention of the Light to the Mote is a person (that is both with us and in Heaven): finite but divine, i.e. angelic.'

Tolkien was not proposing a serious theological formula here. He certainly never published any suggestion like this. A man of great modesty in his way, he said to Christopher that he did not know if his idea was even 'legitimate'. Rather, the vision of his son, caught in the ray of God's light, protected by his guardian angel, gave Tolkien some comfort, and he and Christopher were on such good terms that they could share such spiritual speculation. There is a beauty in Tolkien's idea, perhaps best seen as a poetic image. And yet it is certainly true that there are many things we do not know about angels, so there is room for speculation, provided you always remember that it's speculation.

Surely, too, there is room for poetic vision, like that of Tolkien's.

A suggestion of a different kind, that angels perhaps played a role in messing up the world, or the fallen angels did any way, is provided in the entertaining volume *Café Theology*, by Michael Lloyd. His idea, which has been explored by other writers, is that perhaps the fallen angels, who were at large and active in the world even in the earliest times, are responsible for the crookedness of the world. Lloyd is not disputing the doctrine of original sin or the fall, the rebellion by humanity against the goodness and generosity of God. But the serpent was there in the Garden of Eden.

I find speculations such as these fascinating. I agree with Billy Graham's assertion, in his book *Angels: God's Secret Agents*, that Christian leaders don't talk enough about angels. The happy things in Christianity are so happy, the good things so good, I can't think why we would want to downplay any of them. In fact Billy Graham was spurred to write his book partly by his own reflection that he had never heard a sermon preached about angels.

In preaching on angels, there would be no need for Christian churches to get too speculative about them, because the things we know about them for sure from the Gospels and the other books of the New Testament are powerful enough. We know from numerous passages in the Old Testament and the

New Testament both that the angels are very numerous, there are legions and legions of them. We know that they don't marry. Jesus uses the example of angels to help instruct us a little about heaven. Jesus was asked by those who did not believe in the afterlife what would happen if a man and woman married, the husband died and the woman then married his brother. The example they gave was of a woman who married seven brothers in this way. It was a Jewish custom that if a married man died but left no children, his unmarried brother might marry the widow. So, in heaven, who is married to whom? Jesus replied: 'When they rise from the dead, men and women do not marry, they are like the angels in heaven.' This suggests, incidentally, not that in heaven the goodness of marriage on earth disappears, but rather that people are suffused with a more universal love, which incorporates everything good in life. But we are inquiring here not about heaven but about angels, and this is a nugget in our information lode regarding angels. They are pure spirits and they do not marry. Pope John Paul II, the greatest pope of modern times, commented in 1986 that: 'The pure spirits have a knowledge of God incomparably more perfect than human knowledge.'

The paradox of the greater serving the lesser, angels serving men and women, fits perfectly with everything we know of Christianity and of Jesus himself. There is a Christian cloth here which may look different in different lights, but is made of the same material throughout.

As to the number of angels, it's a very big number. There are passages in the Old Testament that seek to quantify the number, but naturally they are not precise, nor meant, I suspect, necessarily to be taken literally. Their point is just that angels are very numerous. Much of the most straightforward information on angels comes in the Letter to the Hebrews. The authorship of this letter is traditionally attributed to Paul, although scholarly opinion has moved against this. I entertain the greatest doubts about scholarly doubts. Generally I trust the judgement of the ancient Church more than I trust the judgement of modern scholars. Because doubts about the authorship of Hebrews were present in the early Church it's reasonable to put that in the doubtful category as to authorship, but certainly it is a canonical part of the Bible, and the Church attests to the authenticity of its content.

Hebrews tells us a good bit about angels. At one point, the letter to Hebrews (12:22) says: 'What you have come to is Mount Zion, the heavenly Jerusalem where the millions of angels have gathered for the festival, with the whole Church in which everyone is a firstborn and a citizen of heaven.'

The Book of Revelation tells us that one of the core tasks of angels, as of people, is the worship of God, specifically, singing the praises of God. Leaving aside the complex and somewhat mysterious elements of this extraordinary book, which has to be read in the context of the apocalyptic literature that was popular at the time, just consider this one excerpt: 'Then I looked and I heard the voice of many angels surrounding the throne and the living creatures and the elders; they numbered myriads of myriads and thousands of thousands, singing with full voice: Worthy is the Lamb that was slaughtered to receive power and wealth and wisdom and might and honour and glory and blessing.'

It may be that one primary work of angels, so to speak, is to help us poor human beings, but they also know, love and worship God. It makes sense that this is the heart of their own being. There is long tradition that the celestial hosts are lost in perpetual adoration of God and the singing of his praises. That can sound a bit dull, like being in church forever. Mind you, if you automatically think that dull, you possibly have never heard the most beautiful church music. But let's pause for one other take on this business of angels lost in perpetual adoration.

Viktor Frankl was an Austrian psychiatrist who spent three years during World War II in Nazi labour camps and death camps. His wife, Lily, died in the Nazi Bergen-Belsen concentration camp. She was 24. They were separated, in different camps when Lily died, and Frankl had no word of her. Frankl's account of his time in the camps, or rather the spiritual and psychological insights it gave him, is the content of his book *Man's Search for Meaning*. This book, which I quoted in Chapter 1, has been important to me since I first read it decades ago. I have often re-read it. It is one of the most influential books of the twentieth century and in its way profoundly encouraging, although it deals with the Nazi concentration camps, surely the most evil and dehumanised institutions that modern humanity has ever contrived.

Once, during a long march to labour, slipping on ice, stumbling repeatedly, kicked and abused by guards, Frankl found a particular consolation: 'My mind clung to my wife's image, imagining it with an uncanny acuteness. I heard her answering me, saw her smile, her frank and encouraging look. Real or not, her look was then more luminous than the sun which was beginning to rise.'

All that Frankl wanted in that moment was the chance to contemplate his wife's image. He reflects that even if a man is reduced to nothing, when his only task is to endure his suffering as best he can, he can still, through the contemplation of the one he loves, achieve fulfillment. For the first time in his life, Frankl says, he understood the words 'the angels are lost in perpetual contemplation of an infinite glory'.

It has been said that human beings can seldom achieve the angelic disposition, the angelic motive, the love for the sake of love. Frankl surely approached something of this in his desire, in the midst of the Nazi horror, just to have the chance to contemplate, to love, the face of his wife. As it says in the Song of Solomon: 'Set me like a seal on your heart . . . for love is as strong as death.'

The other place in humanity where we can see a kind of perfect innocence is in very small children. One of the strongest themes of Jesus' life is his love of children. His harshest words, the outer limit of his warnings and anger, are saved for those who corrupt children, or hurt them. All people can be forgiven, but sins against children are terrible sins. More than once Jesus instructed his followers that to enter the kingdom of heaven, they should become as little children. There are several aspects of this. Children were powerless in the ancient world and the recurring theme of Jesus is that status and power do not help you enter into his kingdom. But surely Jesus also had in mind the innocence and vulnerability of children, their trusting contract with the adult world that it will look after them and protect them and nurture them.

In one passage in Matthew (18:10) Jesus says: 'Take care that you do not despise one of these little ones: for I tell you, in heaven their angels continually see the face of my Father in heaven.'

The care for people by angels extends far beyond children. But this remark of Jesus' underlines how much value heaven places on children. Their angels in heaven—'their' angels—continually see the face of the Father.

Angels are our friends.

Surely—surely—we need all the help we can get.

CHAPTER 6

Paul the apostle, Christ's Lenin

So also our beloved brother Paul wrote to you according to
the wisdom given to him, speaking of this as he does in all his
letters. There are some things in them hard to understand,
which the ignorant and unstable twist to their own
destruction, as they do the other scriptures.

Peter in the Second Letter of Peter

It is hardly too much to say that Paul
invented Christianity as a religion.

Larry Siedentop, *Inventing the Individual:*
The origins of Western liberalism

Paul has always caused trouble in the Church.

Ernst Käsemann

The conversion of Paul marked a change
in the course of Salvation history.

Pope Francis, homily, May 2019

Saul of Tarsus, known to history as St Paul, was a difficult,
stubborn, passionate, obsessive, energetic, courageous,
brilliant, cosmopolitan, intellectual, practical, confronting,
compassionate, in-your-face, ever helpful, blunt, forgiving,
demanding, generous and loving man. His radical change
on the road to Damascus, from persecutor of Christians to

Christian convert, is perhaps the most significant religious conversion in history.

He was uniquely the master of three separate worlds—the Jewish world into which he was born in Tarsus, in southern Turkey, and to which he was intensely devoted; the Greek world, whose language he mastered and whose classics he read, and which was culturally all around the Mediterranean 2000 years ago; and the Roman world, of which Paul, unusually for an early Christian disciple, was a full citizen.

He didn't just master those three worlds, know them intimately, understand them deeply. He took the elements he wanted out of all three—Jewish monotheism and interaction with a personal God; Greek rationality and the depth of Greek philosophy, not least on the nature of humanity and the first causes of the universe; and Roman globalism and order. These ingredients he transformed by combining them with each other. And then he transformed them again, fusing them into his own transcendent vision of Christianity, based on the teachings of Jesus and Paul's own visionary encounter with Jesus.

It was a unique and explosive cocktail and it has exploded continuously down the long corridors of history for 2000 years.

Paul was the Lenin of the early Church—not morally of course. There could hardly be two more different moral visions in history than Christianity and communism. And Lenin was a murderous revolutionary and tyrant, whereas Paul was an apostle of love. But in the two men's intensity, and abilities, there was something similar. Intellectually, Paul understood Christian beliefs at a uniquely profound level, what you might call the theory of the early Jesus movement; he was also an organisational genius. Lenin did this for communism, understanding and developing the theory of his movement, understanding instinctively and intimately too the dynamics of conflict that would bring it to power, and working ferociously to make it happen. He knew what the objective was, and eventually he worked out how to get there. Paul, too, married theory and practice, vision and implementation, theology and mission. And like most of the great human engines of history, Paul had tremendous, tremendous energy.

Lenin is not the only historical comparison that comes to mind. Paul was in some ways the Abraham Lincoln of the early Church, though of course he was never anything like its president. But he shared key traits with Lincoln. Lincoln understood, if not immediately then pretty quickly, with the greatest moral clarity, the overriding need to abolish slavery, not just stop its spread. He gave expression to this in uniquely powerful language, language that forever defined the moral purpose, the moral grandeur, of this historic task. And he also understood, when many on his side wanted to find a compromise, that slavery could never be ended without the destruction of the Confederate Army. All this, Lincoln achieved, at the cost of his own life.

Paul had no military policy, and he sought no political over-throw, so where is the comparison? The philosopher Leszek Kolakowski, in his seminal work *Religion*, characterises the kind of Christianity that Paul led as possessing: 'the tough self-confidence and self-identity of revolutionaries who did not belong to, and refused to negotiate with, the pagan world and were building within it an alien enclave.'

Paul did not present any military challenge to any pagan society. Had he done so, he would have been crushed instantly.

He didn't offer any movement of civic disobedience. But he played the long game and he knew exactly what he was doing. Instead of mounting a military or political challenge, he revolutionised the inner identity of pagan society. He tore its mind out. And in his lucid, penetrating, unprecedented writings, he left a blueprint of how it was done. N.T. Wright, in his masterly biography of Paul, argues that Paul was inventing a new way of being a human being. The purpose was spiritual, but it finally had political consequences as well.

A.N. Wilson, in *Paul, the Mind of the Apostle*, has called Paul 'the first romantic poet'. I make these secular comparisons— Lenin, Lincoln and romantic poets such as Wordsworth, Shelley and Keats—to underscore the point that Paul was a giant figure of global history. Wright argues persuasively that Paul should be studied not just in Biblical scholarship departments, but much more broadly in faculties covering history, politics, philosophy, psychology, literature. Indeed, if you don't believe that Christianity is true, then Paul's accomplishments are even more astounding, because then you would have to conclude not only that he operated without divine assistance, but that he just made it all up out of whole cloth, pulled it together somewhere from the genius of his own mind.

I am among the many hundreds of millions of people who have had great admiration for Paul (my parents named me after him, Gregory Paul). But to appreciate Paul's distinctive genius properly, it is necessary to say right away a couple of things that Paul was not.

Paul was not the founder of Christianity. Jesus Christ was the teacher of all Christianity. The person of Jesus is the centre of the Christian faith. Paul was not God, nor a god; Paul was a supremely talented and devoted man. Paul did not distort or reverse or fundamentally alter any of Jesus' teachings. Paul was a faithful apostle of Jesus. The early Church was well-established before Paul became an active missionary. There were branches of the Church that pre-existed his activism and were following the same teachings he later explained and elaborated so distinctively. The Christian community in Rome was substantial long before Paul visited there. The early Church flourished in many areas that he never visited, such as Egypt.

These paragraphs seem churlish to Paul. They are not meant to be. But it is necessary to clear the air because many of the most crazy modern misinterpretations of Christianity, and many of the bizarre conspiracy theories of history which feature Christianity, cast Paul as either an evil, moralising genius who misrepresented the benign, easygoing Jesus; or conversely a benign genius who fitted up the revolutionary, political Jesus with a lot of kumbaya love stuff he never really contemplated; or as a universalist genius who transformed Jesus from someone who never wanted to go beyond his own tribe into a leader of a global movement with universal aspirations, and so on.

Paul would reject, with vigour, and if necessary with whiplash rhetoric, each of those monstrous caricatures. Paul was a supremely faithful servant of Christ, and understood better than anyone that the whole of Christianity is focused on the person of Jesus Christ.

It is also the case that Paul was not the only figure of great consequence in the early Church. He and Peter could not have been less alike. The tradition is that Peter was poorly educated, Paul was an intellectual. Peter was a rural fisherman, Paul was a city slicker, semi-professional. Peter was a local boy, Paul a cosmopolitan. And so on. Yet they both put their vast talents and whole human personalities, transformed by the love of Jesus, to the service of the Christian message. Not only that— they became friends, real friends.

The passage at the start of this chapter from the Second Letter of Peter, in which he tells his readers something they already know, that Paul's letters can be a bit difficult to grasp at first reading, is not Peter having a shot at Paul. Absolutely the reverse. It is, perhaps, Peter saying that Paul's letters sometimes need a bit of interpretation. But look at the status that Peter gives to Paul. Paul, according to Peter, is 'our beloved brother'. And lest anyone have any funny ideas about the status of Paul's writings, Peter, the head of the Church, the man chosen by Jesus himself as the rock on which he would build his Church, this Peter describes Paul's writings as 'scripture'.

This must have been a big help to Christians in the decades, and centuries, that followed as they tried to work out exactly which writings they would include in the canon of the New Testament, which would become ultimately our Bible. Peter tells them: Paul's in. End of discussion. It also reflects the genius of the early Church, that the talents and contributions of such widely diverse characters as Peter and Paul, and so many others, could be brought together and made to work effectively.

Paul is famous for opposing Peter on an important issue: whether new Christians needed to convert to Judaism as well as to Christianity. Peter went back and forth on this a bit. Peter was the first of the apostles to sit and eat with Gentiles, but he vacillated a little, later on. Paul was clear from the start. New converts didn't need to become Jewish as well as Christian.

Ultimately, Paul's forceful advocacy won the day and Peter embraced Paul's policy. So did the whole of the early Church. But there were also occasions where Paul acknowledged Peter's authority and subjected himself to it.

We know a great deal about Paul, for someone in the ancient world who never held an official position beyond that of informal Christian leader, and who was a tent-maker by profession. It's part of the paradox that confounds much modern commentary. The early Christians and their writings are among the most thoroughly well-established, and well-attested, of any that we have from the ancient world.

Paul grew up in Tarsus, which was a thriving and diverse metropolis. He was the first urban intellectual to become a big figure in Christianity. He was deeply committed to his Jewish heritage and religious outlook. His father was a Roman citizen, though we are not quite sure how this came about. The family, we presume, were Pharisees. Certainly Paul was. Paul was a devoted student of the Torah, the Jewish scriptures.

Paul was a good tent-maker. We know this because in his later missionary travels he often earned his own living by plying his craft wherever he found himself. Before his conversion, Paul was enraged by the early Jesus movement, first known as 'the Way'. He thought it heretical and a threat to his community's identity. The Acts of the Apostles recount the first Christian martyr, Stephen, being stoned to death with Paul present, looking on and approving of this murder. Acts then recounts Paul energetically persecuting Christians, putting many men and women in jail.

Paul was a natural activist and always intense in whatever direction he was heading in life. He was on the road to Damascus to find more Christians to bring to heel when the most important and dramatic event of his life unfolded. Suddenly there was a flash of light, Paul fell down and a voice said to him: 'Saul, Saul, why do you persecute me?' Paul asked who the voice was and the answer came: 'I am Jesus, whom you are persecuting.' Paul found that he had lost his sight. His companions took him into Damascus and three days later a Christian came to pray over him and baptise him. He regained his sight and for the rest of his life was a passionate Christian believer.

Paul tells his own story several times, once in his Letter to the Galatians, one of the most striking of Paul's letters. Galatia was a Roman province near present-day Ankara in Turkey. Paul wrote his letters, which now form a major part of the New Testament, generally to churches he had founded or visited or planned to visit, often to rule on some internal dispute, or settle some difficult matter of belief or practice. There are also a couple of letters to the Church at large. They are the earliest Christian writings. Wright dates Paul's conversion to about three years after Jesus' crucifixion. He puts Galatians as the earliest of Paul's letters. Some other scholars think the first letter to the Thessalonians pre-dates it. Wright puts Galatians as early as 48 AD, a couple of years earlier than some other scholars.

There is scholarly dispute about Paul's authorship of some of the letters attributed to him. As I suggest in Chapter 2, the ability of scholars to determine absolutely a fact, by reasoning on the basis of stylistic differences or other critical speculation, seems to me likely to be pretty limited. In more than 40 years of journalism I have employed radically different styles of writing, and indeed chosen quite different words for the same ideas, depending on whether I'm writing a news story, a formal newspaper editorial (which job I did for several years), a feature article, an opinion column, a light-hearted piece for the Review section of the paper, an academic paper for a foreign affairs anthology and so on. About a thousand years ago I wrote some newsletters for an industrial data firm and even once wrote some press releases for IBM. No one could match the writing styles across those genres to identify any authorship.

Alfred Deakin, when he was prime minister of Australia, secretly wrote two separate regular columns for London newspapers on Australian politics. In one he often criticised the prime minister (that is to say, himself), in another he might disagree even with that view. He intentionally made the columns a bit different stylistically. Two thousand years later, could someone work out definitively who was the author of those columns on the basis of stylistic differences or commonalities, especially if they only had a dozen or so of the columns to make judgements about?

I also know speechwriters who can achieve a perfect mastery of the voice of the politician they are writing for. All of this establishes nothing other than that it is difficult, if not impossible, for critical techniques, even computer analysis of language patterns, to establish a definitive view of authorship (especially given how few Biblical texts we are dealing with).

So what is a non-scholar to make of all this? It's right for Christians to avoid clericalism, it's also right to avoid scholarism. It is important not to ignore crucial scholarship, but also important not to be intimidated by scholarly opinion. My rule of thumb is that the closer a judgement is made to the time of composition the more faith in it I will have. If the early

Church was confident about the authorship, and the doubts came in only 1800 years later, I'm inclined to go with the early Church. So, with the partial exception of the Letter to the Hebrews, I think if my house were riding on the result, I'd put my money on Paul being the author, either directly or through instructing a scribe, of the letters that bear his name.

Either way, Paul's earliest letters date from the late 40s or early 50s, barely 20 years after Jesus' crucifixion. As I have argued elsewhere in this book, they demonstrate incontrovertibly that the earliest Christians believed that Jesus rose from the dead and is the Son of God. They do this irresistibly as history. Paul was writing to established Christian communities about established Christian beliefs. Even if you think what Paul was writing was all wrong, its value to history as testimony is plain.

When devout Christians read the Bible they tend to take a few verses at a time and meditate on them. That is a sound and good way to approach the Bible spiritually. But it diminishes something of the pleasure of reading Paul's letters in particular. And when professional critics and scholars approach the Bible they are often drawn automatically to textual disputes, dating and authorship controversies, studies of social context, the existing scholarly debate and the rest. And when the enemies of Christianity talk about the Bible you can be almost certain they haven't read more than bits and pieces, which they can fling, out of all context, as evidence against the reasonableness or goodness of Christian belief.

But the best way to read anything, at least the first time you read it, is one book at a time, but reading a whole chapter or substantial section all the way through, preferably in one sitting. Even many churchgoers have encountered the Bible mainly through excerpts and readings. Once, at least, it's worth reading the individual books of the New Testament, one at a time, from start to finish. Naturally the priority for New Testament reading is the Gospels. But Paul's letters are fantastically rewarding. Even the longest is only a little over ten pages. You can certainly read them a letter at a time, one letter per sitting. Of course some of the theological matters are profound and have had scholars and many others writing and interpreting and debating for nearly 2000 years. But no one should be intimidated by the Bible. Least of all should they be intimidated by the layers of scholarship built up around it. Paul's writings are among the most influential in human history. Often they are among the most beautiful. Most of the time their meaning is plain enough. And they sparkle with his personality, sometimes loving, sometimes prickly. Read them for sheer enjoyment first.

Come with me for a stroll through some of the highlights of Galatians. First there is a warm, generous and theological greeting, which invokes Jesus 'who gave himself for our sins to set us free from the present evil age'. Then Paul gets straight into his dispute with the Galatians. Someone's been leading them astray, giving them false teaching. And he's not too happy about it.

But Paul's transcendent vision of the new creation, creation made new by the triumph of Jesus, and the presence with him always of the risen Christ, keep breaking through. At one point, quite early (2:19), Paul describes his relationship with Jesus, which is a relationship available to all believers: 'For through the law I died to the law, so that I might live to God.

I have been crucified with Christ, and it is no longer I who live, but it is Christ who lives in me. And the life I now live in the flesh I live by faith in the Son of God, who loved me and gave himself for me.'

Who loved me and gave himself for me—just let those words settle for a second. How powerful they are. This is the relationship of the Christian to Christ. This is a theme Paul returns to again and again in his letters. He experiences the love of Christ and he puts his life entirely at Christ's disposal. In some ways, Paul's direct testimony of receiving the love of Christ, even though Christ is physically absent, is more powerfully expressed than by any other of the New Testament writers, even those who knew Jesus personally before and after the crucifixion. In this way, Paul is a representative of all modern Christians. He is a democratic Christian, a 'mystical democrat', as G.K. Chesterton described him. Paul in some sense stands in place of modern Christians. We weren't there with Jesus in Jerusalem either. Paul shows how intimate a relationship a Christian believer can have with Jesus.

This was one of the big psychological, spiritual, what we might call pastoral, challenges of the early Church—how to keep the passion for Jesus and his message alive, when those who knew him started to die off. In any event the number of converts and new Christian communities became too numerous for them all to have contact with those who knew Jesus personally, either before the crucifixion or in his risen state.

No modern Christian would claim the gifts or insights of Paul, but Paul is nonetheless, inadvertently as it were, making a claim for the immediacy and authenticity of the Jesus experience for all who seek it, not just for an elect or a privileged priesthood.

Having said that, in more crotchety passages early in the Letter to the Galatians, Paul insists on his own status as a full apostle, equal to the apostles who were chosen by Jesus, or the man who replaced Judas, or to any of the followers who had walked with Jesus in person. He does this partly on the basis that he was given his message through a direct experience of Jesus.

Nonetheless there is a wonderfully double-edged quality to Paul's account of his relationship with the Christian leadership in Jerusalem. He is certainly open to paradox. When Paul first experienced conversion he immediately began proclaiming Jesus, but then he went away for several years to Arabia. Then he came back, visited Jerusalem, and went back to Tarsus for several years. The most notable feature of this is how long Paul really prepared for his later missionary life. Even when he was persecuting Christians, Paul would have known a lot about them and their claims. After his conversion, he would have re-read the Old Testament in the light of his revelation of Jesus. He was probably living in the company of a Christian community in those years so there would have been discussion, reading, scholarship and a deep, rich prayer life. All the way through his letters, Paul emphasises and insists on prayer. Contemplation, prayer, study, some form of community life, Paul prepared himself for the role he was to play.

Straight after his conversion, Paul didn't seek anyone's counsel. He didn't go to Jerusalem to see the leaders of the movement he had so recently been harassing. Perhaps there was a tinge of embarrassment, not that he gives any hint of that. But after Arabia, finally the time came for his first trip, after his conversion, to Jerusalem. He went there to visit Cephas

(Cephas is the Aramaic word for Peter). And he spent fifteen days with Peter. The only other apostle he saw in that time was James. It would be a wonderful thing to have a record of the fifteen days of conversation between Paul and Peter.

The timings of some of his moves are a bit unclear. After a gap of several years, Paul went back to Jerusalem, in response, he records, to 'a revelation'. Despite his immense operational self-confidence, so to speak, Paul was submitting himself to the authority of Peter and the other acknowledged leaders. He put before them the Gospel he was preaching. He did this in a private meeting 'in order to make sure that I was not running, or had not run, in vain'.

Later, he writes, Peter, James and John, 'recognising the grace that had been given to me, they gave to Barnabas and me the right hand of fellowship, agreeing that we should go to the Gentiles and they to the circumcised' (all Jewish males were circumcised). Finally, Peter, James and John, 'the acknowledged pillars' as Paul calls them, asked only that 'we remember the poor, which is actually what I was eager to do'.

That is a moment of sweetness and light. It's Paul being part of the team, seeking approval for his plans, checking even his theology with higher authorities.

But then Paul recounts a ferocious dispute, which is central to the early Church: the future of Christianity and the unfolding even of secular history from that point. A substantial group within the early Christian movement still insisted that to become Christians, Gentiles had to convert to Judaism, follow all the traditional, ritual laws regarding food, who they were allowed to eat with, and other behaviours, and be circumcised.

Paul thought this was theologically wrong, against the spirit and content of Jesus' teachings, and ultimately the early Church agreed with him. But it also would have been catastrophic in practical terms in spreading the Christian message, to ask all adult male converts to submit to circumcision.

Paul's interpretation was right and it was consistent with Jesus' own teaching, his willingness to associate and indeed eat with anybody and his clear teaching that purification was spiritual, not a matter of physical rituals. This is what Paul had taught to the Galatians, and part of the reason for writing to them was that some folks had told them the opposite, that new Christians had to be circumcised and follow all the ritual rules of traditional Judaism.

Neither Jesus nor Paul deprecated the traditions and laws of Judaism. No Christian should ever disparage Judaism, the chosen vessel of God for revealing himself to humanity. Judaism is Christianity's older brother and dear friend. Jesus and Paul believed the laws of their ancestors had prepared humanity for the coming of the Messiah. These laws were transcended now in the new law and the new creation.

So having just told the Galatians of his kind, close, deep attachment to the Jerusalem Christian leadership, Paul then tells them, in stark terms, about his disagreement with Peter (Galatians 2:11): 'When Cephas [Peter] came to Antioch I opposed him to his face, because he stood self-condemned; for until certain people came from James, he used to eat with the Gentiles. But after they came, he drew back and kept himself separate for fear of the circumcision faction.' The irony is that Peter was the first of the apostles to routinely eat with Gentiles, but apparently changed his practice back after it caused dissension in the ranks. Galatians contains quite a lot on this controversy, and Paul certainly lets himself go a bit, at one point saying, though obviously not of Peter and obviously metaphorically: 'I wish those who unsettle you would castrate themselves!'

That's a pretty vigorous bit of polemic for an apostle of love in a letter of instruction to a fledgling church. We can't really know at this distance if there was an element of humour in it. Part of the attraction of Paul's letters is the honest, sometimes raw, humanity that thunders out of them. And they express at different times so many different emotions, Paul as the tender friend, as the kind teacher, as the stern rebuker, as the scorned leader and finally as himself a Christian witness through his own life.

Paul was deeply attached to this particular truth, that ritual purification and the like was no longer necessary in Christ's new creation, where purification would come in the spirit, as he was deeply attached to the truth generally, and he won the Christian movement to his interpretation. Even without Paul, I think that would have been the Christian interpretation eventually. But history is not determined by its 'ghostly ifs'. It's determined by what actually happened. And to some extent, Paul made it happen.

This internal Christian dispute shaped global history.

That's a big statement. It's also true. No one, surely not even the Christian leaders involved, could have realised this at the time. It led Paul to make in Galatians one of his most import-ant and revolutionary statements: 'There is no longer Jew or Greek, there is no longer slave or free, there is no longer male and female; for all of you are one in Christ Jesus.'

In *Inventing the Individual: the origins of Western liberalism*, Larry Siedentop titles his chapter on Paul: 'The world turned upside down'. Siedentop, whose book is the most magnificent, sweeping and convincing book of history I've ever known, is not given to exaggeration. Siedentop traces the emergence of liberalism over the centuries directly to the introduction of Christian universalism. Obviously many Christians over millennia did not follow the best Christian teachings, but it is the revolutionary egalitarianism of Christianity, spiritual and ultimately civic, which transformed the world and provided all the universalist categories which animate our thinking today (at least when that thinking has not gone haywire).

Paul's is the most extravagant and clearest statement of universalism that ever appeared in the ancient world. The most important organising principle of the ancient world, Siedentop argues, was inequality and hierarchy. Social and functional hierarchies were regarded as not only necessary but natural. Social hierarchy merely gave expression to the order of nature. Men were superior to women. Masters were superior to slaves. Adults were superior to children. Citizens and landowners were superior to those without citizenship or property. Citizens were superior to foreigners. Firstborn were superior to younger siblings. This was all obvious in the ancient world.

In most of those relationships, there was not just social inequality but actual ownership. Masters owned slaves, husbands effectively owned wives, fathers owned their children. The primary unit of immortality was the family. It was the family, not the individual, who lived forever.

Christian teaching, as expounded by Paul, revolutionised all that. It didn't, initially, seek to change the laws. But the focus of immortality in Christianity was the individual person. Slaves and women were just as much in an immortal relationship with God as were masters and husbands and property owners. Paul and Peter both frequently state that God shows no partiality. A slave was as likely to find salvation as a master, more likely, given Jesus' preference for the poor and the dispossessed.

The early Christians had no power to abolish slavery or to effect any other civic change. All they could do was determine how they behaved themselves and how they saw God and creation. Right from the start they assumed that slaves—that everybody, from all the nations—were offered salvation in the embrace of Jesus Christ. People were free to reject salvation, but once this enormous leap had been taken, that all human beings are essentially standing in the same status before God— all the social structures of the ancient world were threatened.

Not only that, human agency became central to the out-working of life on earth, and life ever after. This hadn't been the case in the ancient world before. Meaningful agency was restricted to heads of families and officials and the propertied.

These can be complex theological grounds. Different Christ-ians have different views about aspects of salvation. But God doesn't force anyone to accept grace or to believe, to have faith. At the very least, human beings have to be open to God. That's their choice.

So Christianity was extraordinarily liberating and empower-ing for ordinary people in Paul's time. It asks them to have faith in Jesus, to die to the sins of the flesh and in exchange to inherit the cosmos. And the way Christians lived, not killing their infant daughters, practising sexual restraint, viewing marriage as an institution of mutual love, caring for the sick and the poor, finding fellowship with each other no matter what their social or ethnic backgrounds—this too became immensely attractive to people from all backgrounds and classes.

The rejection of polytheism and the espousal of monotheism were also liberating. Local despotisms maintained themselves with local gods, who were aligned with local powers. One, true God, whose message of love and repentance was the same for high and low and for people of all the nations, once widely adopted as a belief, radically disordered the old social patterns.

One true God also threatened the divine vanities of imperial Rome, ever more inclined to claim godly status for the emperor. Christianity, in which Paul taught followers to obey the laws and be good citizens, was nonetheless radically destabilising for the ancient world.

Similarly, the moral life that Paul, following Jesus, exhorted was alien to the pagan world. Wright records the famous second-century Roman physician Galen noting that Christians had two very strange attributes: 'they believed in the resurrection of the body; and they didn't sleep around.'

This reflected the new dignity that Christians were trying to win for every human person, and for every human body.

Tyrants have always hated Paul's universalism. The German Nazi leaders Adolf Hitler and Joseph Goebbels detested Christianity altogether and planned in time to liquidate it completely. Both had a particular hatred for Paul. Tom Holland, in *Dominion*, quotes a definitive Nazi judgement on Paul: 'It is the Jew Paul who must be considered as the father of all this, as he, in a very significant way, established the principles of the destruction of a worldview based on blood.'

Paul's universalism has to be internalised by every Christian. No Christian can ever have an excuse in any circumstance for racism. Every human being is created by God and participates in the saved and glorified human dignity of Christ's new creation.

Paul understood, and taught, that while the second coming of Jesus could be at any moment, the new creation had already begun. Jesus had won the battle against death and evil. In this new creation, Christians were free from old laws of purification and ritual, but there was a new law. In Galatians (5:14) Paul says: 'The whole law is summed up in a single commandment, You shall love your neighbour as yourself.'

But this freedom from ritual observance certainly did not free Christians from the normal moral law and ethics of the Ten Commandments. In the next paragraph (Galatians 5:16), Paul also declares: 'Live by the spirit, I say, and do not gratify the desires of the flesh.'

For Paul, grumpy as he could sometimes be, the love of Jesus was at the centre of everything, and to live in Jesus was to live in love. His most famous statement on love, perhaps the most famous statement in human history on love, comes in 1 Corinthians 13:1: 'If I speak in the tongues of mortals and of angels, but do not have love, I am a noisy gong or a clanging cymbal . . . Love is patient, love is kind, love is not envious or boastful or arrogant or rude. It does not insist on its own way; it is not irritable or resentful; it does not rejoice in wrongdoing, but rejoices in the truth. It bears all things, believes all things, endures all things. Love never ends.'

We ought to note, too, among these magnificent sentiments, how much Paul had to be concerned with practical matters.

As is evident in the Acts of the Apostles, it was soon not enough for Christians to pool their money and their resources. They had to earn new money and new resources. There were mouths to feed. People had to work. You can't give charity to the poor if you have absolutely nothing to give them. A small but persistent strain of business in Paul's letters is one of the oldest church activities—fundraising.

In Paul's astonishing life he was beaten and whipped and attacked many times. We do not know how often he was in prison, but it was more than once. While his faith was transcendent and his courage and energy boundless, yet he too had dry moments, times when he nearly despaired, as he recounts in one of his letters. He had times when he wondered if anything he'd done had any good effect.

And yet there were other times when he was buoyed up by the faith of the churches he'd established, or even the churches he didn't establish. In the beginning of his Letter to the Romans, perhaps his masterpiece, Paul declares: 'I thank my God through Jesus Christ for all of you, because your faith is proclaimed throughout the world.'

Paul wearies over the years. His faith doesn't weary but his body grows tired. He has truly poured himself out for the Lord and for the early Church, and really for all of humanity. We must never think that because good people bear suffering nobly, that they don't really suffer, that it doesn't really hurt. This is true of the closest and best of Jesus' disciples. As we reflected in Chapter 4, think of Joseph's humiliation and confusion and distress when first he found that Mary was pregnant. Think of everything that must have concerned Mary as she went to see her cousin, Elizabeth.

When Paul was whipped or assaulted or hungry or tired or just disappointed, his status as an apostle didn't mean he didn't feel these things. It just meant that he chose to bear them and found consolation and happiness in the love of Jesus and the love of his fellows.

In his final letter to Timothy, towards the end, in comments just before a lot of personal business and arrangements, in a letter written from prison, probably not long before he is executed, under Emperor Nero, Paul allows himself to look back in reflection: 'I have fought the good fight, I have finished the race, I have kept the faith.'

He could little know that the revolution he had begun, the writings that would become a profound influence on the future of the Church and of human society, the people who had received Jesus' message through him, the ethic of universalism— these would all reverberate through the rest of history.

Instead, he was preparing for his last journey, surely to glory, with the Lord.

PART 2

CHRISTIANS AND THEIR NEW WORLDS

CHAPTER 7

Smuggling Christ into popular culture

We are, whether we like it or not, in a situation where
transcendence has been reduced to a rumour.

Peter L. Berger, *A Rumor of Angels*

Just bear in mind the popular American television shows,
Jane the Virgin and *Blue Bloods*, the films *A Beautiful
Day in the Neighborhood*, *Deepwater Horizon* and *Ride Like
a Girl*, and the Pulitzer Prize winning, 2005 novel, *Gilead*, by
Marilynne Robinson. We'll return to them all in due course.

How can Christians inject Christianity back into popular
culture? Especially, how can they do this in creative story-
telling? Popular culture has turned against God, especially
against the Christian churches, and pretty often against
Christians themselves, over the last 50 years.

It's quite a bit too simple to say that for fifteen or sixteen
centuries—from, say, fourth-century Rome—Christianity
dominated Western culture and then it got abolished as a
meaningful cultural insight into the human condition, and
became first more ignored than explored, then more attacked
than celebrated, in popular culture.

But while that formulation is a bit too simple, it's also
broadly true. If you look at Academy Award Best Film lists

for nominations and winners from, say, the early 1940s, to the mid-1960s, from *How Green Was My Valley* to *The Sound of Music*, you see a strong representation of Christian-themed films. Many films without an explicit Christian theme have an affirmation of Christianity as their background. This doesn't mean boring, one-note unanimity. The themes and backgrounds are hugely varied, and as critical as you like. Some Christian films explore the heroism or consolation of faith. Others, among the most effective, explore the gap between belief and life, but still affirm the truth of Christian faith, even as it may be sometimes dishonoured, or partially dishonoured.

Similarly, bestselling book lists, fiction and non-fiction, were filled with Christian titles from the early 1940s to the mid-1960s.

Western culture deserves to have Jesus in it, and should really have him at its centre. Much Western cultural product has become bland and repetitive, or, in seeking ever-greater intensity, violent and nihilistic and sometimes depraved. In Ross Douthat's splendid book *The Decadent Society*, he argues that much popular culture has become literally decadent, bored and repetitive, technically proficient but lacking inspiration. It's still clever in execution, in some ways ever more so, but it lacks purpose, originality, meaning and grandeur.

It's easy to lament the lost artistry of popular Christian culture from as recently as 50 years ago. But lamenting the past is mostly pointless. The more intriguing question is how Christian writers and artists, or even non-Christian writers and artists who think Christianity has something important and worthwhile to say, can speak into the confused and hostile culture of today?

In Australia, as in other Western nations, we have reached a cultural moment which is simultaneously post-Christian, Christian and pre-Christian. I list the conditions in that order because that is the order in which they newly appeared over the last 70 years or so.

First, the post-Christian strand. The God is Dead movement has been going for a long time. For several hundred years, rebellion against the idea of God has been a well-credentialled, even in a sense venerable, artistic and intellectual position. For example, consider the eighteenth-century quartet— Voltaire, Thomas Paine, David Hume, Edward Gibbon. In the last 50 or 60 years it has become the dominant outlook. Pew surveys, census results, broad academic studies and a million other indicators show a steep decline in Christian belief in Western Europe, North America, and Australia and New Zealand.

Second, the Christian strand is still strong, for at the same time as there is ambient decline, Christianity is resilient, in the West and elsewhere. Outside of the West, Christianity is booming, but even in the West, as overall numbers decline, there are strongly growing Christian movements, not least among young people. Christians are now a minority in most parts of the West (they are still a majority in the United States, though declining) but they are destined to be a big, lively and tenacious minority. It is reasonable to list this Christian strand as historically new, and sociologically new, because it is now operating, in the West, in a historically new cultural environment of hostility to Christianity. So it is the familiar Christianity but made unfamiliar by the completely unprecedented cultural context in which it now operates.

And third, perhaps the most novel development of the three, is the pre-Christian strand. This is genuinely new. It is possible to grow up in the West now and never meet Christianity in any serious way, certainly not in your schooling. When I was a kid the Christmas movies we always watched were *It's a Wonderful Life* and *Miracle on 34th Street*. Now, the most popular Christmas movies are *Home Alone* and *Love Actually*, neither of which makes any significant reference to the Christian element of Christmas at all.

Pre-Christians are quite different from post-Christians. The post-Christians still possess a certain common language for conversation with Christians, because they still have some familiarity with the central story and idea of Christianity. And of course, even as they condemn Christianity, they use Christian moral categories to do so. On the other hand, as this familiarity becomes ever more attenuated and simultaneously more hostile, it is as if the post-Christians have been inoculated against Christianity, they are immune to it.

The pre-Christians often enough have mildly pagan vices (sometimes not so mild), but they also have pagan virtues, such as an instinctive openness to the natural law, and, most especially, no necessary, pre-existing prejudice against Christianity. They haven't necessarily heard that it's boring, and grown to dislike it instinctively, because they haven't really heard of it in any meaningful way at all. They substitute secular sentimentality for religious inspiration or even religious sentiment, a very common substitution in our culture. That means they may be more open to the Christian message than the aging, fading post-Christians.

Popular culture is, as I say, pretty anti-Christian these days. Very frequently, perhaps mostly, Christian characters on TV and in movies are agents of vice, repression, sexism, reactionary social attitudes and the rest. Sometimes they are regarded as crackpots, or harmless duffers. Right-on popular culture really only approves of Christians if they abandon all distinctive counter-cultural Christian doctrinal belief and exhibit their Christianity only through orthodox expressions of the prevailing zeitgeist, combined with a gooey niceness. The grand old days of Spencer Tracey and Gregory Peck playing lantern-jawed, physically courageous, morally heroic Catholic priests, or Walter Pidgeon a fine Protestant minister who is the very embodiment of integrity and wisdom in *How Green Was My Valley*—that's all long gone.

This is a tragedy for popular culture in four clear ways. One, Christianity is true, and art should seek the truth, even if, as so often, it decides to argue with the truth. Better to argue with something worth arguing with than with nothing at all.

Two, Christianity offers the deepest sense of hope in the human condition, and art and culture should seek hope.

Three, art which ignores the religious dimension of humanity cuts itself off from a huge swathe of human experience and reflection. It puts itself in a straitjacket. It isolates itself from the great rivers of human sentiment that run across the ages.

And four, the Christian perspective injects depth and meaning into normal, even quotidian, human affairs. It also does this, of course, for tragedy, and for beauty. Much contemporary narrative art lacks depth and meaning to a remarkable degree.

However, there are some happy surprises. So before we think of what might be, and what should be, let's look at a few examples of where Christianity has had an unexpected positive presence in contemporary popular culture.

I cannot tell you how much *Jane the Virgin* surprised me, and how much I enjoyed it. I assumed from the title that it would contain some comic mockery of Mary, the mother of Jesus, or if not that, then at least of the very idea of virginity.

I started watching it by accident and found it beguiling. I was astonished at how positively Jane represents Christianity. It's a sitcom and naturally much of the plot is absurd in the normal sitcom way. Jane Villanueva is a young Latina woman, of Venezuelan background, living in Miami with her mother and grandmother. The family are Catholic, the mother a tad libertine, the grandmother more conservative. Jane, superbly acted by Gina Rodriguez, whose charm in this character is irresistible, decides to remain a virgin until marriage. But a deranged doctor artificially inseminates her by accident. The rest of the many episodes over many series follow Jane's pregnancy, the birth of her son, her marriage, her husband's sudden death and all the romantic and family entanglements of her life.

This could easily be the setting for all manner of anti-Christian ribaldry and mockery. But it is certainly not that—quite the reverse. In the later series there is a bit of lecturing on gender ideology and some mildly left-of-centre, party political stuff. But mostly it stays true to its story and characters. Jane's decision to remain a virgin until marriage is not mocked but affirmed, not as a universal moral principle but at least as a decision that she has every right to make and which is a good decision for her. Just that much alone is mightily counter to Hollywood orthodoxies.

Because it is self-consciously making an effort to sympathetically represent a Latino community, and to honour Latino traditions, it has a pro-Christian, even pro-Catholic, outlook. It's a very funny show, which mixes traditional family comedy with a bit of crime melodrama. At the same time it celebrates and satirises the Hispanic form of the telenovela, with a narrator who plays all kinds of unobtrusive but marvellously funny tricks with narrative conventions. Jane's absent father turns out to be a Latin American telenovela star himself and he becomes the brilliant comic scene-stealer. It's a long time since a TV series such as *7th Heaven*, which centred on a Protestant pastor and his wife and seven children, and was a big hit in the late 1990s, could present Christianity in such a positive fashion.

In Jane, Christian faith is not just a Latino cultural artifact, it's a positive spiritual force. When Jane's mother is diagnosed with cancer the whole family spontaneously drop to their knees and pray the Lord's Prayer in Spanish. When Jane reaches a point of temporary deep discouragement, she ponders taking her young son out of religious education class. Don't do that—her atheist second husband objects—your religion is part of what has made you such a wonderful person.

Before trying to draw lessons from this lovely piece of television, consider a second exhibit, the long-running police and family drama, with its own touches of family comedy, *Blue Bloods*. There are endless US TV cop shows. They are part of the background of all of our lives. *Blue Bloods* is a bit different in one surprising respect: Tom Selleck plays Frank Reagan, the New York Police chief. Reagan, like Selleck the actor, is a Catholic. As with *Jane*, the Christian faith is not just a cultural oddity, a generational hangover, something to tolerate at best, or to leer at and spoof. It's a central and positive part of who Reagan is, and who the family is.

Reagan is not perfect. He makes mistakes and often apolo-gises for them. But he is the series hero, an all-round good guy, good cop, good dad. When he goes into church, he kneels and prays. He deals with New York churches as the political power they are or were, but he also respects and shares belief. At one strangely affecting point, out on his home's verandah, he lights up a cigar. He points at his adult son: 'Don't tell your mother I've been smoking.'

The son looks understandably perplexed. Reagan is a widower. He has not remarried. The son's mother is dead. How could he tell her about Reagan's dereliction with the cigar?

Reagan answers his son's implicit question: 'You pray, don't you?' So there is the New York Police chief exhibiting such a strong belief in the communion of saints that he believes his son could disclose something, otherwise hidden, to his dead mother in prayer. I wouldn't begin to analyse the theology of that, and it's possible that on some level Reagan is joking, though that's not how it seems. But it's still a sharply vivid incursion of the spiritual life into a TV series that otherwise aims at mainstream realism. It couldn't be a stronger contrast to the odious, murderous, lecherous and frequently sadistic Tony Soprano's claim, in *The Sopranos*, that he is a 'strict Catholic'. This claim is meant as exaggerated hypocrisy, and something like it is found in many TV cop shows and gangster soap operas.

What do the happier examples of *Jane* and *Blue Bloods* tell us? In both cases the religious dimension has an ethnic shield, so to speak. Respecting the minority ethnic culture involves respecting its religious sensibilities. The Irish New York cop is such an old, old stereotype I'm a little surprised it still has that kind of cultural power. And given that Irish Americans have substantially lost their Irishness, and much of their religious identity as well, I'm also surprised it can still provide a TV justification for religious belief, as opposed to post-religious alienation.

The Latino identity is probably more powerful in America now. And if you want to portray Latinos honestly, in the round, you do have to make some room for faith and religion. The fact that the politics of *Jane the Virgin* as a series are moderately but clearly left of centre is a good thing in its way for reinforcing this point.

Moderate politics of centre left or centre right are not adjudicated on by Christianity. It is possible for faithful Christians to vote Conservative or Labour in Britain, Republican or Democrat in the US, and Liberal/National or Labor in Australia. The centre left of politics in the West has been in danger of moving too far to the left, gratuitously accommodating attacks on religion and alienating religious voters. This has chased religiously observant voters, and even many only passively believing Christian voters, away from centre left parties.

The characters of Jane Villanueva and Frank Reagan both strike me, for the most part, as admirable Christians doing their best (Jane maybe goes a bit weird in the later series) and I'm sure one votes Democrat and one votes Republican.

A by-the-way observation, immigrants to Western societies are overwhelmingly more likely to be religious than the inhabitants of the societies they enter. They can refresh Western Christianity.

But here are two primary artistic and cultural lessons from *Jane* and *Blue Bloods*. If the arts are to faithfully represent and examine social realities, they must allow for, represent, explore the religious dimension of human life.

And second, while proportionately they may be declining in Western societies, Christians are still a big part of the market.

However, having program makers just seeking to cater to the Christian market commercially doesn't always help with communicating anything of substance about Christianity. Thoughtful viewers might well reflect on the positive view of Christianity that Jane and Reagan embody. Therefore, these programs can be helpful to Christianity. But there is a whole strain of TV and movie productions, and novels too, which contain a little Christian decoration, but no substance at all.

Consider, now, the Netflix series *Sweet Magnolias* (forgive me if you haven't heard of it—I watched a lot of TV in COVID lockdown) about three women friends in an affluent southern-US country town, Serenity. It's a perfectly unremarkable, mildly entertaining, sweet and syrupy three-women-buddies sort of series. A lot of the characters are Christian enough to go to church and even mention their Christianity. A Christian minister figures favourably. Yet all share in the more or less unconstrained promiscuity of modern television orthodoxy. And there is no suggestion that this provokes a single nano-second's reflection or hesitation or conflict in any of the characters. The only questions are: how do I feel about this action, will it make me feel better? I suppose I should qualify that characterisation by acknowledging that the characters engage in promiscuity outside of marriage, rather than full-scale adultery. The husband of the series lead has cheated on her while they were married and the series frowns on that. But provided neither party is actively married at the time, any sexual relationship is okay. The behaviour may be realistic enough—I'm no expert on American small towns—but the premise of the show seems to be that there is no counter-cultural moral content in Christianity at all. It's one thing not to be prudish. It's another thing to wholly embrace promiscuity as a positive lifestyle which poses no moral or ethical problems for the believing Christian. This is artistically unsatisfactory in part because it is propounding something which is not consistent with human truth, but it's not culturally true either. Plenty of Christians misbehave routinely, but they normally at least feel some ambivalence, if not outright regret, about it.

On the other hand, this does seem to embody what sociologists call moralistic therapeutic deism, which is Christianity dumbed down to the idea that there is God and we should be nice, but not much else. The term 'moralistic' in this context doesn't impose any moral obligation, or provide any moral inspiration, to the Christian beyond whatever the society already approves of. Christianity then becomes nothing more than a non-directional counsellor. Its only normative message is: I'm okay, you're okay, and the only question it asks is: how does that make you feel? That kind of Christianity is so anaemic that it generally cannot sustain itself, even as a social reflex or modest convention of manners. If that's the Christianity of popular culture, it will have a feeble existence and I would guess a short half-life. A sensible response to that kind of Christianity, of the bland leading the bland, is to say: I'd rather be at the beach.

An approach at its base not dissimilar to *Sweet Magnolias*, though very different at the surface, is to be found in the popular 2002 novel *The Monk Downstairs*, by Tim Farrington. This is a perfectly acceptable middlebrow romance novel which uses Christianity as a species of exotica. The plot is straightforward. A monk from an undisclosed order of Catholic priests leaves the monastery and abandons his priesthood. He rents an apartment in the basement of the house of a divorcee with a small child. Inevitably, quite soon, they fall into a passionate love affair. The monk, pretty gloomy at leaving the monastery, soon enough is as chipper as a songbird. All his existential, metaphysical and spiritual problems are solved by getting it on with his landlady. By the novel's end they are heading towards marriage.

Along the way there is a good deal of incidental stuff on monastic meditation. But this is Christianity reduced to *Eat Pray Love* at best. In fact, it makes *Eat Pray Love* look pretty profound. The plot is believable and okay at one level. But the monk keeps his faith, and remains a Christian mystic, while engaging in his happy, promiscuous affair. He even conducts some priestly sacraments for his new love, even though, as an ex-priest, he is strictly forbidden from doing this. The Catholic rules on this are a bit complicated but quite clear. Theologically, in the Catholic tradition, a priest is always a priest. The priesthood is a permanent condition, but men who leave the priesthood lose the Church's permission to administer the sacraments. In an emergency an ex-priest is allowed to administer the sacraments. Say an ex-priest is involved in a car accident and a Catholic is dying by the roadside and begs for the sacrament of reconciliation, confession of sins and forgiveness of sins. An ex-priest could do that and the Church would approve. But in *The Monk Downstairs* the priest, fully conscious that he is breaking all the rules, performs the formal sacrament of anointing the sick, which is quite different from just praying for the sick, simply because his new love doesn't want to get an outside priest to attend to her mother. Again this is believable enough at one level. A monk might well rebel against the rules, have a passionate affair with his landlady and live happily ever after. But *The Monk Downstairs*, in the shabby new tradition of moralistic therapeutic deism, has it both ways. He remains a serenely reconciled and happy Catholic, indeed an adept at the deepest fruits of mysticism, while breaking the moral rules and the church rules.

This novel reduces Christian mysticism to an Oprah Winfrey chat on mindfulness, a kind of mental zoning-out technique, a sub-Buddhist meditation on nothingness, always accessible and apparently impervious to how you actually behave or what you actually do.

While the monk in this novel was a monk, he presumably spent his life in contemplative prayer directed towards the God of the Bible. A decision by the monk to reject all of that would be credible. A human weakness which gives in to desire ahead of all his monastic and priestly formation—that is also credible, all too credible. What is frankly unbelievable is a decision that all of that Christian belief doesn't matter, but that the ex-monk is still a deeply practising Catholic, at peace with himself, the Church, the Bible and God. Does he think the Ten Commandments were a stenographer's error? The monk would be intimately familiar with all of the New Testament. Jesus in the Gospels, and Paul at length in his letters, make it clear that a life of sexual morality is required. Christians have been wrong in the past to give the impression that they are obsessed with sex and even more wrong to look as though they think sexual morality is the whole of morality, or even the most important part of morality. A healthy Christianity has an outlook which is not prudish. But it is not valid or true or reasonable to come to the conclusion that Christianity makes absolutely no moral demands at all involving consensual sex among adults. *Sweet Magnolias* and *The Monk Downstairs* describe a Walmart/Kmart consumer Christianity which you get very cheap, because it literally costs nothing.

This is the opposite of many of the great Christian novels of the twentieth century and earlier, which often pivot on the contradiction between desire and morality. The desire needn't be sexual desire, it can be desire for power, or money, or fame, or pride, or drink, or drugs. But if there were never a conflict between desire and morality, there would in fact never be anything which constituted a moral choice.

Two of the greatest Christian novelists of the twentieth century were the Catholic converts Evelyn Waugh and Graham Greene. Their Christian novels often pivot on the conflict between morality and desire. In Waugh's *Brideshead Revisited*, the tragic scenario is that Charles and Julia are in love but cannot be together because Julia is already married. For a time they have an adulterous affair but finally Julia breaks it off because she wishes to live according to God's law. Charles desperately hates this—he hopes her heart might break—but he understands. Ultimately he, too, comes to God.

In its way, Christian belief ultimately consoles both Julia and Charles, but it also makes demands of them. Oddly enough, *Brideshead Revisited*, though lush and sumptuous and hugely enjoyable, and almost insanely successful, is nowhere near Waugh's best novel. His best explicitly Christian novel is the Sword of Honour trilogy—*Men at Arms, Officers and Gentlemen* and *Unconditional Surrender.*

Waugh was a pretty weird guy with a lot of odd views. As a political commentator, especially in often irony-laden and self-caricaturing interviews, he was a broad reactionary, but as an artist he was a subtle interpreter of humanity and society. A friend asked him once how he could claim to be a Christian at all, given his frequently awful behaviour. His answer was that if he were not a Christian, she would scarcely recognise him as a human being.

The Sword of Honour trilogy follows the story of Guy Crouchback during World War II. The famous critic Cyril Connolly regarded it as the finest novel to emerge from World War II. Waugh's outlook is idiosyncratic, rooted in history and even a bit eccentric, but it is highly and explicitly Christian. At war's outbreak, Guy is a disillusioned, 35-year-old Englishman, of an old but obscure Catholic family, living in Italy. His glamorous, beautiful wife long ago left him. Guy is honourable, decent, restrained, a little awkward, a little passive, but wanting very much to do something useful with the rest of his life. He often prays in the course of this novel but has no beatific vision. His prayers most often concern his own shortcomings and his chief request of God is that he find something useful to do.

It is true that part of Guy's melancholy is the deep wound of his marriage and that he does not consider remarrying because it is against the rules. But that is not the crux of the novel. The alliance between Hitler's Nazi Germany and Stalin's communist Soviet Union, in Guy's view, brings the two most evil forces of the twentieth century together. The war against them seems to offer Guy salvation. He immediately volunteers for the army.

The novel functions in part as a strange love song to the British army, with which Guy slowly falls out of love. The army, in its declining integrity, serves as a metaphor both for the Catholic Church and for the whole of Western Christendom, which Waugh saw as being in the process of losing their vitality. By the end of the novel, Guy realises how foolish and self-indulgent it was to think that military service would bring him personal salvation. The dialogue about the purposes and morality of war is subtle and many sided.

Along the way, in between bursts of sheer Waugh comic genius, there is an acute, early diagnosis of some of the deepest pathologies of Western modernity. The odious Trimmer, a coward and liar and general rat, is promoted, wholly fraudulently, as a war hero. In Trimmer, Waugh foresees with astonishing diagnostic accuracy the essential deformity of modern celebrity, celebrity without achievement, purpose, value or moral direction. To balance this, however, there is the character of Guy's father, Gervase Crouchback, the most sympathetic, and the most wholly good, character in the entire Waugh opus. Crouchback Senior is filled with spiritual hope and purpose and goodwill. The dialogue between the father's cheerfulness in spirit, and Guy's slightly self-indulgent melancholy, is one of the great explorations of the novel.

Despite his contrarian nature, even Waugh was not immune to the fashions of his time, and he was fond of finishing his books on a humanly unhappy note. But he couldn't altogether bring himself to do that in the Sword of Honour trilogy, because in the end the deepest theme of the book is Guy Crouchback's moral survival. This is a recurrent theme of Waugh's, almost a Christian existentialism—the plight of the civilised person cast among barbarians in an increasingly barbaric world.

It's difficult to imagine a Christian view as clear-eyed as Waugh's finding its way into popular culture, such as best-selling novels, now (but not impossible to imagine, as we shall see), and certainly the television mini-series of the Sword of Honour trilogy was a lamentable failure to do justice to any of Waugh's themes.

For a direct expression of an explicitly Christian world view, consider the American film *A Beautiful Day in the Neighborhood*, and for an explicit presentation of an incidentally Christian view, consider the Australian film *Ride Like a Girl*. The American film is one of the loveliest I have seen. It penetrates the heart in unexpected ways. It concerns the life and work of Fred Rogers, a mildly conservative, soft-spoken, Presbyterian minister who went into children's television and created an institution, *Mister Rogers' Neighborhood*, which ran on US TV from the late 1960s to 2001. Tom Hanks plays Mr Rogers, and was nominated for an Academy Award for the performance.

Mister Rogers' Neighborhood was directed at kids from pre-school to pre-teen. Unlike almost any other TV show of that type, it dealt with moral development in children, and confronted tough issues like death, anger and loss. And yet everything about the show was positive and warm and good. Numerous American friends have told me that Mr Rogers was the most important adult in their lives, from about the age of five to eleven, after their parents. Rogers was a lifelong Republican and moderate conservative but didn't intrude politics into his public persona. Everything he did was based on Christianity but he introduced it quietly and subtly.

The movie describes the unlikely friendship between Rogers and an *Esquire* writer sent to interview him. This is semi-fictionalised to structure a dramatic arc, but it's basically true. The journalist is hard-bitten and cynical—how extraordinary for a journalist!—and initially thinks Rogers is too good to be true, that over time he will puncture the facade and get to the grimy reality behind it. But it turns out there is no façade: Rogers is just good. Rogers helps him get his life back together. The journalist hates his dad. At one point Rogers says to him: just remember, your dad played a big part in making you the good man you are today. Rogers' favourite prayer, his whole attitude to life, is contained in three words: thank you, God.

Rogers is not perfect. He had some troubles with one of his sons. He prays, reads Scripture and swims every day to channel his energies. But he is always kind. The film is engrossing as a story, but it is a singular departure for Hollywood, for there is a consoling, quiet, meditative quality about it. There is a restraint which is not awkwardness, but rather something like grace.

I'm not quite sure why this is, but one of the most difficult things in art is to make a normal, good person interesting. Art finds evil easy to dramatise. Similarly, super-heroic goodness, wartime sacrifice or some such, is inherently dramatic and ready-made for film. But the life of steady goodness, which is the way goodness so often comes, is much harder for the arts.

The less overtly Christian film *Ride Like a Girl* nonetheless has some of the same qualities. A gentle, attractive film, it tells the story of Michelle Payne, the first female jockey to win the Melbourne Cup. She is the youngest of ten children and her widowed father, Paddy Payne, is the film's other lead. In terms of Christian content, the family are Catholic Christians and go to church on Sundays and it means something to them. The parish priest is a friend and helper, especially when tragedy strikes or threatens to strike.

You get a positive glimpse of Christianity as part of life in a film like *Deepwater Horizon*, about the massive 2010 fire and oil spill in the Gulf of Mexico. Towards the end of the film the surviving oil rig crew, almost entirely hard-bitten, physically tough, manual oil workers, drop to their knees on their rescue ship and recite the Lord's Prayer, to mourn their dead and to give thanks for their own survival. That is a positive way for Christianity to be seen. The film is not about religious issues. It is about life and death. Ordinary people generally turn to God at such moments. Mark Wahlberg, the driving force behind this film, is himself a believing Christian. He did some pretty bad things in his youth and he has apologised for them. Such a scene of prayer in such a big, mainstream film is surely helpful. It doesn't in itself mean that people will turn to Christianity, but it's a positive signal that this Christianity means something, and can strike a claim to cultural credibility which ought to be recognised more often.

In the movies about Fred Rogers and Michelle Payne, the film makers could not possibly have told the respective stories without including the Christian element. So here is one big hint for Christians. If you lead lives that are so extraordinary that artists want to explore and recount them, and you are seriously Christian, there is a very good chance that Christianity will get a positive treatment in the stories that result.

Though there's no guarantee. Contrast these two films with the lamentable, woeful, unspeakably lame (I may be understating things a bit there) movie *Tolkien*, about J.R.R. Tolkien, author of *The Lord of the Rings*. Tolkien's great tale of Middle Earth was one of the most widely read works of fiction in the world in the twentieth century, with more than 150 million copies sold. It is often claimed to be the biggest selling novel of any type in the twentieth century. Central to Tolkien's life, imagination and work, infusing every aspect of his being, was his profound Christianity. Yet this wretched film approaches Christian belief a little as Queen Victoria is said to have responded to the idea of lesbianism—she'd heard of it but didn't really believe it existed. It is a small consolation that this aimless film, released in 2019, was a commercial flop. It followed the example of a big Oxford University exhibition on Tolkien a few years earlier, which also didn't mention his Christianity. Both the film and the exhibition were effectively acts of cultural censorship of Christianity. They are representative, and in their way deadly. They are almost part of the culture of death, because they deny the root of life, and the animating spirit of all Tolkien's art and activity.

Tolkien was immensely influential in the conversion of his close friend C.S. Lewis from atheism to Christianity. Not only that, his Christian vision is all through *The Lord of the Rings*. It was also all through his extraordinary life. Tolkien was orphaned at age twelve and his mother had decreed in her will that a Catholic priest, Father Francis Morgan, from the Birmingham Oratory, who had greatly helped the family during her widowhood, be his legal guardian. That in itself was an astonishing decision as the family had other relatives. But Tolkien's mother didn't trust them with her son's religious formation (she was Catholic, her family were Baptists).

Tolkien and his younger brother lived in boarding houses near the Oratory and went to the priests' house for breakfast and after school, went away on annual holidays with Father Morgan, and, though lonely without their beloved mother, thrived in the life and companionship of the good fathers. Later Morgan used money from his own family to subsidise Tolkien at Oxford. Tolkien had won a scholarship, of course, but it wasn't enough to cover all his expenses, so Morgan made sure there was enough money so that the young Tolkien could enjoy a normal undergraduate life.

The one rift between boy and priest testifies to the depth of Tolkien's honour and religious devotion, his regard for his guardian, but also his determined romanticism and his extraordinary will. Tolkien fell in love with the girl who would be his wife, Edith Bratt, when he was still in high school. Morgan, unromantically but not entirely unreasonably, forbade the relationship until Tolkien finished his education. So for a couple of years the two young people had no contact. On his 21st birthday, Tolkien wrote to Edith, to say: time's up on our forced separation, let's get married! Having not heard from him for years, Edith was by then engaged to someone else. Tolkien travelled to see her and immediately won her back, and they married when he was still in effect impecunious (and later maintained a friendship with her ex-fiancée). Then Tolkien went off to fight World War I. All this did not lead to any lasting estrangement from Father Morgan, who was like a father to Tolkien. In a letter to his grandson, Michael, in 1965, Tolkien wrote: 'I have met stuffy, stupid, undutiful, conceited, ignorant, hypocritical, lazy, tipsy, hardhearted, cynical, mean, grasping, vulgar, snobbish and even (at a guess) immoral priests in the course of my peregrinations, but for me one Father Francis outweighs them all . . . I first learned charity and forgiveness from him.'

You would think that Tolkien's unconventional, heroic romance with Edith, or the deep, enduring relationship with Father Morgan, or even more the Christianity which drove *The Lord of the Rings*, would offer magnificent material for any dramatisation of the life of the greatest creative mind of the twentieth century. Instead we got a lame, schoolboy drama and an extended, ineffective dream sequence about World War I.

Tolkien's Christianity has been whited out of popular culture's treatment of both *The Lord of the Rings* and its author. Tolkien himself was explicit that while it was not an allegory, his great creation was a Christian book. In 1953 he wrote to a friend: '*The Lord of the Rings* is of course a fundamentally Christian and Catholic book . . . the religious element is absorbed into the story and the symbolism.'

How is *The Lord of the Rings* a Christian book? There are countless Biblical echoes, countless uses of Biblical imagery. Orcs are fallen elves, as demons are fallen angels. Aragorn, who delivers his people from Sauron, is a Moses-like figure. Tolkien saw his wizards, Gandalf chief among them, as inspired by angels, their job essentially to help lesser, rational creatures— hobbits, elves and men—to resist and battle evil.

Much more deeply, the story opposes good and evil, but it also sees, in Sauron, the personification of evil, that evil is an active, dynamic person trying to bend history.

The tale sees salvation for the whole of the good come through the hobbits, halflings, among the least of creatures. Despite the great battles, salvation does not come primarily through kings and warriors. Literally the first shall be last and the last shall be first. Even Aragorn long occupies a much lower status before he becomes the king. When the book first came out in the 1950s, a time of much greater Christian and Biblical cultural literacy than our own time, the shrewder critics saw much of this straight away. Bernard Levin, who later became a famous columnist for *The Times*, reviewed it for *Truth* and observed that it was reassuring to see that 'the meek shall inherit the earth'.

One of the subtlest theological points in *The Lord of the Rings* comes at its climax. The deep Christian theme that in order to save your life you must be willing to give up your life runs throughout. The ring carriers, specifically Frodo, and before him Bilbo, have to be willing to renounce the corrupting power of the ring. (Warning: the next sentence here is a plot spoiler if you haven't read the book.) But even Frodo, simultaneously the bravest and the most innocent and the best of the characters in the entire saga, when it comes to the completion of his mission, cannot bring himself to throw the ring into the fire which will destroy it. Instead Gollum, tragic little figure, both good and bad, who has followed Frodo, leaps forward to steal the ring for himself and then falls into the fire to his death, with the ring, thereby unintentionally destroying the ring. The earlier act of decency by the hobbits in not killing Gollum enables the ring to be destroyed. But Frodo's failure to give up the ring voluntarily, after his magnificent heroism in bearing the burden of the ring for so long, is the key. Tolkien is clear that even the best mortal creature cannot resist evil alone, but needs divine assistance.

Tolkien never preached in public and didn't enter religious or political controversies, although he had strong views on some

issues. But he was a devoted husband and father and grandfather, so his letters are full of his faith, both in an everyday
way and in special and difficult circumstances. The letters to
his sons, especially when they are in the armed services in
World War II, are straight-from-the-shoulder advice. This is
how to pray when you are far from home and from church.
This is how I found military life in World War I and this is how
I prayed. Never forget the assistance that your guardian angel
is ready to provide. He also wrote to his sons about marriage,
always referring very tenderly to his wife, their mother, but also
saying that a man needs to have a certain control of himself,
and to understand his own failings, if he is to be a faithful and
decent husband.

I don't think Christians make enough of Tolkien's Christianity. He is after all one of the towering cultural figures of
the last century. Here is one practical suggestion. A volume
of Tolkien's correspondence was published in 1981 and it
runs to some 460 pages in a large, hardback format. Tolkien
was incapable of writing a lazy or disfigured sentence. It is all
good. Much of it, naturally, concerns *The Lord of the Rings*
and the often intricate answers he provided to people seeking
more detail about the characters. However, a substantial
minority of the letters deal directly with Tolkien's Christian
beliefs. An enterprising Christian outfit should distil these to
a volume of a quarter or so of the length of the 1981 book,
keeping no letters purely about *The Lord of the Rings* unless
they are primarily concerned with the Christian dimension,
but keeping all the letters of advice to his sons and daughter,
and what correspondence there is with C.S. Lewis, especially
where he disagreed on a point of theology with the great

Christian apologist. Such a volume could be called *Tolkien on Christianity*. It would encourage and inform Christians, may even be an accessible pathway to faith for those who love Tolkien's work but don't know Christianity, and it would be a sign-post for popular culture: Hey! Look at this! Did you know this genius was a profoundly believing Christian?

Of course the very fact that Tolkien posed a certain challenge to his readers—to have the moral and Biblical and historical sensibility to sympathise with the deep Christianity underlying his mythical creations—meant that this Christianity was always going to pass quite a few people by. I read *The Lord of the Rings* first as a teenager and was completely absorbed in the tale, felt that I was present for every step of the adventure. The fear instilled by the Black Riders, later revealed to be the Ringwraiths or Nazgul, on their first appearance is one of the most vivid memories I have from a lifetime of reading novels. I can't say I understood every moral or theological implication of the book the first time I read it, but certainly it seemed to inhabit a moral universe I was familiar with. And I could sense, even then, the Biblical thinking which infused it.

But it is likely that more explicitly Christian creative works will have a more direct impact on the popular culture and on individual human beings. It is rare now to find a widely popular creative literary work, popular in the secular culture as well as among self-describing Christians, which is explicitly Christian in its themes.

One of the most important exceptions is the dazzling novel *Gilead*, by Marilynne Robinson, which won the 2005 Pulitzer Prize. It is, I think, the best Christian novel of the 21st century. To describe its structure will give you no sense of its beauty or power. The year is 1956 and the Reverend John Ames, a Congregationalist minister in Iowa, deep into his seventies, is preparing for death. He married Lila, his second wife late (his first wife died not long after their wedding 50 years ago) and has a seven-year-old son, Johnny. He writes an account of himself, mixed with bits of good advice and much rumination, for the son to read when he's older.

It sounds as though it could be lame, preachy, wordy, lacking drama. It is instead a luminous treatment of a human life, enthralling and lucid, almost hypnotic in the depth in which you enter this life. Part of Robinson's genius is to get Ames' tone of voice just right. In a novel told in the first person, as this is, the distinctive voice of the narrator is one key to plausibility. Even if an event seems unlikely, or a judgement is one you might disagree with, it carries great credibility if you can hear the voice clearly and recognise the character in the voice, if the voice itself is convincing. I am a lifelong fan of the Richard Hannay adventure novels written by John Buchan, of which *The Thirty-Nine Steps* is the most famous, and most frequently filmed. The plots teeter on the very edge of preposterous, barely possible and almost insanely unlikely. The stories are told in the first person by Hannay, and because Buchan captures Hannay's voice perfectly, and because Hannay is so likeable, so good to spend time with, the novels remain readable and enjoyable even as they defy credibility.

There is nothing that defies credibility in *Gilead*. Ames recounts his violently abolitionist grandfather, also a preacher, who took up arms to fight slavery and, as his son put it, preached the town of Gilead into the American Civil War. The son, John Ames' father, reacted with a Christian pacifism.

Although this seems to be a novel concerned with the inner life of an individual rather than the outer life of a nation, you realise later on that the first part of the novel has acted, among many other things, as a kind of ethical contest or moral dialectic between the activism of the grandfather prepared to encompass violence in a transcendently just cause, ending slavery, as opposed to the seraphic pacifism of the son, who surely hates slavery but objects to bloodshed in any cause.

Ames is preoccupied with theology, whether he's behaved well, how he might have better helped his community. He is transcendently grateful to God for sending his wife and then his son into his life after decades of more or less self-imposed loneliness after the death of his first wife, his childhood sweetheart.

His best friend is the Presbyterian minister John Boughton. Boughton's son Jack, who has behaved badly, exploited women, fallen to drink and disappointed everyone in his life, comes back to Gilead after many years away. He is seeking refuge, and redemption of a kind. To Ames' distress, Jack strikes up a friendship with Ames' wife, Lila, and son, Johnny. Ames is scared that after he's gone, Jack Boughton might intrude on the life of his wife and son, might even marry his Lila.

The fear that Ames has for his wife and son when he is no longer there to help them is a powerful dynamic in the book, and it conflicts with his desire not to condemn Jack Boughton unfairly, to exercise charity towards Jack. Should he at least warn his wife what kind of man Jack Boughton is? Ames believes absolutely in the goodness of his wife, who before marriage had a hard life that he only hints at. He fears that she has a kind of innocence that could be exploited. He can see that his wife feels sorry for Jack Boughton, perhaps even identifies with some of his isolation. Then he reflects: 'It is one of the best traits of good people that they love where they pity. And this is truer of women than of men.' This sometimes gets women into difficult situations, he believes. But he can't find a good way to warn against it, 'since it is, in a word, Christlike'.

He also reflects, in writing to his son, that if Jack Boughton threw Ames himself down a flight of stairs, he could work out the theology of forgiving him before he hit the bottom of the staircase. But if the young Boughton should harm Ames' son, why, then his theology might fail him. Ames never rails at any misfortune of his own, but there is pathos, tragedy even, in being 77 and having a much younger wife and a seven-year-old son. And yet Ames' overwhelming sense is of gratitude for the life and wonder he's experienced.

Ames understands his own fallibility. He also understands that all Christian belief is mediated through personal experience. He reflects: 'It is religious experience above all that authenticates religion for the purposes of the individual believer.'

This meditation by a deeply religious man on the meaning of life and the welfare of his wife and son leads to distinctive, intriguing, religious speculation which is most unusual in modern novels. Ames wonders at length about what heaven will be like. He believes in heaven and he believes it will not disappoint. Will he and his son meet as two vigorous adults, rather than as a boy and an old man? That would be fine. But then again he would love to meet his son as a small child, to have his son leap once more into his arms. I don't think I've ever read more speculation about heaven in any novel. Yet it's not forced or artificial or overdone. Ames will soon die and he's wondering, in the most practical way, about his future, about his family's future.

It is a failure of modern Christianity that we almost never talk of heaven. Christianity believes in the four last things: death, judgement, heaven and hell. They are all indispensable parts of the human condition and the Christian message. Every human being will face them. Perhaps it is a tragic loss of genuine belief in the metaphysical reality of the spiritual which has led Christianity to move away from talking about any of the four last things.

This has long been a tendency of the modern condition. The great Australian-British Catholic writer and apologist Frank Sheed was once asked by the Jesuits to preach a sermon in a New York church. He chose to preach on heaven so that at least once in his life he would have heard heaven mentioned in a sermon in church, even if he had to preach it himself. Robinson achieves sustained, intelligent reflection on the nature of heaven from a Christian minister in a commercially and critically successful novel. That's almost a miracle in itself.

At one point Ames reflects on the beauty of a line of oak trees. He has been so busy admiring existence that he hasn't had time to enjoy it properly. He feels like a child who has just opened his eyes to see the wonder of things and knows nothing of them, and now must close his eyes again. All this human beauty is so real, surely somehow in heaven it will persist. Yet impermanence is an essential part of human beauty, while heaven is eternal. Ames reflects: 'I can't believe that, when we've all been changed and put on incorruptibility, we will forget our fantastic condition of mortality and impermanence, the great bright dream of procreating and perishing that meant the whole world to us . . . I don't imagine any reality putting this one in the shade entirely, and I think piety forbids me to try.'

Theologically, Robinson is asking this question: our mortality is part of our goodness, how will immortality preserve that part of our goodness tied up with mortality?

One lesson for Christians seeking to enter creatively into the mainstream culture is that if you are good enough, the culture may not wish to ignore you after all. Robinson's subject matter is determinedly theological. She doesn't compromise on what is important to Ames or what she believes will be interesting to the reader.

Although there are sentences of pure, sweet perfection, Robinson does not go in for the purple passage or needlessly use the hundred-dollar word. Hers seems a voice characteristic of the American mid-west. Yet while her novel is explicitly Christian in outlook, it doesn't ask you to accept Christianity, at any level, in order to appreciate Ames' view.

One novelist who was immensely popular in his day, Graham Greene, did occasionally and daringly do just that. The Greene novel I love best is *The End of the Affair*. Greene is sometimes credited with restoring a real sense of evil in the British novel. He certainly did that in his dark and terrible *Brighton Rock*. He is also sometimes credited with celebrating failure, and you could argue he did that in *The Heart of the Matter*.

But while he was seldom cheerful, he did always acknowledge hope. *The End of the Affair* is his best novel in my view and his most explicitly and fully Christian novel. It contains miracles which don't let the reader off at all. If you provide for this book the willing suspension of disbelief which all novel reading involves, you have to provide an at least temporary suspension of disbelief in Christian miracles as well.

The plot involves a simple set-up of morality versus desire. Maurice Bendrix, a novelist, is having an intense affair with Sarah Miles, the wife of a senior but personally ineffectual civil servant, Henry Miles, who is nonetheless in his way a gentle and kindly fellow. The scene is grimy World War II London, and Greene evokes its tackiness and seediness, its tiredness, well. He always conjures place superbly. Bendrix's flat is bombed and it seems he's dead. Sarah is distraught and, unknown to Bendrix, promises God that if Bendrix lives, she will give him up. Miraculously, Bendrix, who seemed dead, comes back to life. Sarah keeps her word to God. They separate, Bendrix is very bitter and soon enough Sarah dies. Bendrix gets hold of her diary and finds in it a long, passionate dialogue with God.

Sarah's act of renunciation, her promise to God, lead her nearly to despair but also into an intense relationship with God, and finally to an intense love of God. After her death, several miraculous cures are effected. The most dramatic concerns a man with a disfiguring birthmark across one side of his face. He too falls in love with Sarah. She rejects his romantic love— she is still married and determined to be faithful to Henry—but she kisses the mark on his face. This is a striking echo of Jesus touching the leper to cure him. A few days later the man's birthmark begins to disappear, and ultimately he is free of it.

The novel is always effective and involving, but it really soars, really becomes something remarkable as a work of art, when we get to Sarah's dialogue with God in her diary. This is writing in an altogether different register. She pours herself out to God: 'Let me forget me. Dear God . . . if I could love you, I'd know how to love them . . . I don't mind my pain. It's their pain I can't stand. Let my pain go on and on, but stop theirs . . . If I could love you, I could love Henry . . . If I could love a leper's sores, couldn't I love the boringness of Henry?'

After Sarah's death, Henry and Bendrix are reconciled to each other, all jealousy between them disappears and they begin to care for each other in friendship. Bendrix finds that he believes in Sarah's God. This brings him no happiness. I was reminded, the first time I read it, of C.S. Lewis in his absorbing memoir *Surprised by Joy*, finding that, initially, coming to believe in God was extremely unwelcome to him. Bendrix thinks for a minute that he hates God. He blames God for taking Sarah away from him. At the end of the novel, Bendrix thinks that he is too old and tired to learn to love, and asks God to leave him alone. But he has gone from dismissing the possibility of God, to actively disbelieving in God, to accepting that God is real, to blaming God for his misfortune, to finally recognising that God is love. The next stage would be to welcome divine love explicitly into his life. It is clearly a trajectory of hope, and that is where Greene leaves us.

The End of the Affair has been made into two excellent films, one in the 1950s starring Van Johnson and Deborah Kerr, and one in 1999 with Ralph Fiennes and Julianne Moore. Although the latter movie was nominated for Academy Awards, I think the 1950s film was better, and was perhaps the finest screen performance by the much underrated Van Johnson, one of the most effortlessly likeable men from the golden era of Hollywood.

It's very seldom now that you find Christian miracles in mainstream creative works—films or TV or novels. Once they were not uncommon. *Miracle in the Rain* in 1956, also with Van Johnson, was just such a one, where a soldier comes back from the dead to see his grieving sweetheart and return a coin she had given to him, as proof, perhaps, that he was there, to reassure her that love lives on. But there were many such movies with miracles. These were much rarer in literary novels.

The contemporary reluctance to credit Christian miracles is a paradox because in every way the culture has become more credulous about everything but Christianity, truly living out G.K. Chesterton's observation that when you stop believing in Christianity you don't believe in nothing, you believe in anything. Magic realism has introduced all sorts of strange occurrences into fiction—a human character becomes a salamander, a bird becomes a man, and so on.

In serious popular culture now, if a miracle is even considered a possibility there is normally an each-way bet. So there will be a natural explanation available, as well as a miraculous explanation. Sometimes there is only the appearance of a miracle. In *The Healing Art* by A.N. Wilson two cancer patients have their diagnoses mixed up and the one who is clear is given a false death sentence. After visiting a religious site she finds herself clear of cancer. This clever, wry book is overall sympathetic to Christianity, but it cannot quite trust the reality of the divine intruding into everyday life via a miracle.

Most Christian writers stop short of explicit miracles not, I think, because they don't believe in them, but because most people don't experience unequivocal miracles in their lives.

Some Christian novels, nonetheless, can reach to the extremes of human behaviour, encompassing almost the miraculous, without ever requiring the reader to accept direct divine intervention. One of the greatest Christian writers of the last hundred years is the Englishman Piers Paul Read. His bestselling book is *Alive*, a non-fiction account of Uruguayan air-crash survivors in the Andes forced to resort to cannibalism of fellow passengers who died in the crash, in order to survive. It sold five million copies.

In one of his great novels from the late 1980s, *The Free Frenchman*, set in World War II, the protagonist prepares for battle and expects to die. A Christian of decidedly rackety habits, he can nonetheless face death confidently because while he has not always lived a good life, 'he has sought the good'.

This is not only a phrase of great power but also acute moral understanding. It may be difficult to conclude overall that you've lived a good life, but more likely you can say that you've sought the good. I have been reading Read's novels ever since the 1980s. He was considered a foremost English literary novelist, winning all the big prizes except the Booker. His star has faded a little now, unfairly I think.

In one of his most Christian novels, *A Married Man*, a bored husband, John Strickland, idly reads *The Death of Ivan Ilyich* by Tolstoy while on holiday at his in-laws. He has given up serious reading because he's a busy barrister, but also he doesn't think books have any effect on people. But Ivan Ilyich makes him dissatisfied with his loving wife, good children and happy circumstances. To relieve this baseless and egocentric dissatisfaction, Strickland embraces pretty hollow political activism and a reckless promiscuity. Complications arising entirely out of his dereliction lead to his wife's death. Strickland himself discovers the bodies of his murdered wife and her own newly acquired lover. In an agonising scene, he remarks to his dead wife's brother: 'We weren't as unhappy as it must seem.'

There is a great power in this lament, for it is really a plea that Strickland's whole life, especially his marriage, was not worthless, notwithstanding the terrible murder he indirectly causes. The plea is that though he has caused such misery, not all his life was like that. There was beauty in his marriage, though for a time he was too stupid and self-absorbed to see it. This book was made into a more than good TV series starring Anthony Hopkins, one of the first big breaks of his career.

I got to know Piers across several stints I had in London. He is a man of deep faith, great warmth, remarkable erudition and absurd modesty. He is happy to talk about the controversial elements of Christian belief and all the affairs of the great world. But really I think he does that more to oblige visitors than anything. His faith is a central part of his daily life and he's really more inclined to talk about the readings at that day's mass. I found him a person of very easy companionship. It was like meeting up with an old friend. We had read so many of the same books, seemed somehow, between London and Melbourne, to have so many common friends, and without wishing to slander him by association, seemed to find that bond of friendship which arises from points of the deepest sympathy in outlook.

Read is also comfortable, artistically, at that 'dark and bloody crossroads', in Lionel Trilling's phrase, 'where literature and politics meet'. My favourite of his novels is *Polonaise*, set mostly between the world wars and then continuing for a little after World War II, in Poland, Paris and England. It concerns mainly three characters, Stefan, his sister Krystina, and her husband, Bruno. Stefan begins as something of an idealist, but becomes a corrupt and increasingly nihilistic figure, with a gift for writing but nothing of consequence to say, a kind of avatar of the modern age.

Exhibiting eloquence without substance, naturally Stefan is celebrated in the 1930s, that low, dishonest decade, as W.H. Auden put it. The 1930s that Read evokes bears more than a passing resemblance to our own time: 'The literary and artistic circles in Warsaw grew more varied, frivolous and obscure, and Stefan, now freed from ideological restraint, became known as the most seriously frivolous and lucidly obscure of all young writers of the Polish avant-garde.'

When a culture becomes seriously frivolous and lucidly obscure, as ours has, it is ever more difficult for the overtly Christian artist to find a place. The most sympathetic character in the novel is Bruno, a communist, though he, like Guy Crouchback, is purged by terror and pity in the war, only much more severely, and finds comfort in going back to mass. Bruno is killed by the Nazis, trying to save Stefan's abandoned family. The novel traces a long arc ending in Stefan finding his way back from perversion and decadence to belief and purpose, finally in defence of Bruno's daughter. There is terror in this novel, terror and corruption and despair. There is also beauty and redemption and hope. Read was rightly compared to Dostoevsky in reviews of *Polonaise*.

Australian Christian novelists have often been a little oblique in their religious purposes. I am thinking particularly of Chris Koch, who wrote the finest work of the imagination by a Western author about Indonesia, *The Year of Living*

Dangerously. It concerns a group of Australian journalists covering Sukarno's mad last year as president, in 1965, and his overthrow by Suharto.

This is the most artistically successful Australian novel I know. Reading it when it first came out, I felt the tropical sweat running down my back and could smell the sweet, clove cigarettes that once were Jakarta's characteristic aroma. This novel determined the course of my life because, from the moment I read it in 1979, I wanted to work in Indonesia and Southeast Asia. I did a lot of that in the next 40 years.

Koch became one of my closest friends for the last four decades of his life. He was a profoundly believing Christian, but the Christian outlook of his novels was often implicit rather than explicit. Nonetheless, it was unmistakable. In *The Year of Living Dangerously* there is a typically Kochian, Socratic dialogue between the protagonist, Guy Hamilton (played by Mel Gibson in the Academy Award–winning film, his first big role) and his assistant, Kumar, who is a communist. Kumar says the West no longer has any solutions to offer Asia: 'We will win, because we know what we believe and you believe in nothing but your pleasures.'

Another way for a Christian writer to dramatise questions of religion is to place the religiously anaemic culture of the contemporary West in close contrast with a more vibrant religious culture. In *The Year of Living Dangerously*, the cameraman Billy Kwan, a Christian convert who is undergoing multiple crises, comments: 'Lately, I have a feeling the Church has spent its passion. If it has, there's no place for me. There's something rather fine about Islam, don't you think? The passion's still there. I'm attracted to it.'

Of course, you cannot really have any acquaintance with Asia, which is something Australians should all want, without a sense of its vast religious hinterland.

Only once did Koch explicitly reveal his Christian purposes as a novelist. In an essay, 'Mysteries', in his collection *Crossing the Gap*, Koch wrote: 'This is all that a Christian novelist can do, in the end: to salvage joy wherever it's to be found, among the rubbish and waste and pathetic incongruities of life; and to show as well the results of its displacement; to identify those counterfeits that come to us in its place, whispering their lies of fulfillment, power and love.'

That was Koch's manifesto and it's noble. No one could admire him more than I do. Yet I do think some Christian novelists do more than that, or different.

Finally, the Christian novelist who has moved me the most is Willa Cather, like Marilynne Robinson a Christian woman from the American mid-west, Nebraska to Robinson's Iowa. Her two greatest novels, *My Antonia* and *Death Comes for the Archbishop*, are more like a magnificent celebration of life than conventional novels.

She wrote a hundred years ago, but her prose leaps off the page to grab your attention. Like Robinson, she won the Pulitzer Prize. Every sentence yearns for and finds a greater truth, a higher truth, a truth both more sublime and sweeter. Also like Robinson, she doesn't really offer a normal plot, not even necessarily psychological development. She renders instead the patterns of life and the most intimate depths of the human heart in prose which seems simple but has a cumulative power that I find just breathtaking.

My Antonia is a pure celebration of a good person, who survives her fair share of misfortune and even betrayal, not only survives but somehow radiantly triumphs, not by finding a good life, but by transforming a life that might look shabby from a distance into something radiant. I was completely bowled over by *My Antonia*, completely smitten by the heroine, happy, as was the novel's narrator, her friend, Jim Burdon, just to be in Antonia's presence. Like many Christian novels, it is a story of moral survival, but much more than that, of the transformative circle of grace that a human being can create. Cather was born a Baptist but became a faithful and serious Episcopalian. Yet in *Death Comes for the Archbishop* she somehow penetrates to the most secret chambers of the heart of two good priests. This great book, set in New Mexico in the nineteenth century, has rightly been described as less a novel than an act of prayer. I have never encountered a more flawless work of art.

Popular culture needs the presence of Christ, because good culture should always have a concern for truth and beauty. It might seem hard for Christians to get popular culture interested in Christ. But Christians have some advantages. Art, especially narrative art, is always, like journalism, on the lookout for good material. Christians have the best material there is for their stories. The proper subject for narrative art is the truths of the human heart. And at the centre of every human heart, even if unknown, is God. Christians only need to tell their stories well. The world will surely listen in time.

CHAPTER 8

Christians who keep giving

Immense love does not measure, it just gives.

Mother Teresa

In a gentle way, you can shake the world.

Mahatma Gandhi

Watching a television program changed Gemma Sisia's life forever, and the lives of thousands and thousands of others. Or maybe not. Maybe her extraordinary life would always have taken something like the course it did. Maybe the TV show was the occasion, not the cause. Gemma grew up on a huge sheep and cattle property near Guyra, just north of Armidale in the northern tablelands of New South Wales, and she had the kind of large country life, the big bush experience, which makes Australian legend, but which is becoming an ever-smaller slice of our nation.

She was born Gemma Rice, the fifth of eight children, all the others boys. Plenty of older brothers to compete with fiercely in farm work with cattle and sheep, and mastery of horses; and plenty of younger brothers who sometimes needed a hug and a bit of big sisterly mothering. The Rice spread was huge, 100,000 acres, and there was plenty of work to do.

Gemma's parents, Sue and Basil Rice, were Catholics, religious—their family home has a dedicated prayer room—and life for young Gemma was a rumbustious country adventure, though there was also a big stress on education and culture, learning a musical instrument, taking elocution lessons. It's a kind of big country life in some eclipse today.

'Our thing was horses,' Gemma tells me.

'On weekends we were at agricultural shows and horse jumping and travelling on country show runs. I thought this was completely normal. Gee, we were blessed. It was the best childhood. But every Sunday, wherever we were, mum and dad would find a church for mass. I still go to mass. I've never abandoned the faith.'

Gemma is 49 when I talk to her. We connect via Zoom. She is in Tanzania, near the city of Arusha, at the School of St Jude, which she founded 20 years previously, and I am in distant Melbourne. In our long discussion she takes me, via her laptop, on a bit of a tour of some of the school. I meet some of the people working in the office, have a look at the playground where I see hundreds of African kids running around enjoying themselves at lunchtime. It looks like a happy playground looks anywhere.

This school—three schools now—has become Gemma's life's work. The three schools—one primary, two secondary—have nearly 2000 students between them, more than half of them boarders. The students share only two things in common: they are very poor, and they have some academic ability.

Oh, and a third thing—because of Gemma, they will get as good a school education as almost anyone in Africa.

The road from Guyra to Arusha was long and winding, lots of stops along the way, and yet you have a sense that something like this was always in Gemma's destiny.

'When I was in Year 9 there was Live Aid, and I thought I'd just love to go to Africa and help.' Live Aid was an international concert organised by the Irish singer Bob Geldof in 1985 to raise funds for relief of the famine in Ethiopia.

Gemma's parents sacrificed a lot for her education and that of her brothers. Her dad, whom she loved with all the energy of an only daughter, was eventually forced to return to legal practice because the land didn't furnish a sufficient financial living for the family. But with all that Gemma, like her brothers, went to boarding school in Sydney for the last two years of her schooling.

She attended St Vincent's College in Potts Point. She admired the nuns. If anything, she was a bit more conservative theologically than they were and had many good-natured arguments with them about various issues: 'I really loved Sister Margie. She was the last headmistress of the school who was a nun. I said to her once that I was thinking of entering the convent. She said if I did that she'd leave.

'What attracted me to the nuns was the idea of service. I also liked the poverty part, living in poverty, living a simple life.' She found herself drawn to the service and outreach activities the school undertook, and those of some outside groups as well.

'It was the mid-1980s and the time of AIDS. I'd go [to] the hospice near the school and all these gorgeous young men were dying of AIDS. They'd been ostracised by their families and they were desperately lonely. We'd go there for a few hours and just keep them company. I loved working on the soup vans as well. I love the good feeling you get when you've helped someone, it's better than anything.'

Gemma worked hard to get into medicine at university but didn't quite make it. She reflects now that if she had got into medicine, she may well not have gone to Africa. It's very unlikely she would have founded the School of St Jude. So she enrolled in a science degree at the University of Melbourne, where she lived at Newman College, in the very same room her beloved father had occupied as an undergraduate. She was still determined to go to Africa to help out, but she wasn't quite sure how to do this. Sister Margie had told her the Sisters of Charity, who ran St Vincent's, had no establishment in Africa.

While she was at Newman College Gemma met Sister Kay, a nun from the Sacré Coeur order, who ran a school in Uganda: 'She inspired me. She told me about what she did in Uganda. She came back to Melbourne for cancer treatment. She told me she really needed maths and science teachers. She helped me to get a place in Uganda.'

And so, with very little idea of what exactly she would encounter, after graduation and a teaching qualification, Gemma travelled to Uganda to work as a teacher at the nuns' school. She lived with the nuns for several years and for a time thought that she might join the convent herself as a nun. But, while her admiration for the nuns has not dimmed, she realised that she herself was not meant to be a nun: 'It was pretty obvious pretty early that it wasn't for me. I like my independence. I didn't know there was any way I could be in Africa except with the nuns.'

She seems to have approached Africa a little like she approached Guyra, a great place for adventure, lots of people to get to know, lots of opportunity to help. With a friend from the Ugandan school, she went to Tanzania for a short safari holiday. Her safari driver, Richard Sisia, fell in love with her almost instantly, it seems. While she rebuffed him at first, and it was years before they married, she soon enough fell in love with him too, and they would have four children together. Though she spent a couple of years back in Australia before they married, and people tried to fix her up with 'blokes with utes', farmers and prospective family men, and her mother was initially against her marrying Richard, she truly loved him. They waited for each other.

Having met many remarkable Christians, I've found that there is no one, set way that Christian faith expresses itself, except that it always involves love and selflessness. With Gemma, her style and approach to life are not contemplative, or chapel pious, though she certainly goes to church and in every way is a believing Christian.

Without wishing to seem either blasphemous or theologically eccentric, I am reminded by Gemma's life of a lecture I once heard on the nature of God. The lecturer, the famous American scholar Robert Barron, in trying to explain the necessarily mysterious, commented that God is not really a noun, God is a verb. It's not so much that God exists as that he is actively being, he is the verb 'to be', rather than the noun 'existence'. That's a longwinded way of getting to the idea that Gemma Sisia as a person strikes me overwhelmingly as a verb, a doing word, rather than a noun, a name word.

Her life as an undergraduate didn't threaten her religious belief but was pretty kinetic, as the military folk might put it, and full of intense social activity, especially attending every Bachelor and Spinster Ball she and her brother could get to all across eastern Australia. Many young people drift away from their religious beliefs at university. This didn't happen to Gemma: 'I discovered college life, and seldom went to lectures. But I've never lost the faith. If anything, the faith gets stronger in hard times. At uni, there was a 30-minute mass at lunchtime. I could go to it because it was only 30 minutes long. I just found I had a better week if I went to mass. My brother Ben and I once drove from Melbourne to Armidale for a B&S ball on a Saturday night and we didn't get to sleep at all, so we went straight to mass on Sunday morning in the [Armidale] cathedral, with me in my taffeta dress and Ben in his dress shirt.'

Gemma has had one particular, and unlikely, helper all through her life, especially in everything she has done in Africa. That helper is St Jude, the Apostle, the patron saint of desperate situations and hopeless causes.

'I swear I have a direct line to the man,' she reflects, as she shows me the statue of St Jude which sits on her desk. Now, I don't want anyone to think Gemma is a heretic, an idolater or a polytheist. When she asks St Jude to help her, she is not asking him to exercise any independent, magical power. She is asking him to pray to God on her behalf, in a normal expression of what Christians call the communion of saints.

Having said that, it is astonishing how big a role St Jude has played in her life, and in her school. 'In about Year 9 you start challenging your parents and teachers. I was slagging off at the saints. My mother loved St Anthony [the patron saint of lost items] but I never found anything through St Anthony. And St Christopher [the patron saint of travellers] didn't stop me crashing my Valiant. I was saying these saints aren't much help. But my nan told me about this saint, St Jude, who is not very busy because people always get him mixed up with the bad apostle, Judas. So they're reluctant to ask for his help.'

The first time Gemma remembers asking for St Jude's intercession was after she'd had a fall from a horse that resulted in a serious injury: 'I was show-jumping at the state championship after [recovering from] a very bad fall and having been hospitalised. My prayer was around keeping me safe. Of course he kept me safe and I actually won the event so he did more than keep me safe.'

She has become close to St Jude and relies on him a good deal. Catholics have a form of prayers called a novena, which means a prayer or devotion repeated once a week for nine successive weeks. Gemma explains to me that you're not supposed to use the novena to St Jude for regular or trivial matters, but only in extreme cases. And in an emergency you can say an hourly novena, repeating the prayers, which are quite short, over nine successive hours, reciting the prayer at the beginning of each hour.

Towards the end of her university course, Gemma's intense socialising meant she was way behind in her study. Her friend Sara came round to her room for study nights just before the exams. At Gemma's urgings they prayed the hourly St Jude novena. The next day, Gemma was not even going to attempt the genetics exam because she hadn't been to any of the genetics lectures. But her friend prevailed on her to give it a shot anyway and—miraculously?—she passed. That may all seem trivial, but passing allowed her to enrol in an honours year in science, in which she studied much more conscientiously, and then in a teaching qualification. This paved the way for her eventual career in Africa.

There is nothing remotely sectarian in the way Gemma leads her life or runs her schools. Protestant, Catholic, Muslim, no particular faith at all—children of all backgrounds are welcome. And she has had staff—270 Africans now work at St Jude's—and volunteers of all faiths and none. Everyone's welcome who makes a real contribution.

Gemma's Christianity is intensely practical, and this Christianity lives, and is defined, exactly and fully in the life that she leads. But nor is she the slightest bit embarrassed or shy about her beliefs. She would as soon apologise for them as apologise for her family. Her Christian belief is there in every part of her personality. On one occasion, early on in the school's life, the school desperately needed a new bus. She prayed hard for St Jude's help and she told one of her non-believing colleagues that she was sure something, meaning St Jude, would come through in time. Sure enough, the fledgling school received an unsolicited, large donation that week, which bought them a new bus.

'I have a deal with St Jude,' Gemma tells me, 'if ever we can't meet the annual budget I'm changing the school's name.'

If Gemma's style of Christianity seems a bit strange to you, don't be too narrow-minded or too censorious. Or too prescriptive. It powers a magnificent life of service, and nothing is truer of belief than the life it inspires. Her familiarity with St Jude, which may strike you as flippant, or superstitious, or even irreverent, is the way someone talks about their close relatives. Not only that, life is often untidy. Christianity is sometimes untidy in response. It has more styles, and more mysteries, than any one of us can make out. God has his ways, and these are very diverse.

When Gemma first returned to Australia from Uganda she wanted to continue to make a contribution to Africa. She was convinced that raising education levels would be central to reducing the poverty which so afflicted girls and women in particular. So she raised money to help schools and provide scholarships. But in time she found a lot of the money was not being properly used. It was being raised for one purpose in Australia but finally being used for another purpose in Africa.

She developed the idea of founding her own school. Initially she thought this would be in Uganda. Once when she was visiting Richard's family, before they were married, his father said to her: why don't you build a school here in my village in Tanzania? We are poorer than Uganda and I will give you two acres of land. So that's exactly what Gemma set out to do.

She had no idea what it would cost and no experience of building at all, much less building in Africa. So she went back home to raise the money. She tells the story often. She had her first donation of $10 and no experience and no official backing and she dreamed of a wonderful school. It was about the most unrealistic ambition she could possibly entertain. Naturally, it was a matter for St Jude.

In one perfect piece of providence, Gemma hooked up with the Rotary clubs around Armidale and across New England. They had faith in her—and after meeting her, who wouldn't? The Rotary clubs became her main fundraising source. Rotary clubs are a magnificent, under-celebrated tradition of service in Australia. I have had a bit to do with them myself and they strike me as mainly good-hearted, small-business people and professionals—accountants, pharmacists, lawyers—who get together to enjoy each other's company, hear interesting speakers and make a positive contribution, through the work they do themselves and the works they support through donations and fundraising.

When Gemma finally got round to building her school, a group of volunteers from Rotary went to Tanzania to physically build the first classroom for her. The school opened in 2002 with three students. The two criteria for entry have never changed—the students must come from a family with genuine financial need and must pass an entrance exam which shows they have some academic ability.

The next twenty years were an epic journey for Gemma and her schools. The schools are now several clusters of beautiful buildings spread over two big campuses. She started very small. Initially, she and Richard lived in a single room that he built for them. Many of the earliest Australian volunteers at the school camped in tents in Gemma's garden and essentially lived with her and Richard while everybody pitched in to get everything going, from scratch.

Gemma had to convince the local community, and all the authorities, that her project was credible, that she was not just another fly-by-night non-government organisation that would pack up and leave when the going got tough. The sheer drive and effort involved in the whole thing were prodigious. Once a year she came back to Australia to do an exhaustive round of fundraising speeches. She tried to get people to sponsor individual students and build up the school's numbers that way.

There were early crises over money, over wells that were half dug and then abandoned, over builders who couldn't build straight walls, once or twice over staffing. Now, as she says, she has 'three very stable schools' but they were born of relentless effort, almost superhuman energy and a determination never to give up.

There were plenty of lessons along the way. Just saying the students are poor doesn't cover the whole circumstance of their lives and how that affects their education. She found that many couldn't concentrate too well because they were hungry. So she started to serve them a lunch. Now every student has a hot meal and a snack every day, and the boarders get breakfast and dinner as well.

Gemma shares the credit with everyone who has helped her but it's been her project and her responsibility. Early on, she found she really did need to personally supervise every load of bricks, every delivery of concrete, every serious expenditure. And a woman doing all this, much less a white woman with no pre-existing connection to the area, involved its own set of hurdles.

There have been bouts of malaria, times of missing mum and dad and brothers and friends, times of discouragement: 'People can think it's glorious working in the third world, but sometimes things get really hard. It's lonely, it's gruelling, everyone's in need. Things get very tough. There's a saying I love which has helped me a lot—this too will pass. Sometimes I chop the day into blocks, and say to myself, I've just got to get through to twelve o'clock, and then three o'clock, and then six.'

Much as she loves it, if she felt the school was hurting her relationship with her husband or her four children, she would give it away. She keeps a precious family life, entertaining any VIPs at lunch rather than dinner, seldom going out at night. Mostly, she's at the school all day and at home with her family in the evening: 'It's pretty hard to get me out of the house at night.'

She and Richard have raised their children in Christian belief: 'That's very important to us.' Her oldest son is staying in Australia when we speak, and she wonders how his faith will go: 'Coming from Africa, it's a very God-fearing culture, whereas in Australia I feel you're a bit ostracised for going to church.'

In Tanzania, Gemma tells me, when something good happens, a person will say: 'God is good' and the answer is 'all the time'. So that's an affirmation of faith every day—God is good, all the time. Though the school is not denominational, when necessary, Gemma has had the whole school saying the St Jude prayer. Every teacher has a copy of it. She puts a lot of trust in that saint's help. In 2021, when I talk to Gemma, the schools need a combined income of about $6 million a year to function. Most of that comes from Australia, none from any government, but there is now substantial support from American donors too: 'I'm blessed being able to connect people in need with people who can help.'

Gemma is excited because the first kids to leave her school have graduated university and some are now teachers. Soon the first doctors among St Jude's alumni will go into hospitals. Poor kids with brains, street smart and tough in their way, but hearts full of love as well, who just needed a chance. Every year, St Jude's is inundated with applicants: 'We get kids from 400 kilometres away who've never been in a car before, never seen Arusha before. Now they're students here, and without this school there's no way they could get this kind of education.'

Gemma strikes me as not altogether comfortable talking so much about herself, but there is no other way she could raise the funds that her schools need. Her motivation, I suspect, hasn't changed from Year 9, or from St Vincent's when she went to sit with AIDS sufferers and keep them company. As she said, 'I love the good feeling you get when you've helped someone.'

To my surprise, I find that Gemma Sisia has helped me too, for she's made me proud to be a human being.

* * *

Frances Cantrall was a normal young woman attending Schoolies Week on the Gold Coast. That sentence needs a little explanation. She wasn't normal by the standards of Schoolies Week. But it is the institution of Schoolies Week itself which has become a little abnormal, not Frances Cantrall.

Schoolies Week has become a kind of bacchanalian blow-out for high school students after they finish their final exams. Nothing wrong in principle with young people gathering for fun and letting off a little steam. But the event has become an occasion, sadly enough, for excessive drinking, illicit drug-taking, exploitative and hurtful sexting, sometimes dangerous physical stunts, random violence, and a culture of casual or even drunken hook-ups. It is now often an ugly scene.

Cantrall was there to offer the kids an alternative, to engage them in conversation about love. She was there to talk to them about a word they would surely never normally hear—virtue—and to suggest to them how they should expect to be treated in relationships, and how they should treat others. She believes you should love people and use things, not the other way around. She was scheduled to meet some others from her group, the Culture Project, a bit later that night, but right then, at the start of the conversation, she was the only person from her outfit on the beach.

She didn't feel isolated, she certainly didn't feel intimidated. She's a contemporary young person, at ease among lots of other young people. Her approach was to strike up a conversation with a young person, or a small group of them, and ask them: what is love? She walked towards a girl who looked approachable. But two young blokes wearing death metal T-Shirts were in the way. They decided they'd rather talk to Frances than have her talk to someone else.

She recalls the moment: 'I asked them: so what is love? They said to me: love is shit. So I tried another tack. I asked them what they were passionate about and they said death horror rap gore music. I'd never heard of this so I said can you give me a demo? They screamed out a horrific song which was about eating a baby. They said to me: we're very counter-cultural, you know. I said I'm counter-cultural too. So for six hours we just talked. They'd had really tough lives. One had lost his father to suicide. One had lost someone close to methamphetamines. They really said their plan in life was just to have some fun and then end it. Of all the people I've talked to, I thought they were the most resistant to what I was saying. But a year later I got a letter from one of them saying: you saved my life that night. I was just blown away. But you see, we all have an ache, a hunger, to hear the truth.'

This modestly astonishing incident cries out for some context. When I speak to Frances Cantrall she is, at 27, the founder and now a veteran organiser of the Culture Project. She spends her life ministering to her generation about love and integrity, virtue and respect, the integrated human person, and the reality of who you are as a human being and where you came from.

How did all this come about? Cantrall grew up in a small country town in the Hunter Valley, near Newcastle in New South Wales. She was raised in a Catholic family, practising but not fanatical, and has five brothers. She first learnt that there was such a thing as abortion when she was twelve. The sister of a friend had such a procedure. Cantrall investigated the matter in the way precocious twelve-year-olds do: she looked it up on the internet, read some books, talked and prayed, and by fourteen was organising seminars and talks to offer women and girls an alternative to pregnancy termination. Also at fourteen, she received her first death threat, delivered over the phone to her mother.

But really, she thinks the ball got rolling in her life even a bit earlier than that: 'Growing up, my parents would tell my five brothers and I that we were created for a purpose, something only we could do and if we didn't do it, then our world would miss out. A bit like a missing piece in a jigsaw puzzle. One of my most cherished memories is the birth of my sister, Rosie. She was born when I was ten years old. Rosie had health problems so I tried making a bargain with God. I had ten years of life, Rosie only had a couple of days. [The bargain was] that He should take me instead. When I realised I couldn't die instead of Rosie, I decided that I wanted to live the life for the two of us, that I wanted to figure out what her purpose was and to live it really well.'

Her aunt wrote a poem for Rosie, expressing the tiny baby's view of her few days of life. It finished with the lines:

Did you hear me whisper?
I spoke the words He asked me to
Love one another, as I have loved you!

This poem had a big effect on the ten-year-old Frances: 'I remember reading those two lines and it clicked. Love! That was Rosie's purpose, it was one word, it sounded easy, until the second day when I wanted to punch my brother. As I journeyed with friends and came up against the big questions of life, I realised that the issues we see in our culture are all symptoms of the same core problem. We have forgotten who we are and what we are created for. As human beings we were never made to be used, to be objectified, we were made for love. The reason I started the Culture Project was that I believe every human being is worth love and the only way anyone should be treated, including how we treat ourselves, is with love. If we did this, if we lived this, we would have a different culture.'

Nonetheless, Cantrall's road to founding this remarkable little organisation, the Culture Project, went through its own distinct stages, which now in hindsight may seem inevitable, but certainly didn't strike her as such as she was living through them.

Her family are townies, but they have cattle on agistment, so they live something of the farm life. She had been to a small school in a small town and was determined to go to a big university. Fate intervened: 'I was kicked by a cow.' This resulted in an injury which kept her away from her scheduled enrolment at the university of her choice in Sydney.

She journeyed down to Sydney a little later to enrol. A friend had talked her into visiting Campion College, the independent liberal arts college in western Sydney, on the way. Campion is a magnificent institution which, like many American liberal arts colleges, focuses on a 'great books' curriculum. Students spend the first year, intellectually, in the ancient world, studying philosophy, history, literature and theology. They study the same subjects in the second year, but this time in the medieval world. And then the third year they spend in the modern world: 'I got off at Toongabbie railway station and it was cold and miserable and I didn't want to be there. But I spoke to some of the faculty and students and I just felt such a sense of peace, I knew I had to go there. It was a place I was able to learn and to grow.'

She kept up her activism and at one point, while Cantrall was still an undergraduate, a young woman who was pregnant got in touch with her. The young woman wanted to keep her baby but was under all kinds of pressure to terminate the pregnancy. Her boyfriend was threatening to bash her to force her to miscarry so that he wouldn't have to pay child support. Cantrall helped her find alternative accommodation and ultimately the young woman had the baby. Cantrall was so moved by this experience, she wanted to leave Campion then and there and go into full-time activism: 'I'm a very impatient, prideful, stubborn person.' But wiser counsels prevailed, and she finished her degree.

There was the opportunity to do one semester as a visiting student at Our Lady Seat of Wisdom College in Canada, like Campion, a liberal arts college in the Catholic tradition. She spent a month undertaking training with an outfit called

Generation Life, which later became the US Culture Project. Although Cantrall's group takes inspiration from the US Culture Project, there is no formal connection. The Australian group that she runs is independent and all Aussie-made. There was one other Australian at the US training, and he and Cantrall were both offered the chance to continue working in the US. But they both had one more semester to go in their degrees and a big commitment to doing something for Australian young people.

Now the Australian Culture Project has, in Sydney's west, a house for boys, a house for girls, and a small office. Those who want to get deeply involved do a missionary year, an immersion year of full-time study and reflection and educational activities. Cantrall knew from her studies in history that a small group had set out to change the culture once before, so she modelled her organisation on the four pillars of Benedictine spirituality: prayer; formation; community; work or ministry.

By the time I speak to Cantrall, they've had some thirteen young people go through at least one full-time year of ministry and study, including lawyers, teachers and nurses. Some then stay on for a second year, some go back to their old workplaces, some have found a vocation in religious life. Beyond these thirteen, the Culture Project has attracted hundreds of volunteers.

The full-timers are indeed full time. They are supported by donors, but not big, rich donors. Mostly they are supported by friends and family. Each full-timer raises a salary substitution amount of sponsorship, enough to keep them going for the year they give to the Culture Project, a modest stipend composed of donations from different people who believe in the Culture Project.

The full-time year can be quite intense. The young people involved style themselves 'missionaries'. If the group warrants it, there can be deep study. Attendees are encouraged to attend daily mass, to set aside a 'holy hour' during the day. Then there is communal prayer, which is crucial to the life and spirit of the place. That's prayer taken care of. Each is encouraged to have a spiritual director, someone to advise them in the life of the spirit. This is either a priest or a nun. Nuns at two convents support them in spiritual ways, sometimes hosting them for spiritual retreats, or praying for them, though these nuns are not involved as spiritual directors.

Everyone is also very active in ministry: 'Our approach is to engage students on the level of the culture and share stories and ask questions that awaken their desires of what they were made for.' The group makes presentations to schools (always with teachers present), to university groups, youth groups and also turns up in pubs and at beaches, wherever young people are. They run a series of Restore Nights, which typically feature a guest speaker and fortnightly Culture Catch-Ups. A little like the Alpha program, which Nicky Gumbel in London pioneered (and which we will explore a little in Chapter 12), the emphasis on the discussion is respectful exchange, listening to young people as well as talking to them.

The simplicity and directness of their approach are important: 'This generation is really wary, very cynical—are you trying to sell me something? Are you trying to shove Christianity down my throat? We always start by asking "what is love?" and the students and young people themselves will get back to asking about God. The problem is we've forgotten who we are and what we're for. We came from God, who is love, and we'll return to God, who is love.'

Sometimes they are called in to talk to a group of kids who have experienced profound bullying, or an epidemic of sexting. The symptoms they see in their own generation are many—depression, loneliness, bullying, pornography, abusive and exploitative relationships.

The Culture Project bases its approach on the 'Theology of the Body', which was a course of lectures and reflections given by the late Pope John Paul II. He emphasised that every person shares in the body of Christ and that every human being is to be treated, and to treat themselves and others, with dignity. John Paul II not only put the human body on the highest level of dignity but saw its very existence as a divine revelation. He said: 'The body, and it alone, is capable of making visible what is invisible, the spiritual and divine. It was created to transfer into the visible reality of the world, the invisible mystery hidden in God from time immemorial, and thus to be a sign of it.'

The Culture Project is attempting something a lot of Christian groups have tried and found extremely difficult, and that is to communicate a counter-cultural message of substance in terms which are not only intelligible to contemporary people, but which instinctively appeal to them. At one level it's easy enough for Christians to proclaim their counter-cultural message. But doing so in the traditional way is frequently unsuccessful. For the circumstances they confront are ones in which the culture, or large parts of it, have been immunised against the Christian message, often against any Christian utterances at all. Traditional Christian language is either not understood or has been radically de-authorised. In coping with that, or reacting to it, Christians can easily go to the other extreme, and speak to the culture in such soothing, inoffensive and approved contemporary terms that their message finally has no substance, no distinctiveness, at all. It neither challenges, nor helps, the culture. To find an entry point into contemporary culture for Christianity, and a language with which to speak effectively to today's young people, and then to tell them about the timeless Christian truths in all their splendour, fulfillment and challenge—that is a remarkable achievement.

Cantrall and her colleagues at the Culture Project want to restore the culture, starting with their own generation. There's no easy or instant way to do this, no way it can be accomplished by mass media campaigns or internet brilliance, though such techniques have their place. It has to be done face to face, person to person, like the early Christians. She and her co-workers believe they have one profoundly important qualification for the work: 'The reason we're called to share this message is because we're the ones that need to hear it.'

* * *

Jenny George has high achiever written all over her. She is a former dean of the renowned Business School at Melbourne University, has a brace of higher degrees and could no doubt be earning as much money as she liked in private industry. Instead, when I interview her, she is the CEO of Converge International, a company which grew out of one Christian charity and is owned by another Christian charity.

George has high-profile professional achievements, but alongside them has always devoted a big chunk of her prodigious energy and talent to actively living out her Christianity. Converge International was originally an organisation providing chaplains. Now it provides health and wellbeing services, especially in the areas of mental health, to hundreds of Australian organisations. In the five years that she has been CEO, George has tripled the wealth of the company. She is not going to get rich out of this, however. The business pays dividends to the charity which owns it.

Among many other things, it provides about 40 chaplains to various organisations: 'We find that chaplains are better than counsellors at building relationships. Many of our chaplains are also counsellors.'

George grew up in an intensely Christian family in New Zealand: 'Everyone in my family was actively Christian. My four grandparents had come to faith as teenagers. I grew up in the Open Brethren [often known in popular culture as the Plymouth Brethren]. In the Brethren there are no paid ministers, everyone mucks in. My dad preached every third or fourth week. My mum did about twenty hours a week of pastoral work. The Brethren expected that your life would look different. Women didn't wear trousers, people didn't smoke or drink, you gave away a large part of your income, you gave away a lot of hours of work.'

George is an Anglican now, but she doesn't deprecate her Brethren past. Whatever criticisms you might make of the Brethren, its life involves something many Christians baulk at, and that is really allowing their Christian beliefs to rule their lives.

'My mind was shaped [as a child] by C.S. Lewis. I read the Narnia stories by about nine, *The Screwtape Letters* by the end of primary school and the rest of the books by fifteen, including the difficult ones. In *The Abolition of Man*, Lewis takes early issue with postmodern relativism.'

She also read *Why I Am Not a Christian* by Bertrand Russell. She was surprised that such an intelligent man could provide such a caricature of Christianity, attack a version of Christianity she couldn't recognise.

The Brethren don't go in for infant baptism. George made a decision at twelve years of age—often, it seems, a critical age in a person's development—for adult baptism: 'The NZ version of the Brethren became quite open. It became similar to the Baptists, the main difference being no paid ministers, and much more emphasis on communion.'

One of the distinctive features of the Brethren is that they see Scripture, the New Testament in particular, as their only creed. They emerged originally out of Anglicanism because they were dissatisfied that Anglicans, and other mainline churches, had lost sight of the purity and simplicity of trying to imitate the life of Christ as closely as possible. Of course, the way they interpret this is often controversial. Even George's grandparents did not vote, for example, such was their intentional standing aside from much of mainstream society. But her grandfather did place a religious tract into every letter box on the South Island of New Zealand, completing this monumental task in his 90s.

George did her first degree at the University of Canterbury in New Zealand. She became involved with the Navigators, originally a US Christian group, which had a big following in the military and emphasised memorising verses of the Bible and maintaining other spiritual disciplines. A very bright student, George later went to Stanford University to study postgraduate maths, which led in time to a PhD. There she joined a regular Christian Union group. These are the mainstream evangelical Christian campus groups and emphasise Bible study and Christian fellowship. Stanford was full of brilliant international students and George credits her time there with giving her something of an international education.

There she met the famous Catholic anthropologist, literary critic, theologian and philosopher Rene Girard. His distinctive contribution is to see human rivalry arising out of mimetic desire, or the wish to imitate someone we admire, or more specifically to have what they have. This rivalry leads to conflict, which results in the need for a scapegoat to take the blame, either the weakest party in the dispute or some innocent party whose persecution can create a war-solving unity for the warring parties. The sacrifice of Jesus in his death both provides the ultimate scapegoat, removing the need for other scapegoats, but also proclaims the innocence of the victim, glorifies the victim and undermines the scapegoat-blaming and -hating culture of violence.

George found Girard a charming man, but more than that, she worshipped at the same church as he did. She could appreciate his ideas more deeply after coming to know him as a good and decent human being. She describes the whole experience as 'mind-opening'. It was important to her that Girard not only preached goodness but was a good man, treating the people in his life kindly and with love, uniting therefore, as Christians should, belief and practice.

After Stanford, with her PhD in business and applied mathematics, she came to Australia with an academic career in mind: 'I don't actually like research so much. I like thinking but I'm more pragmatic and less precise than the ideal researcher. I love what we do here at Converge. I was in academia at Melbourne for 17 years, always at the Business School. I was Dean from 2009 to 2011.

'At the age of 40 I found I was pregnant with my first baby and stepped back a bit. In 2016 I came to Converge and it combines Christianity with a business role. The work we do is deeply rooted in the Christian idea of the person. The idea of mental health at work is deeply rooted in Christianity. Work is good for us.'

When she took over, George penned a theological reflection on what it meant for an organisation like Converge to be living Christian values. The first thing it meant, she wrote, was that Converge would work for the betterment of everybody, Christian and non-Christian alike: 'God's common grace, his work in the world, is extended to all.' She quoted the Gospel of Matthew (5:45) that 'He sends rain on the righteous and the unrighteous.'

Then, in answering the questions of what Christian values Converge aspires to, she nominated three: 'People—we believe that every individual has value and dignity and should treat others as they would like to be treated. Work—we believe that work is good and that meaningful work gives human beings purpose and satisfaction. Health—we believe that people suffer when they are alienated from their environment, from other people and from themselves, and improving mental health requires reconnection to healthy relationships and meaning-ful work.'

Converge operates all around Australia with some 270 employees and about 1800 contractors. Its first impetus came from the desire to help returned servicemen from World War II, then the Korean War, with all the issues they had in coping with their wartime experiences.

When George came to live in Australia she also had to work out where she would worship. In Palo Alto, the Catholic church she attended sang the liturgy: 'I fell in love with the liturgy. I had overcome the anti-Catholic prejudices of the Brethren.'

But she couldn't accept, theologically, the role of the pope, or of Mary, in the Catholic Church, so she ended up an Anglican, in a church with a very high, or formal, liturgy. At the same time she was involved in a parish which was ministering actively to Somali refugees. She met her husband, Matt, at this church, where he was an assistant minister. He later became the vicar at St James Old Cathedral Anglican church in West Melbourne.

When Matt and she first went to St James it had 20 worshippers on a Sunday. In a time of steep decline in Christian belief in Australia they have built that up to 80, and still practise a deeply traditional and musically rich liturgy: 'The anti-liturgy people are likely to be baby boomers, children of the [19]60s who don't want anything linked to history. Millennials are much more open to something which is 300 years old.'

So George is certainly a committed and well-informed Christian, living out social action, professional involvement and an active prayer life all in an entirely Christian context.

But she too suffers her doubts and is often enough assailed by the temptations of atheism: 'There have been plenty of times when I've felt like I just don't know if any of this is true. There's no compelling argument involved. I just look around the world and feel I'm not feeling particularly close to God. I've got through times like these through a series of things I tell myself. One is that I've gone into this [Christianity] in the past and found it reasonable. I remind myself of my twelve-year-old self who made this commitment. I feel almost like it's a marriage vow. I made a promise, there might be times when I'm not feeling it. It's very much like a marriage. I surround myself, through the choices I make, with spending time with Christian friends, so I'm getting enough Christian input from enough Christian people.'

She repeats this phrase which seems to have taken up a helpful residence in her mind: 'It's very much like a marriage, sometimes you're feeling it, sometimes not. It's relational, and you know it's going to get better.'

Paradoxically, perhaps, it's not the fact that the culture these days is unsympathetic to Christianity which might contribute to the cold periods in George's religious feelings. In a sense, it's the opposite: 'It's not what the culture might say about whether my actions are lining up with the culture. It's more likely that I'll feel [religiously] sceptical if there's no difference between my life and the culture around me, for example, if I'm not giving away a significant amount of money to Christian causes.'

Without wishing to verbal George, she is giving expression, I think, to a deep insight here. Christianity isn't always meant to make you comfortable. In our culture, so many people have told me in their different ways, if Christianity is not making you feel a little uncomfortable, and a little different, it is less likely that you'll hold onto it.

This thoughtful, alert, conscientious, intellectual and activist woman prays in two main ways—in the liturgy of her church, and in song. During the COVID period her parish organised three daily prayer sessions over Zoom—8.30 am, 5.30 pm and 9.00 pm. These prayer sessions are both liturgical and Scripture based.

Her other chief method of prayer is singing in choir, as well as privately playing the piano and singing hymns. The role of music in Christian life is intimate and central. Church music is the language of prayer for many people.

And then there are other times when George engages in mental prayer. That would seem quite a lot of prayer, and yet she says to me that she doesn't feel she prays enough. Very few Christians ever feel that they pray enough, yet they pray much more than people might realise. Though she has moved into a form of worship that emphasises high liturgy, George has kept some of her Brethren customs, such as memorising parts of Scripture.

Ritualised liturgy itself leads to the memorisation of Scripture passages: 'There is an aspect of ritual which is about the words seeping deep into your bones. With dementia patients, often liturgy or music seems to cut through and make a connection.'

I first met George at a small, informal Christian dialogue. I was impressed by the razor-sharp quality of her intellect and the directness, the cut-through, of her speech. She wasn't unfriendly. Everything she said was jovial, collegial in spirit. Nonetheless, her words were like a scythe cutting through the verbiage of the rest of us. I thought then: this is a formidable woman shaping her life to the service of the Lord. Characteristically, George is alert and analytical about all the trends in the culture, but she is not dismayed by them, and they don't really affect her approach, even to the public dimensions of her Christianity: 'We have to be faithful in the moment. I'm still infected by my evangelist approach.'

It's not as important to affect the culture, she says, as it is 'to be faithful and affect people. It's a soul-by-soul battle.'

CHAPTER 9

Light, and shadow, in the hearts of leaders

Not only does the democratic state of mind spring from the inspiration of the Gospel, but it cannot exist without it.

Jacques Maritain, philosopher and author of
The Rights of Man and Natural Law

Scott Morrison gave his life to God, committing himself to the service of Jesus for the rest of his days, on 11 January, 1981. He was twelve years old. He remembers the day and the moment with perfect clarity. He has never gone back on this promise.

When Morrison became Prime Minister of Australia in August, 2018, he made religious history of a kind. He was the first member of a Pentecostal church to become Prime Minister of Australia and the first Pentecostal to become a national leader in any developed nation.

There had been national leaders who were Pentecostal in Africa, but not before in a wealthy, first-world society.

The nation has got to know Morrison as a man and a political leader. But they saw the Pentecostal dimension of his faith explicitly on one rare and striking occasion. Easter, 2019—there is Scomo on our TV sets and in the newspapers, in an open-neck shirt, right arm high in the sky, palm forward, eyes closed, swaying in song and prayer, at the Pentecostal Horizon Church that he and his family have attended since they moved into Sutherland Shire on Sydney's southern beaches.

It is an arresting image, one we've not seen before. Prime ministers at prayer are normally solemn, not to say po-faced, in the front pew of an Anglican or sometimes Catholic cathedral, at Christmas or Easter, well dressed in a suit and tie. We almost never see them in their own regular worship, and if we had done in the past, it wouldn't have been like this.

TV cameras are normally present only for a civic occasion— state funerals and the like—or for a PM visiting a specific faith community, maybe the Lebanese Maronites or the Greek Orthodox.

Horizon Church asked Morrison if they could welcome the cameras in and he agreed.

I have known Morrison moderately well since just after he became his party's Shadow Minister for Immigration in 2009. In the normal way, as a foreign editor, I typically get to know foreign and defence ministers and their shadows. But I've always written a lot about immigration issues and often know those ministers and their shadows as well.

Morrison is an easy person to relate to because he is very direct. When he was immigration spokesman I talked to him a great deal. I have always been a strong supporter of a big and non-discriminatory immigration program, including a big refugee component, but I've also generally been opposed to people-smuggling and illegal entry. Morrison held similar positions, only more so, so we had a lot to talk about. However, this chapter is not about politics. People of goodwill, and certainly Christians, can disagree on these issues vigorously.

I might be completely wrong on everything I think about this issue. I profoundly believe that God and Christianity do not adjudicate between mainstream centre-left and centre-right politics. Christianity has a lot to say directly about life issues, because those are issues of basic human rights. And it has a lot to say about extremes—it would be completely impossible to be a genuine Christian and simultaneously a Nazi or a communist.

Often, though, Christianity gives you clear principles but not specific policies. As Morrison frequently says, the Bible is not a policy handbook. So it is abundantly clear that Christians are obliged to help the poor. How they do that is up to individuals and organisations, proceeding from goodwill. It is perfectly legitimate to think you can help the poor by giving trade unions more power to protect the low paid. Alternatively, it is equally legitimate to think you can help the poor best by deregulating the labour market, which might involve reducing union power, so that more jobs are created and fewer people are unemployed and thereby poor.

I have never met an Australian Christian politician I would say is not sincerely trying to live out their ideals and implement policies for the good—from Penny Wong on the left of the Labor Party to Andrew Hastie on the conservative side of the Liberal Party. It's legitimate for a politician to think: these policies are the best way I can give effect to my Christian principles; it's entirely wrong, except in extreme cases, for them to say, only this policy is a Christian policy, or, if you don't follow my policy, you're breaching Christian teachings.

As Kim Beazley used to remark, it was not a sin for someone to disagree with his policies. Morrison is at one with Beazley on this. I have never heard Morrison claim justification for any of his policies on the grounds that they are Christian policies. Yet Christianity is at the heart of Morrison's life and identity. In this chapter I am inquiring into the beliefs of four national leaders who have served at the highest levels our nation offers— one Liberal, one National, one Labor and one with no party affiliation. I am not primarily interested in how their beliefs affected their polices, though that is a perfectly legitimate question.

I'm much more interested in what they actually believe, and how their beliefs have affected their own lives.

Morrison doesn't go out of his way to talk much about his religious beliefs. His public attitude to them seems to me about right. He doesn't hide them, he's happy to share them with people if asked. When it's relevant he'll say a prayer, as for rain in a drought, but his religion doesn't determine any policy matter and he is the prime minister for all Australians, for Australians of all faiths and none.

Actually, when Morrison became PM, the top of his government, though populated entirely by white men, was uniquely diverse religiously. The prime minister was a Pentecostal. His deputy prime minister and leader of the National Party, Michael McCormack, was Catholic. And his treasurer and deputy leader of the Liberal Party, Josh Frydenberg, was Jewish, the first Jewish politician to hold that position. Each man had a continuing active participation in their faith. Pentecostal, Catholic, Jewish—a holy trinity of religious identities, as richly diverse, religiously, as you would find in any modern government.

Pentecostals are a booming Christian denomination, the fastest-growing Christian affiliation in Australia, and the fastest-growing Christian denomination internationally, though other Christian groups are also expanding rapidly in different parts of the world. It's only in the disturbingly non-performing West—Western Europe, North America, and Australia and New Zealand—that Christianity has been suffering serious decline in recent years.

Morrison and I have occasionally discussed religious matters privately in the past. Because I sometimes write about religious faith and experience, a number of politicians over the years have talked to me about religious issues, including a number of atheist politicians curious perhaps to hear a defence of belief. Many of these conversations I wish I could have over again, because for many years I think I was too cagey and wary about what I said. I certainly don't think I offered anyone much help.

After he became prime minister, I spoke to Morrison mainly about foreign affairs. I'm not claiming any special status here. Prime Ministers talk to a lot of people, including a lot of journalists. Talking to Morrison for this book is the first time I've interviewed him about his religion. Morrison was not always Pentecostal. Both his parents were religious: 'I grew up in the church. My mother is still going there. My father went there to the end [of his life]. Church life and community were wrapped up in one for us. My parents ran the church youth organisations for 45 years.'

The church in question was the Presbyterian church at Waverley, in Sydney's eastern suburbs, which later became part of the Uniting Church (which drew together Presbyterians, Methodists and Congregationalists).

Morrison's father was a policeman: 'Dad was in the CIB [Criminal Investigation Bureau] when Roger Rogerson [a famous detective later convicted of murder] was there. Dad was just known as a good cop, a straight-up guy. I asked him once: did you know Roger Rogerson? Yes, he told me, he was quite a charismatic character.'

But as anyone who has ever known and cared about a police officer will tell you, it's a tough and dangerous life. Morrison reflects: 'Dad's faith was a massive way of dealing with that job. I grew up under dad. He had no illusions that the world was a violent place. He sometimes had to deal with the worst of society. The light and passion of his faith helped him do that.'

The young Morrison participated in his dad's church-based musical theatre and even made a few television commercials as a kid. Morrison's parents were conservative Christians and they were deeply involved with their sons' lives: 'My mum said to me, when we were born, like Samuel's mother she handed us over to the Lord.'

Morrison's vibe these days is not essentially touchy-feely. He comes across as an Aussie dad, happy in the Shire, a good bloke at a barbecue. It's a constructed image but it's also true, just as John Howard was truly a cricket tragic, Paul Keating truly loved Mahler and French clocks, Bob Hawke was truly a sports nut who once had a problem with the booze, and so on. All senior politicians work hard to project a specific image. The best find something authentic about themselves to stand at the centre of that image.

One thing to like about Morrison, notwithstanding his knockabout, ocker style, is the straightforward way in which he talks of belief and religious identity when he deems it appropriate to talk about them at all. Ask Morrison if he believes and you get no equivocation, no qualifications, no tortured sub-academic dissertation on the nature of belief. Yes, I believe, he says. It's a representative Pentecostal style. It's a quality Pentecostals share with Muslims, among others: they're not embarrassed about God, they're not embarrassed about their religious customs and beliefs.

Morrison's pride in his father, in both his parents, is immense: 'Dad retired early at 55, after 35 years in the force. He retired as a Chief Inspector. He finished at Hillsdale near Maroubra. His worst experience was the Luna Park fire [in 1979]. Dad had to go there and identify bodies.'

Though they certainly weren't poor, there wasn't that much money in the Morrison household: 'We grew up in his [dad's] aunty's house. Dad and mum would work on the cruise ships, running the kids' program.' This led to Morrison and his brother getting their first experience of the South Pacific, where, incidentally, Morrison's Pentecostal faith is familiar, a point of connection, not a point of difference.

Given his home environment, it was likely Morrison would grow up either a committed Christian, or reject Christianity altogether. But Morrison's choice to be an active Christian was still emotional, intense and entirely personal.

As a child, Morrison attended with his family a huge Billy Graham crusade at Randwick Racecourse in 1979. By the strangest of coincidences, his future wife, Jenny, whom he had not yet met, was at this crusade as well. By an even odder coincidence, so was I. I am nearly a decade and a half older than Morrison, and an evangelical Anglican friend took me and another friend along. I found Graham impressive but I didn't feel drawn to go down to the altar at the end and make a dramatic life commitment. Hundreds, perhaps thousands, of people did so that night, which is how Billy Graham crusades typically finished.

Morrison's brother, Alan, a couple of years older than him, did go down to the altar to make his own life's commitment: 'I have this lingering memory on the night, my brother went down and he was two years older than me. I talked it over with dad. Dad said don't go just because your brother did. Wait till the time is right for you.'

Billy Graham had a big impact on Morrison, nonetheless. He never forgot Billy Graham. Morrison's extremely active parents ran the Boys' Brigade and the Girls' Brigade (a more Christian version of the Boy Scouts): 'When I was in Year 7 there was a pan-Australian camp of the Boys' Brigade. We had one in Nunawading [in Melbourne]. Dad and my brother and I went. There was an altar call at the end. I'd seen my brother do it at the Billy Graham crusade. It was a classic evangelical experience. On that camp I gave my life to the Lord, on 11 January, 1981. I was twelve. I massively felt it that day. It is a confession of repentance. I felt that movement, to get to my feet. I spent the rest of the day sitting with the chaplain.

'When I went through school I was known as the Christian kid. When I went to uni [the University of NSW] I used to go to the Anglican Bible Studies group. My brother started going to the Christian Brethren Assembly at Waverley Gospel Chapel. In my late teens he baptised me there, which meant a lot to me. I met [my wife] Jenny through their youth group. In Year 12 we started going out together.'

Morrison and his wife met when they were twelve years old and started dating in their teens. They had the briefest romantic break-up, long before their marriage, but have basically been together their whole lives. They married in 1990, just after Morrison finished university. Jenny is a nurse. There is nothing false in the tenderness with which Morrison always speaks of his wife. She is a warm and friendly person. As he has said, she really is the centre of his life.

It is well known that they struggled for 14 years, and many rounds of IVF treatment, to get pregnant. But they didn't want it to dominate their whole lives, so they finally gave IVF away and then, miraculously, their two daughters were conceived naturally, with Jenny falling pregnant for the first time at 39.

Morrison comments: 'The biggest blessing is the girls. We never thought we'd have them. God is in the waiting. Faith gives you the confidence. Faith is the source of strength. You try to trust to the Lord. We had many prayers from Christian friends. Abby was born the seventh day of the seventh month, 2007.'

The Morrisons have shared this story publicly, I suspect, for three reasons. People are intensely curious about their lives. Also, their experience might encourage and give hope to others. And perhaps they want to give public thanks for the miracle of their daughters' lives. I suspect a fourth reason as well. I have met Jenny a couple of times and she is, as I say, a warm and gracious, a generous person. It strikes me she might just have an in-built inclination to share the good news.

Morrison briefly considered going to the US to study theology after his uni degree and this would have involved at least the consideration of a career in church ministry. Former NSW Premier Mike Baird did something similar. Numerous politicians considered Christian ministry (Tony Abbott spent three years training to be a priest) or spent a year or two as volunteers in overseas Christian or aid settings (Kim Beazley did that in India, Penny Wong in Brazil). Some, such as former South Australian Labor Premier Lyn Arnold, and former Keating Government minister Michael Tate, went into Christian ministry after their careers in politics. Pat Dodson had been a Catholic priest decades before he became a Labor senator. This is not really surprising. We are much too cynical about our politicians and underestimate the moral seriousness with which many of them approach their lives. Mostly they are joiners and activists, people who really do want to make a difference.

Morrison's journey to the Pentecostals was gradual and fortuitous. It did not involve rethinking any big theological issues. In 2000 he got a job in New Zealand and he and Jenny went to church at the Christchurch Brethren Assembly: 'They were a lot more charismatic [in style]. We had some wonderful pastors and friends there. I love that type of worship.'

Pentecostals are not as well understood outside their own groups as they should be. I confess a bias. I admire them a great deal, their energy, their openness and enthusiasm about their faith. Pentecostals are a mainstream Christian group and their doctrine is orthodox and Bible-based. Things people tend to like about them are a tradition of great music, a positive, cheerful outlook and an energy about their worship and their community personality. Like all Christian movements, like all human movements, they've had their scandals, but that just proves they're human like everyone else.

Pentecostal theology centres on the gifts of the Holy Spirit. Perhaps the central passage in the New Testament that inspires Pentecostals comes in the Acts of the Apostles: 'When the day of Pentecost had come, they were all together in one place. And suddenly from heaven there came a sound like the rush of a violent wind and it filled the entire house where they were sitting. Divided tongues, as of fire, appeared among them, and a tongue raised on each of them. All of them were filled with the Holy Spirit and began to speak in other languages, as the Spirit gave them ability.'

Pentecostals are a rapidly growing denomination with perhaps half a billion followers worldwide. They are also a movement within other denominations. The Catholic Church has its own first cousin of the Pentecostals, the charismatic movement, which also emphasises the gifts of the spirit. The traditional point of theological difference between charismatic and Pentecostal is that the latter has also taught a second baptism in the Holy Spirit. Catholics receive something which is roughly equivalent to a second baptism in the Holy Spirit, in the sacrament of Confirmation.

The gifts of the Holy Spirit have always been part of Christian belief. Modern Pentecostalism grew out of a little, impoverished, mixed-race church in Azusa Street in Los Angeles in 1906. It was led by an African-American pastor, William Seymour, a son of freed slaves. That certainly has the right Christian feel about it as the starting point of a big revival. One of the features that most propels Pentecostal success, I think, is its emphasis on experience rather than intellectualising. Its church services tend to be emotional and uplifting.

The most controversial aspects of Pentecostalism are speaking in tongues and faith healing. These practices are much less strange than they might seem at first blush. Almost all Christians of all denominations pray for the sick and hope that their prayers will be answered. They, too, believe in faith healing. Speaking in tongues happens a lot in the New Testament. Pentecostals believe speaking in tongues is the Holy Spirit enabling them to pray. A friendly sceptic might view it as a kind of free-range vocalisation of the sentiment of prayer. There is nothing in it of superstition or of the sinister.

Morrison takes up the story: 'When we came back to Australia in July 2000 we really appreciated that style of church and we started going to Hillsong church, in Waterloo [an inner city suburb]. It's a bit different from the one in the Hills. It suited us, it was big, we made a lot of friends. Later we went to ShireLive. It's now called Horizon Church. I've never been that fussed about denominations. I just like a community, Bible-based church.'

So how does Morrison feel about the character of modern Pentecostalism?

'There have been a lot of changes in the Pentecostal church. It's mainstreamed a lot. The gifts of the Holy Spirit still take place. It's part of their theology and belief. I could count on one hand the number of times I've heard it preached about. Baptism of the Holy Spirit is basically someone praying over you. I don't speak in tongues. The preaching is very practical, about how you live your life. Twenty years ago it was more doctrine heavy. While those things are still there, baptism of the Holy Spirit is more a prayer, a pastor prays over you. If you feel the need to be prayed over, people come and lay their hands on you. As a new MP I used to quite enjoy going to Catholic churches and experiencing the liturgy there. I like the peacefulness of the Catholic worship. I also love the energy and the exuberance of the Pentecostal worship.'

Morrison tells me there are times when he has felt profoundly moved and comforted as fellow Christians have prayed over him. One highly unusual occasion Australians saw Morrison pray, and talk about praying, came in April 2021 when a video was taken of him speaking to the Australian Christian Conference, the national gathering of Pentecostals.

He told his fellow Pentecostals: 'I've been in evacuation centres where people thought I was just giving somebody a hug, and I was praying with them. God has been using us [Morrison and his wife Jenny] to provide some comfort and reassurance.'

Morrison confirms to me that obviously he only prays with people if they want him to, with their permission. Surely praying for someone cannot be seen as an act of arrogance. Christians are encouraged to pray even for their enemies, as Jesus did, as well as those they see suffering right in front of their own eyes.

And the gesture of touch, the laying-on of hands—it certainly has a Biblical resonance, but it is also a timeless expression of human solidarity.

Morrison also spoke that day of how he seeks inspiration from God in tough times. He recounted being on the Central Coast during the previous election and feeling discouraged: 'I was saying to the Lord, where are you? Where are you? I'd like a reminder.'

Then, in the gallery he happened to be visiting, he saw the image of a giant eagle and as with so many religious people a verse came to him, this time Isaiah 40:31: 'But those who hope in the Lord will renew their strength. They will soar on wings like eagles; they will run and not grow weary, they will walk and not be faint.'

That verse, prompted by the sight of the picture of the eagle, spoke directly to Morrison, as he told the Pentecostals:

'The message I got that day was, Scott, you've got to run to not grow weary, you've got to walk to not grow faint, you've got to spread your wings like an eagle to soar like an eagle.'

This is not Morrison claiming falsely to be the anointed eagle of God, swooping down from the heavens to deliver justice, truth and the American way. It is rather the old, old, good story of a Christian finding inspiration in the word of God when he feels weary.

Morrison also quoted at length from the moral insights of the late Rabbi Jonathan Sacks, whom he joked read the Old Testament more than the New. He spoke of community as the focus being 'not on you, but the person next to you'. He spoke of many things, but I mustn't get distracted by politics.

Instead, let's return to the discussion of Morrison's faith.

How does Morrison pray privately?

'I try to pray every day. When I can I'll get down on my knees. Getting down on your knees is a sign of complete dependence in your life. Other prayer is conversational, in the garden at home or wherever. Prayer is an important act of submission and acknowledgement. It involves humility, obedience, submission, faith and thanksgiving. The Bible is massively important to me. It's got easier now that it's on your mobile phone. This year I've been reading the Old Testament. I'm currently reading about Ruth. I read parts of the Gospel regularly. Faith is not passive. Faith is an active process of engaging with God. Generally I won't talk about it too much. It's got nothing to do with politics. It's really relevant to me. I couldn't function without it. My faith informed my life.'

It's important to try to understand exactly what Morrison is saying here. Faith is central to Morrison and he brings his whole personality and values and principles to politics. But faith does not dictate his specific policies. Therefore, he thinks it's unfair, if someone disagrees with his policies, to attack his faith, or to claim he is trying to impose his faith on others through his policies.

Sometimes this sort of thing gets on Morrison's nerves: 'One former politician on a plane gave me a gobfull about my faith and my decisions. I said to him—you can judge my policies as a Liberal and you can judge their efficacy. You can't judge my relationship with God. There's a lot of prejudice and ignorance. It's like going surfing or going to the football. The fact that I go for the Sharks doesn't affect how I put the Budget together.'

Morrison is assuredly not equating Christianity with supporting a particular football team. He does seem to be saying that being a Christian, like supporting this football team or that, does not predict or determine what policies you will support on most issues.

Morrison took tough decisions about boat people when he was Minister for Immigration. I often talked to him about those matters and I know he worked seriously and sometimes agonisingly through the ethical issues. He believes that what he did was morally justified and in the national interest. But at times he struggled emotionally with the grim situation and with the consequences of these decisions. At home with his beloved Jenny he was in tears over the moral gravity of the decisions he felt he had to make.

'Do I search my soul and spirit when I make a tough decision? Yes. The Bible is not a policy book. I do believe I did the right thing. It's not that God told me to do it. I always had a practice of visiting every detention centre in Australia. You've got to accept the moral consequences of the decisions you make.'

Generally, Morrison finds not only acceptance but warmth from most people over his faith: 'In the mainstream community there's no prejudice. In the commentariat there's a lot of prejudice, and on the political fringes. Generally people are perfectly cool with my faith. If I'm trying to engage with Islamic or Jewish or Hindu communities, it's a point of connection. There's a very easy meeting of people of faith. I've formed a lot of really good friendships with leaders in the Pacific.'

People write to him a lot about these issues: 'The letters I get are amazing and it's a lovely thing. People send me all kinds of things. That's been a tremendous encouragement for me. It's not something I politicise. People send me books, devotional studies, they knit things, it's lovely. I don't mind it when people come up and talk to me about it. If there's one thing Christianity teaches you it's about your own vulnerabilities. I'm not there to judge people's souls.'

Does Morrison believe in eternal life? 'Absolutely.'

Will he see his father again? 'When we go to glory. I absolutely believe it.'

Will we be judged on our lives? 'Of course, we all are and we've all failed. That's why Jesus came, to save, not judge. The doctrine of grace says that none of us gets there on our own. Of course I absolutely believe in eternal life.'

I believe he does.

* * *

The road to Australia's most unlikely YouTube, webcast and podcast sensation is long and strange. It begins at Tamworth airport in northern New South Wales. John Anderson, the still ludicrously handsome former deputy prime minister (Germaine Greer once said he was the only Australian cabinet minister she wanted to bed) meets me in a well-used family four-wheel drive. Punctiliously courteous, he spends five minutes apologising for being 30 seconds late.

I knew Anderson only very slightly when he was a politician. I met up with him later, in odd circumstances, really. He was staying with an old friend of his, the distinguished medico Professor Bruce Robinson, in Perth. Bruce is an old friend of mine too and he had lying around his house a copy of a book of mine, *God is Good for You*. Anderson read it while he was there and rang me to suggest we catch up. This began a long and rich conversation between us and led to the invitation to come and stay at his property for a few days. We are nearly exact contemporaries, born eight days apart, a few hundred metres from each other in different Sydney hospitals.

My visit takes place during a terrible drought. As we drive away from Tamworth and its town water the land gets drier, more distressed. An hour on the road and we stop for coffee at Gunnedah, then it's back on the road, another 45 minutes west, through Mullaley, the last in a series of down-at-heel little towns before arriving, at last, at Anderson's beloved cattle property, Newstead.

It should be beautiful, and 12 months later when the drought has broken, Anderson texts me photos in which rivers of grass swirl majestically through his land. But during my visit the land is devastated by drought, and bleak, the odd little patch of green reflecting maybe an hour's rain a week ago. And the property is all but bare. The family destocked months ago, selling cattle when they were still fat and valuable, before they cost a fortune to feed. Anderson's wife, Julia, and his daughter-in-law Alex, wept as they loaded the last cows onto the trucks.

'It's a strange thing to come back here and not want to drive round the paddocks just for morale,' Anderson reflects.

You cannot understand Anderson, a sixth-generation grazier and farmer whose family has been on the land since 1840, without understanding something of this property and all that it has meant to him. His family represents a rich vein of Australian life which has been, as an influence on our nation, on a long, slow path of decline. But that is not the most compelling aspect of Anderson in his maturity. Astonishingly, Anderson became a super-hit on the internet, preaching, among other things, Christian belief and Christian values. This is quite a feat, given how poorly his property, like much of rural Australia, is served by modern communications. While there, I can only access the internet by hotspotting on Anderson's mobile. As if rural life is not hard enough, we handicap it in a thousand extra ways.

Anderson founded a website through which he has been viewed by millions of people worldwide. It follows a straight-forward formula—he asks people he admires to join him in conversation, something between an interview and a fireside chat. He does the interviews in a little studio in Sydney, paid for by a couple of business backers. He takes no salary from the venture himself. And now there is a vast reservoir of material on his website. His first such interview, with

Canadian psychologist and life values guru Jordan Peterson, was viewed by more than a million people. They talked about values and culture and what it means to live a good life: 'I hadn't met Jordan till that morning. I was fascinated with his love of history and his deep, passionate, earnest interest to help young people reground themselves. He was involved with young people he'd met in Melbourne, who were really looking for reality. The conversation went for an hour and 23 minutes and I told him we'd get that down to something reasonable but he said, no, don't edit it. He told me young people are not reading books now but they will listen to content on a podcast. Leave everything in, he told me—all the content, the tears, everything. And of course he was right.'

Part of the popularity of the website comes from Anderson frequently discussing Christian belief. He also talks about culture, values, life, meaning. Of course he engages politics, too, but I'm not concerned with that here.

As it happens, some months later Anderson decides to nominate for politics once more, offering himself as a Senate candidate for the Nationals. He later talks this over with me and even here my sense is that his motivation is at least as cultural as it is political.

One of his most popular guests was Peter Hitchens, the Christian apologist brother of the late famous atheist Christopher Hitchens. Popular Australians include John Howard and Kim Beazley. The conversations can go for a long time—90 minutes is common—so he'll get an author who has written at length about the unity of Christianity and science, or the crisis in the Western understanding of fatherhood, and really dive deep down into those issues.

And of course the net is so accessible and so international. Anderson's biggest audience is in the United States, followed by Australia, Canada and Britain. People watch his interviews on YouTube, or on his website, or download the podcast. Christians routinely lament that today's culture is turning against them. One of the best things they could do in response is create high-quality cultural content themselves. That's just what Anderson has been doing.

After six years in the job, Anderson stood down as deputy prime minister in 2005 and left parliament in 2007. This was genuinely for family reasons, but, as with all the best politicians, there is this relentless hunger to contribute something more, this search for a way to make a difference—it enters into their souls, perhaps it was always there from childhood. The website, and a new willingness to get involved in public advocacy, are Anderson's way of making another contribution.

We talk for a while in his library, a formal, serene room that is full of books—many of them on Christianity—though in truth the room itself is now not much used. As with most country homes, life revolves around the kitchen. And it is in the living area flowing from the kitchen that Anderson has his computer and from where he does most of his non-farm work. Son Nick and his wife, Alex, now run the 1800-hectare property and live in their own cottage nearby. Mostly, Anderson and his wife live in the big house, which is spacious rather than grand, on their own.

On my first night, Anderson invites a dozen close friends for a sit-down dinner on the front lawn. They are doctors, pastoralists, neighbours, and their conversation, focused on public affairs and international relations, is thoughtful, sophisticated, well-informed. Their interests and their culture are outward-focused, curious, urbane. They talk easily about their properties, but underneath everything is a throbbing anxiety about the drought.

People in the bush work hard, but they have time to think and to read. In my time at Newstead, I never see the television go on. Anderson's wife, Julia, is away; daughter Laura is staying. Julia's absence makes its own contribution; you learn something of a man from the way he speaks of his wife. The tenderness and respect with which Anderson speaks of his wife tells me something of her, and of him.

You might think that Anderson's Christianity is predict-able—after all, he's a conservative cattle grazier from a long line of conservative cattle graziers. But the road to his Christian convictions has been long, longer than the road from Newstead to Canberra. And it involved a period when he didn't believe in a good God, a time of anger with God. Anderson's basic attitude to life is gratitude. He expresses this sentiment often. But life has dealt him some savage blows. His parents married late and his mother died from cancer when he was just three. He has just a couple of wispy memories of her. One was when mum and dad and young John drove all the way to Tamworth to pick up a new truck and he was given the special honour of riding home in the truck with dad. But he remembers mum on the drive in.

There followed a series of governesses for Anderson and his little sister, but he has fond memories of only one of them. Anderson's dad was a good man, but he never fully recovered from his World War II injuries. Under tank fire he tried unsuccessfully to pull a young bloke into the trenches beside him. The young fellow died and Anderson's father copped fearful shrapnel wounds that should have killed him. In his childhood, Anderson would hear his dad in the middle of the night screaming out: 'Get down! Get down!'

Still, Anderson's father did his best by his kids. Every afternoon he would make some time to spend with them. A little before he was fourteen, home from The King's School in Sydney where he boarded, Anderson was practising cricket with his dad on the front lawn of his house. Even today Anderson looks a sportsman. He was once destined for high honours in cricket. Quite a distance away from Anderson and his dad, Jane, his younger sister, was playing with a kitten. Dad was bowling and young John hit the ball perfectly, in the sweet spot. Dad had been a fine athlete himself and John could sense his pride in his son's perfect shot. Good shot, John!

But suddenly his sister looked up, saw the ball speeding towards her and turned her head. The ball struck her on the base of her skull and she died.

Anderson rarely talks of this incident, but he will do if he thinks it might help someone who has suffered similar tragedy. One day, on a rambling walk around his property he tells me more of how he felt about it: 'My childhood ended that day. It was shattered. For a long time afterwards I was thinking— can this pain ever end? I was never suicidal. I was at King's School, where people were considerate. But the concept of a God who loves me and can love made me angry. I believed in an impersonal God.'

The pain didn't go away. He learned to live with the pain.

The death of his sister, even now, is never far from Anderson's mind. There is hardly a day when he is not conscious of her.

It made him seek out his own answers to life's basic questions: 'Blaise Pascal is right—we hate religion because we fear it might be true. At Sydney University I had a great lecturer who one day said to us—you have three choices, embrace your fathers' faith; reject it; or sit on the road. I made an intellectual decision that day that it was better and more rational to believe than not to believe.'

That was Anderson choosing life, when death in its manner beckoned.

The best bit of luck Anderson ever had came when he met his wife: 'Partly because I'd had such a shattered family life myself, I really craved the family life that Julia brought me.' All of this, and that restless inner voice so many politicians have, led Anderson to public service. He was thrilled to become leader of the Nationals and deputy prime minister, but truly hated being away from Julia and the kids for extended periods: 'Politics is murder on the family.' So, at the age of 50, he gave up politics to return to the farm and the family he loves.

Like so many people on the land, Anderson is well and deeply read. He is an evangelical Anglican, not pushy but forthright. And he has, in that evangelical tradition of bearing personal witness, a willingness to confront the deepest feelings, the deepest issues, and deal with them directly. The style is slightly different from the Pentecostal style. It is not so exuberant, tending more to the sober, even the grave, but it is still direct. All of his life experience, and all his Christianity, Anderson fed directly into his website.

For the measure of its success is not just quantitative—how many people view a particular interview—but qualitative, what effect does it have on individual lives. Anderson is especially thrilled that so many young people have responded to it. His direct interactions with viewers of the webcasts are telling: 'One girl got in touch and said she had been drifting into atheism and dreaded telling her mother about this, but then she listened to Jordan Peterson and others on the website and they brought her right back to the faith.'

Anderson has been willing to engage directly with people, especially concerning Christian issues, who respond to his interviews. Two cases are illustrative: 'One young fellow wrote in and said he was a uni student studying X, Y and Z and felt overpowered by the progressive postmodernism that he felt he was surrounded by. But he told me he'd discovered the website and that allowed him to reground himself. Then he said: since you're responsible for all this would you allow me to buy you a cup of coffee? The two met in Sydney and became fast friends. Anderson has become a mentor to the young man.

The most intense interaction concerned a young boy who had been involved in a farm accident in which a close mate had died. The boy felt responsible for his mate's death. His uncle emailed Anderson to say both the boy and his father were in a bad way. Perhaps he was thinking there might be an email in return, a word of encouragement, even maybe a phone call. Julia was away for a couple of days and there were plenty of spare bedrooms on the farm. So, though the farmer lived far away, Anderson suggested the family drive up and spend a day or two with him at Newstead. Their time on the farm involved some burnt steaks and plenty of tears.

Anderson took the father and son on a walk around the farm and showed them exactly where the accident had happened all those years ago with his sister: 'I said to the young fellow—I'm showing you this in a way I haven't even showed my wife. I told him the whole story because I wanted him to know he was not alone in his experience. At one point I said to him— your dad believes in you, I believe in you, you've got to believe in yourself, you must draw on the belief that others have in you, just like I had to myself all those years ago.'

Creating the website, and coming back into the public domain, also meant for Anderson 'coming out' more openly as an active Christian. Australian politicians, and ex-politicians, are generally very modest about their religious affiliations. First, despite the defensiveness politicians have to adopt, they are all deeply aware of their personal flaws and they don't want Christianity to be judged by their lives. Second, they don't want to sound holier than thou, as though they are setting themselves up as paragons of virtue. And third, they don't want to give any succour to religious sectarianism—one faith against another, one denomination against another. And finally, much of the culture and media are often hostile to public religious belief and they don't want new headaches.

But contemporary politics demands authenticity. We want to know ever more about our politicians. And Christianity has been so much under attack. A new mood, I think, of modest disclosure is coming into play. Anderson reflects on the change: 'I think it's true to say I was one who kept fairly quiet about faith in public life. People knew I was a Christian. But recently I've felt a responsibility to own my faith in the public space.'

Perhaps surprisingly, Anderson attracts little hostility: 'My objective always is to be courteous. I haven't really had a negative reaction.' Civility is important to Anderson, something he practises, something he respects. He's worried about its frequent absence in public debate: 'People can still think and they can still feel, but they can't tell the difference.'

During my stay at Newstead, I meet two of Anderson's adult children, Laura and Nick. Like his dad, Nick is a political conservative but is across every latest development in agriculture and talks of farming 'within the environment, not against it'. He loves the family property but says that even if he and his wife weren't living on it for some reason, they would do something else in agriculture. The ease both daughter and son have in dad's company is not something I think you could fake.

Anderson's youngest son, Andrew, was born when Anderson was a busy cabinet minister. Andrew was profoundly disabled. He lived only a few short months and was constantly in and out of hospital. Julia later wrote an essay revealing that while they knew before the birth of the disabilities he would face, the Andersons never considered terminating the pregnancy.

In his eulogy for his son, delivered on 19 August 1998, Anderson said: 'Andrew's life often saw us wondering what we'd done to deserve so much difficulty. His passing sees us wondering what we did to deserve so rich a blessing. This little fellow was quite defenceless and yet he was to totally and utterly disarm us. God taught us something we'd heard about, but not really understood, that his grace is sufficient for us, for his power is made perfect in weakness.'

* * *

Peter Cosgrove was perhaps the most popular soldier in Australia in the last 50 years. Head of the international peace-keeping force (INTERFET) in East Timor, Chief of Army, Chief of the Defence Force, Governor-General—it was a storied military career.

He was a good soldier, obviously, an effective leader. But he also had something quite rare, and that was a genius for communication.

Let me give you just one example. In 1999, Cosgrove was appointed to head the international force in East Timor, after the East Timorese in a referendum had voted overwhelmingly for independence from Indonesia. Order had broken down and brutal militias, who wanted East Timor to remain part of Indonesia, had been killing civilians, looting and vandalising property. Cosgrove was asked on TV how Australian soldiers would deal with the militia, who were capable of such violence. He replied along the lines of: 'They're very good at killing women and children. Let's see how they go against trained soldiers.' It was the perfect answer, exuding both quiet confidence and moral purpose.

On another occasion, much later, Leigh Sales on *The 7.30 Report* was asking him about his memoirs and how he would have acted, as governor-general, in a constitutional crisis. He answered to the effect: 'Well, Leigh, when you're governor-general, every night before you go to bed you say, Lord, don't let the country be in constitutional crisis.'

A straightforward answer, which involves a declaration of prayer, is instantly relatable and moves the discussion onto a friendly plane.

Evelyn Waugh, in his majestic World War II Sword of Honour trilogy, has his hero, Guy Crouchback, marvel at the way senior officers can flow so effortlessly between different modes of relationship and communication—one minute a friend at the bar, another a kindly brother, then after that a commanding officer whose orders need to be obeyed straight away. Cosgrove's bluff military manner is perfectly authentic, but it's also something he works on. It's both defensive—it defuses a lot of controversy—and it's proactive, it's a way of entering into someone else's world on a friendly, even intimate, basis.

He rang me up once to ask about some international matter. We played telephone tag a bit and had trouble connecting. When he finally got through, he began the conversation: 'G'day Greg, you got a minute for an old digger?'

The hero of East Timor, the former governor-general, the bestselling author, approaches me with the line—got a minute for an old digger?

Well, yes, guess what, I got a minute for an old digger.

I have known Cosgrove for many years, not terribly well, though we seem to be great friends when we talk. I wrote a lot about East Timor, and about military matters generally, and in the way of politics and journalism and high military affairs, Cosgrove and I ran into each other periodically. I always took the opportunity to ask him about military policy. Because as well as the bluff good humour, Cosgrove was the master of substance. He was a little like John Howard, or indeed Bob Hawke before him, containing his substance behind an overtly vernacular style.

I remember shortly after he became Chief of the Defence Force, his telling me that one challenge for him would be to get the different military services to integrate much better. The navy would be a particular challenge, he told me. They already feel like they belong to a bigger, classier defence force, namely the US Navy. It was a point of substance, an arresting image, a memorable line, which I often later used, though without attributing it to Cosgrove.

Cosgrove has always been a proud Catholic, though obviously without the slightest hostility to anyone because of their own religious affiliation or lack of affiliation. We are both 'old boys' of Christian Brothers schools and we have a lot of friends in common. I think of these as reasons I always felt so much at ease in his company. In fact, on reflection, I think it had nothing to do with any of that, and I flatter myself in thinking anything on my part had any effect at all. It was just Cosgrove's formidable professional ability to metaphorically disarm people and bring them into his orbit. He would be on terms of similar ease with dozens, perhaps hundreds, of people.

Cosgrove's father and grandfather were soldiers. He went first to a small Catholic primary school in Paddington, in Sydney, then to the big Christian Brothers college at Waverley, near Bondi. Though you seldom hear him talk about religion, when you ask him about it, he's very forthcoming. Cosgrove honours the tradition that spawned him: 'My core was formed by a strong family. There's a moral core which, if you deviate from, you are eating away at yourself.'

What things comprise this moral core, what things must you be aware of? 'Sin, the life hereafter, redemption, love, mercy and compassion.'

It's hard to imagine, but Cosgrove once found the big school at Waverley intimidating: 'I found school a little overawing. I came from a little parish school in Paddington where I was the dux of the school. I went to high school and found there was a lot of smart guys there. The Christian Brothers, some were what I would call muscular Christians. They weren't overwhelmingly religious in their demeanour, but you learnt in the embrace of the Church. They were men of learning, rigour and vigour. They were men's men. We had no suggestion of any misbehaving brothers, no sense that any were predatory.'

Cosgrove has mixed feelings about the Royal Military College at Duntroon: 'It was a very rough and tough environment at Duntroon, it was secular and oppressive. There were church parades [going to services on Sundays] but you were out in the street, you were not in God's house at Duntroon. That and bastardisation, I was a victim of it and later a perpetrator of it. It was not a Christian way to treat people. It was mostly the humiliation factor, reducing human dignity to an afterthought.'

Bastardisation involved the endless humiliation of junior cadets, and their being given countless extra tasks, by senior cadets. Cosgrove as a senior was known as 'a hard bastard'. He regrets and apologises for his ways then and has been fiercely opposed to such practices ever since: 'It came to a head in 1969. It was publicly exposed and banned. I was in Vietnam by then, I read about it in the papers. I came back [to Duntroon] as commandant in 1997 and I looked under every rock and it was not there.'

Cosgrove has been a believing Christian all his life, even, especially, when he served in Vietnam. He was a lieutenant, a platoon commander in a platoon commander's war. He saw real action, was involved in deadly firefights, and was awarded the Military Cross.

Did he pray in combat? 'There were those informal moments of prayer, so frequent as not to be formal. There were those flashes of thought, those thanks to God that you and your men have survived. Even thanks that you'd done your job, which is a bit of a euphemism. Thanks that this poor man in a green singlet who's an Aussie soldier has survived. There was no thought of privileging a Christian over a non-Christian.'

How did it feel after combat to see enemy dead, people he or his soldiers had killed? 'There was sadness at the sight of dead people. They are human beings, they have families too. Not remorse, because you'd done what your country asked you to, but sadness.'

Cosgrove is quite clear. He didn't feel remorse for what he'd done in battle. He did what a soldier is required to do in conformity with the laws of war and the morality of a just war. But he felt sadness, compassion, at the death of the individuals who were part of the enemy force: 'They are human beings too.'

What of the morality of soldiering? 'The first Christians would not resist even to save their lives. But another side says that God has put us on earth for the struggle [of life], to live until our natural end with dignity. Living with dignity means preserving freedoms. You need Christians to defend the rights of others whether they're Christian or not. I came out of a military family grounded in World War I and World War II. These men were Catholics. I presumed the morality [of soldiering] had been worked out long ago.'

Cosgrove was the first Catholic Chief of the Defence Force (CDF), which seems a remarkable quirk in Australian history. But as CDF, and in other leadership positions before that, he was, he says: 'very low key about the way I expressed my faith. I would stress morality rather than Christianity. Unless you quizzed people, you would never know what their religious background was. I made it a practice as an officer never to inquire of my soldiers what their religious outlook was. I wanted concrete evidence of their ability to perform. As I got more and more senior, I wouldn't have had a blind idea who was what religiously.'

As governor-general, Cosgrove attended church more often than at any other time in his life: 'My wife is an Anglican, a strong person of belief. I was proud of being a person of belief. [When he was governor-general] we went to everything—churches, synagogues, mosques. Sadly, we go to a lot more funerals these days' (he is 73 as we have this conversation).

Does he pray today?

'I pray for the kids, the grandkids, for the government—I want them to get things right. I pray for the CDF. They say there are no atheists in foxholes. That's too glib. A lot of atheists have performed very well in foxholes. But it is possibly true that everyone who is terribly scared clings to the hope that if the worst does happen, my spirit may live on. I think of the first responders (ambulance, fireys, police) who see so many people at the last moments of their lives. I'm reminded of the police. Every police family must think about—when so and so goes to work today, are they coming home?

'It's important to believe, and to worry about the hereafter—which gate will you walk through? Life everlasting means a life well lived will be rewarded. I love the thought that I'll meet again the people who have been important in my life. Not for a moment would I hesitate to say I am a man of faith.'

Although Cosgrove is an ebullient man, who seems to believe, like Colin Powell, that optimism is a force multiplier, he is concerned about what's happening to Christianity in his own society: 'I worry about the degrading, or the decaying, of the core of religious belief in Australia. There are people drifting away from faith and I think that's unfortunate. It's attractive to tear down institutions, but if there's no substitute, we're adrift. We can all line up things we want to tear down, but the question is, what then, what's next? I do think there will be a bounce back in belief. I don't know exactly how that will happen.'

Like John Anderson, Cosgrove can't quite work out why debate has become so uncivil: 'The seemliness has gone out of public discourse—so you just pop things out of your mouth.'

One episode of his life brings him no regrets—the mission in East Timor. 'I felt incredibly lucky to be the guy in charge. I'd just been in the job long enough to know what I was doing. [Much longer, though, and he would have been too senior for the job.] I also thought that Australia was doing a great thing in East Timor. There was some risk because plainly the Indonesians would lose face. We had to be careful. The predating scenes [of the militias] on TV were terrible and we had to stop that. But I believed we should be able to under-write the freedom and safety of those people.

'Kerry O'Brien had me on *The 7.30 Report*. He asked me if there was anything I'd like to say to those people whose families were going to be part of this mission. I said "I'll take care of them".'

Cosgrove has no formal vocational or professional role in Australian Christianity, though he was for some years Chancellor of the Australian Catholic University. He lends his name to a number of causes, especially those associated with the military and with Catholic groups he supports. He was energetic, active and highly supportive in helping the splendid Catholic liberal arts college Campion College, in western Sydney, to get going. He lent it his good name, gave it every public recommendation and spoke at its fundraisers. He doesn't regret any of that: 'If Campion didn't exist, you'd have to invent it.'

Although he left the professional military in 2005, you get the sense that Cosgrove is forever part of the military family. He recognises its faults and weaknesses, and the mistakes and even sometimes the crimes of some of its members. But as with all family relationships, you never lose your love.

He sees a special connection between the military and the Australian nation: 'Here we are, a country with a reputation for irreverence, disrespect, a larrikin spirit—who would have thought we'd be so disciplined in the COVID experience?

'Our countrymen and women make magnificent warriors when there's no choice but to be warriors. As people mature in their military vocation, they become more conscious of their responsibilities. Kids at the start in the military have a video game idea of combat. Their training makes them fit and gives them a thin veneer of lethal skills. The more deeply they get into it, the more they realise they're standing on the edge, very often they're a fraction of a second from not coming home. So it becomes vocational and it's one in, all in. They're in a company with unlimited liability. We owe them our love and support.'

That's what Cosgrove offers to those he cares about, and this category includes the whole of Australia—love and support. And prayer. A Christian soldier. It's no oxymoron.

* * *

No one has ever doubted Bill Hayden's basic decency. A sailor, a policeman, then a politician who did a university degree part-time while he was an MP, he came from an older Labor tradition. He could play his politics tough enough, and he held all the highest posts of government our nation has to offer except the prime ministership. He was Social Security Minister and introduced universal health care. He was treasurer. Later, he was opposition leader and came close to winning government for Labor in 1980. When Bob Hawke came to power in 1983, Hayden became foreign minister.

I was just starting out in journalism when Hayden was opposition leader. But I got to know him a bit when he became foreign minister. Hayden could be hard and even ruthless, but there was never anything vicious about his politics. And he seemed to have an innate sense of the tragedy of life.

I really got to know Hayden better when he was governor-general. In 1990 I began two years in Canberra as the foreign affairs writer for *The Australian*. Quite a few times I was invited to Government House for diplomatic dinners and the like. Nothing unusual about that, a foreign affairs journalist going to diplomatic dinners. But on a couple of occasions Hayden asked me to stay behind after the dinner for a drink. Even by then I'd sworn off the booze, so a drink for me was a cup of tea.

Hayden naturally wanted to talk mostly about foreign affairs but once or twice we talked a little about religious belief. Hayden was a conscientious and intellectually serious atheist. In 1996 he was named the Humanist of the Year by the Rationalist Society. But when we talked, the conversation would often drift to God. I felt even then that Hayden was a decent and good man, caught in a continuing crisis of unbelief. The crisis itself was I think a sign of his own deep contemplation, even in the midst of politics and vice-regal life.

Nonetheless, he took his atheism seriously. At his swearing-in ceremony he made an affirmation rather than take an oath on the Bible. He felt his atheism prevented him from taking up the governor-general's traditional role as head of the Boy Scout movement—the Boy Scout promise says, 'I will do my best to do my duty to my God.' He didn't want to deprive the Scouts and he found another way of being associated with them, but he wouldn't make a promise to a God he didn't believe in.

On a couple of occasions, for no possible reason of his own self-interest at all, just out of kindness, really, Hayden has been conspicuously thoughtful and generous to me. My wife and I married in Kuala Lumpur in 1993, then had a wedding party in Sydney a little later. Friends must have told Hayden, governor-general at the time, about this because he sent a completely unexpected and wonderfully warm, humorous, congratulatory message to our Sydney celebration. He then went out of his way several times to invite both of us to Government House together, which would have been a great treat for Jessie as a new migrant to Australia. But we had moved back to Sydney and for family reasons we couldn't both be away from home at the same time in that period, so we always had to say no. And of course, if you say no repeatedly the invitations eventually stop. I feel I missed a chance to get to know a remarkable Australian leader a little better. There was an offer there of something related to friendship from a great man, and I missed the offer.

As governor-general, and then in his retirement, Hayden kept up a lively interest in foreign affairs, so for a time we still had intermittent contact. I had occasionally been a little tough on Hayden on some foreign issues both when he was opposition leader and when he was foreign minister, and later in assessing his record. I was more in sync with the Bob Hawke/Kim Beazley foreign policy tradition in Labor. But there was nothing in Hayden's record seriously to object to. Once, correcting something I'd written, he wrote a letter to the editor of *The Australian* suggesting I was in danger of becoming 'the grumpy old man of foreign affairs'. That was a wonderful Hayden riposte—perfectly gentlemanly within the informal rules of public controversy, drolly ironic given that he was more than 20 years my senior, and criticism laced really with an edge of good humour and gentleness. In the age of the Twitter sewer, which we've reached now, to be gently reprimanded as prematurely a grumpy old man is almost a gesture of friendship.

Hayden had a giant career, and he rightly gets credit for introducing Medibank, which became Medicare. But there's something else he deserves the thanks of a grateful nation for. He was the unsung hero of bipartisanship on refugees. Hayden was opposition leader from 1977 to 1983. These were the years when the government of Malcolm Fraser was actually bringing in substantial numbers of refugees from Vietnam, Cambodia and Laos. They were being resettled from refugee camps in Southeast Asia and they were the first big cohort of Asian immigrants officially encouraged by an Australian Government. Much more than Gough Whitlam or Bob Hawke, Hayden had real compassion for these refugees, even though they were anti-communist and likely to be anti-Labor. As Labor leader, he underwrote community acceptance of refugees. Supporting the admission of these refugees was for a time the consuming passion of my life. Still, I mustn't get side tracked by politics.

Hayden had one last surprise for the nation when, in 2018, he announced that he had abandoned his atheism and was embracing Catholicism, or, as we might put it, Catholic Christianity. His mother had been a Catholic. In primary school he was educated by the Ursuline nuns and he had gone to mass sometimes as a kid. But he had decided quite early that he was an atheist, that he didn't believe in God or the Bible.

In late 2020 I sent him a note asking if I could talk to him about it. With characteristic generosity, he readily agreed, although he was in failing health and it was a draining effort for him to speak at all. Because of COVID we had to speak over the phone—him in Ipswich, me in Melbourne. We put the phones on speaker at both ends. And we caught up that way a couple of times.

There was only one question I really wanted to ask. Why did you come to Christian faith, Bill? 'I couldn't bear the emptiness. In my mind there was an emptiness without belief.'

He also referred me to the influence of Sister Angela Mary Doyle: 'She had been an administrator at the Mater Hospital in Brisbane for more than 20 years. She contacted me when I was in a terrible fight to bring in universal health care. I was worried when I was a minister that she'd be offended by my views on abortion and euthanasia. She never complained to me. Mater was a big hospital. It was somewhere the poor could always get medical treatment.'

Hayden thinks her support was so important that there wouldn't be Medicare today without the role she played in the politics of its introduction.

He tells me she also had a very direct influence on his religious homecoming: 'A few years ago I went down to see her when she'd had a heart attack. The next day I had the sense that I'd been in the presence of a very holy person.'

This had a profound effect on Hayden. In a letter he wrote to friends explaining his decision, he said of Sister Angela: 'I've always felt embraced and loved by her Christian example . . . There's been a gnawing pain in my heart and soul about what is the meaning of life, what's my role in it. After dwelling on these things, I found my way back to the core of these beliefs in the Church.'

As a child Hayden was brutally bullied by his father, who was a fierce atheist, forever sneering at religion. Hayden has said that he could never forgive his father 'for giving mum a backhander and laying her out on the floor'. One of the reasons he wanted to be a policeman was to deal with perpetrators of domestic violence.

Hayden tells me his mother was a great influence on him. She was always a safe haven. Even after all these decades you can hear the tenderness in his voice when he speaks of her: 'My mother had a big influence on me. She was a believer. She'd been ill. She went to church and wisely took out a little insurance.'

When he announced he was coming back to church, coming to religious belief, Hayden received a wide range of letters and messages of support, among others from Kevin Rudd: 'My daughter rang me up very surprised. She reminded me that Gough Whitlam had told me "the Catholics will get you before you go". Whitlam said they've had hundreds of years' experience at this and they can see when someone's gettable.'

To my surprise, Hayden raises an issue with me which I didn't know anything about: 'In 1966 we lost our oldest daughter, Michaela.' Five-year-old Michaela was running across the road to a relative's car after Sunday school and she was run down and killed. In his autobiography, Hayden is typically generous, perhaps heroically so, to the driver of the car, a poor fellow, he says, beside himself with distress, but he couldn't have done anything about it. Hayden exempts him from blame and holds no grudge.

He picks up the story: 'I think I was insane enough with grief to be certifiable. One day I had a dream that I met her [Michaela] in a shopping centre, and she was a mature young woman with children of her own. It had all been a misunderstanding. It took my breath away.'

Dreams like that, are they a blessing, or are they a torture? For a little while they give us a taste of paradise—and perhaps they are indeed a foretaste of heaven—but then we wake up and all the grief begins again.

My own parents lost a baby daughter—my little sister Mary—a few years before the Haydens did. I know little Mary was in my father's mind, and on his lips, until the day he died. The same with my mother. Little Mary was as real a presence to her as her other four children.

Does Hayden hope to see his daughter again? 'I hope so, to see my daughter in the life to come.'

After Michaela died, Hayden did go to see a young Catholic priest who did his best to console him. At the end of their talk, which Hayden appreciated, the priest offered to pray and said Hayden could join in or not, whatever was most comfortable for him. Hayden didn't pray that day, because he couldn't believe. But he remembers the priest's kindness.

Hayden tells me that his wife, Dallas, 'is a believer, most strongly'. There is a paradox in the way he talks about Dallas publicly. He is both loving and reticent at the same time. As long as I have known him he has spoken only with respect and affection of his wife, sometimes paying tribute to everything she has had to put up with. Yet in this most intimate decision of his life, he leaves her role substantially unspoken. But you get the feeling she has accompanied him on this journey.

He takes up the story again: 'It wasn't easy for me to change my belief. I'd been an atheist for many years. My father was such a strong atheist. A critical factor in causing me to come to belief was meeting an old friend, a judge, in the Qantas lounge once. Dallas was with me at the time. He said to me that the non-believer segment of our society is growing strongly. But our moral code is in the Bible and no one has put an alternative. It could be a disaster. That made me rethink my position. It was a long time ago. It played a role in my change. People like me and him who were atheists—I'd go to Humanist Society meetings and all they ever talk about is more money for education. They're not talking about the deepest issues. Humanists should be talking about how do we promote a society that's decent. Humanism should be a life shared with others, and to create circumstances where others can be assisted.'

Hayden fell in love with Christianity when he realised that much more than a religion of rules, it's a religion of love. He saw this in his mother, he saw it in the Ursuline nuns of his childhood. He saw it in Sister Angela Mary Doyle. I'm sure he saw it in his wife of 60 years, Dallas. Blessed was he to be amongst such women.

He goes to church when he can and he prays: 'One of the great things is that most nights I say prayers for people who are in trouble. He might be surprised to hear it, but I say prayers for Graham Richardson because he's in ill health and I pray for his speedy recovery.' Hayden repeats that line: 'He might be surprised to hear that.' It sounds almost as though Hayden has surprised himself.

Richardson was instrumental in Bob Hawke successfully challenging Hayden for the Labor leadership all those years ago. Hayden likes to get rid of grudges and he hates a lynch mob. Although our talk is about religion, not politics, he tells me of his thoughts about John Kerr, who as Governor-General sacked the Whitlam Government: 'I didn't like the way people pounced on him and denounced him. I felt very sad about what happened to him.' Hayden is not remotely endorsing Kerr's actions, which removed Hayden, along with all of Whitlam's other ministers, from office. His comments on Kerr shouldn't be interpreted politically at all. What Hayden is objecting to is mob abuse and lynch-mob justice. Hayden tends to identify with the guy, or the woman, getting beaten up.

Hayden was always a man open to unpredictable friendships. He tells me that Tony Abbott came up to visit him at Ipswich. They sat together over morning tea and talked and talked: 'We were talking of priests who get into trouble. He said the problem is they don't have enough faith. I said to him that morning that I regard him as a friend.'

In our discussion he recalls to me that I myself once trained to be a priest. That is overstating things a little, but I did have a year in a junior seminary, seeing if I might become a Redemptorist priest. From what prodigy of memory and fellow feeling could Hayden possibly have retrieved this detail? He makes other comments, friendly and warm, though we have not seen each other for years and are talking via the disembodied medium of the telephone.

When Hayden came to Christian faith he said publicly that he wanted to vouch for God, he wanted to encourage people to come to God, he wanted to stand for belief, he wanted to help in St Vincent de Paul, he wanted to help poor people.

In all this, with whatever strength he had, he was faithful. And what was his motivation? Surely we can say simply that in Bill Hayden there was goodness, and goodness, and goodness.

CHAPTER 10

The Great Wall of Heaven

The extraordinary popularity of Daoism and Buddhism,
especially during the Middle Ages, bears witness to the appeal
of mysticism and supernaturalism to the Chinese mind.

Christian historian Christopher Dawson

Of course we're scared, we're in China, but we have Jesus.

Pastor Jin Mingri of Zion church, Beijing

Thus, if a foreigner could be found today who, though
admitted to the Chinese banquet, would not hesitate to rant
in our name against the present state of China, he I would
call a truly honest man, a truly admirable man!

Lu Xun

The best way to understand Christianity in China is through the lives and testimony of Chinese Christians. Through contacts organised by Open Doors, an international group which helps persecuted Christians around the world, I had the chance in late 2020 to talk to a number of active Chinese Christians. We talked at length, and freely. The only condition was that I would not disclose their identities. Peony is a softly spoken, warm, gently vibrant woman in her fifties. She lives in a big city in southern China. She doesn't come from a Christian family.

'I was sixteen when a classmate shared the Gospel with me,' she tells me.

'She invited me to join a small Christian fellowship, fewer than ten people. Knowing about God is different from knowing God. I found fellowship in that group and I found God there. I found a peace with Jesus which is difficult to explain. I raised up my hand, it was just beginning. I would say now that the Holy Spirit came to my heart, but I was rebellious and did not obey straight away.'

Peony's parents didn't like her Christianity and, quite soon after joining, she left the Church for a while, went to uni, got a good job with a big company, eventually progressing to middle management: 'I was having a period of difficulties in my life and another classmate approached me and invited me to attend a church service with her. When I attended I just cried, tears after tears after tears. But Jesus was with me in that difficult period. I decided to commit my life to Jesus.'

Peony has not experienced too much direct trouble with the government herself over her religion, but she knows the situation of other Christians: 'Persecution in China varies from region to region and decade to decade. Because I live in a big city I don't feel too much pressure. People in big cities are not negative to Christians. Christians are good people so others don't have negative feelings towards them.'

In the first decade of this century it was the case that if your church group had no politics, no international connections, no nationwide organisation, generally the government would tolerate it. But since about 2016 things have been changing.

Peony continues: 'The situation changed drastically in the second half of 2018. Persecution started strongly in late 2018 and unregistered churches need to conduct services in a very low-profile way now. Registered churches can continue their services, but some churches are forced to amalgamate. Maybe previously you had 100 churches in a district, now it's maybe 30.

'Since the government revised the regulations, a lot of unregistered churches have decided to divide, making their congregations much smaller. I don't believe at this stage the government will target small groups of people worshipping together. I do hear of some pastors being arrested. The authorities seldom arrest lay believers. They may check their ID cards, or take them to the police station just for a few hours.'

Peony has also seen state control of education become much tighter: 'In China all students attend public schools. Ten years ago many Christians tried home schooling. Most were very small scale, just a few students, always less than ten.' That type of private schooling was effectively shut down by the government. The new regulations made it impossible: 'In recent years we feel the state leadership, the Communist Party, really wants to impart socialist values, and values of loving the country, to students.'

So the operations of Christian churches have become very constricted. Big, public appeals to believe, big services with lots of music, big social gatherings, famous pastors with lots of charisma and a media profile—they are all out of the question for Chinese Christians. So how do they spread the Christian message?

'The most common way to share the Gospel today is through personal relationships. But if I work in a government body or institutional sector I have to be very careful. A Christian can be warned not to share the Gospel with colleagues.

Some institutional units get junior colleagues to declare that they are not Christians.'

Peony reflects on the mystery of Christianity's growth in China: 'During the Cultural Revolution [1966 to 1976] Chairman Mao tried to eliminate all religions. But some say that Chairman Mao did actually help the spread of the Gospel in China. Due to God's faithful servants, Christianity did survive and after the Cultural Revolution there was a big revival.'

Peony is an impressive woman and her innocent, pure, good faith animates her conversation. Also a kind of everyday acceptance of low-level persecution—believers only get taken to the police station for a few hours at a time, as though this is something to be thankful for—and a kind of guileless courage, which I hope does not lead her to distress. But let's try now to put what she reports in context. What's the big picture of Christianity, and religion generally, in China?

More particularly, is there any chance that Christianity can do for China what capitalism failed to do? Namely, to soften the harsh Marxist–Leninist and increasingly nationalist atmosphere of the society into something gentler and better? Of course, the purpose of Christianity in China, the purpose of Christians in China, as Christians, is not to effect political or geostrategic change but to bring the Gospel good news to individual Chinese. Naturally, though, having a lot of Christians in a society will inevitably change that society.

The story of Chinese Christianity has been deeply troubled since around 2012 and much more so since 2018. As studies by the Pew Research Centre and many other studies attest, Christianity is the most persecuted religion in the world. Some of that persecution occurs in China. The situation in China is nowhere near the worst situation that Christians face in the world. And the treatment of ethnic Uighur Muslims in Xinjiang is worse, as is that of Dalai Lama–focused Buddhists in Tibet. That is because they are not only religious minorities but ethnic minorities concentrated in specific locations. So they are seen by Beijing always as potential separatists.

The challenge Christianity presents to the Chinese Government is quite different. That challenge resides in Christianity's universalism, which means it has the potential to appeal to tens of millions, indeed hundreds of millions, of mainstream Chinese, ethnic Chinese, all across the nation. And it has done exactly that. Millions of Chinese in cities have become Christians. Many of these people are successful, well-educated, with something to offer. The vacuum in values and meaning which the exhaustion of Marxism has brought about, plus the distant but bitter memories of the Cultural Revolution, and the emptiness in meaning of the naturally welcome material success of recent decades—all these have conspired to make a lot of Chinese open to the Christian message. Another factor predisposing people to look more explicitly for meaning is rapid urbanisation. People who moved to cities were suddenly without the friends and rituals and routines of country life which previously had offered identity and meaning.

If we just take a few steps back from today's controversies, the longer view of Chinese Christianity is one of astonishing achievement and growth. In fact, on any measure, China is one of the most impressive stories of Christian growth across the second half of the twentieth century. This is big news for China, it's kinda big news for the world. It's pretty big news for the Gospel.

Chinese civilisation and culture are one of the great engines of human creativity and development. As the late Pierre Ryckmans, himself a deeply committed Christian of Belgian background, and the greatest Sinologist ever to work in Australia, observed in the introduction to his masterful translation *The Analects of Confucius*: 'whoever remains ignorant of this civilisation, in the end can only reach a limited understanding of the human experience.'

I lived and worked in China for a period in 1985 as *The Australian*'s first-ever Beijing correspondent. I made a feeble effort to learn the language. I sometimes went to Christian worship in Beijing's Catholic cathedral. I got to know artists and academics at the Central China Art Academy. Their work was mostly modern, but I fell in love with traditional Chinese painting. I read in translation some of the classic modern Chinese writers, especially Lu Xun, whose *The True Story of Ah Q* marks him as China's George Orwell. Most of all, I made good Chinese friends. I found that Chinese culture is indeed thrilling because it is coherent and beautiful and yet wholly different from the Western tradition. Underlying culture, humanity of course is universal, but the Chinese culture to some extent shows you a different way of being human.

However, traditional Chinese culture on one hand, and the Communist Party of China on the other, are radically different things. It is the totalitarian ambition by the Chinese Communist Party, ruling the Chinese state, to control every aspect of Chinese culture, civilisation and the Chinese people, which is producing serious tension at home, and finding aggressive outlet abroad.

Nothing is more important culturally for China than the future of religion, especially the future of Christianity.

Determining how many Christians there are in China, and how many believers of other religions, is no easy task. Ian Johnson, author of the splendid *Souls of China*, estimates 300 million to 400 million Chinese are believers in one religion or another. Most of these are Buddhists, Daoists and practitioners of Chinese folk religion. His estimate, full of goodwill but methodically careful, is that, as of 2021, there are 60 to 70 million Christians in China. *The Economist*, in a piece in September 2020, settled on a similar figure. These estimates are much higher than the Chinese Government's official numbers.

Open Doors, which studies information about persecuted Christians pretty closely, estimates there are just under 100 million Chinese Christians. The highest credible estimate comes from Professor Fenggang Yang at Purdue University in Indiana, in the United States. He thinks there may be as many as 115 million, or perhaps even a bit more than that. Some Christians estimate considerably more again than this. In one speech, former US Vice-President Mike Pence talked of 'up to 130 million Chinese Christians' though he didn't explain where the figure came from. Many guesstimates are based on extrapolating heroically from very limited polling data. Polls are unreliable in open democracies. In societies like China they are extremely rough guides at best. The truth is finally unknowable, and even rests in part on how you define belief, but anything north of 100 million seems an extremely optimistic figure.

The vast majority of Chinese Christians are Protestants, with about 10 or 12 million Catholics included in the overall number of Christians. Whether it's 70 million, or 115 million, the total number of believers is nonetheless an astonishing achievement for Christianity in communist China. As Johnson records, in 1949 there were perhaps 4 million Christians in China, 3 million Catholics and a million Protestants. To go from 4 million to 100 million in that time, or even from 4 million to 70 million, during some of the most savage anti-religious persecutions in modern history, is almost miraculous. Perhaps that 'almost' is misplaced. The second-century Christian writer and theologian Tertullian observed that the blood of martyrs was the seed of the Church. There has been plenty of seed in China.

Initially, after the communists came to power in 1949, they tried to reorganise religion under a so-called united front mechanism. A united front in a communist society is a way of bringing in a notionally non-communist organisation, theoretically to work on common projects with the Communist Party, in reality to accept the Party's leadership, to subordinate its own goals to those of the Party, and ultimately to come under more or less complete control by the Party. Christianity was seen as a foreign religion and all the foreigners were thrown out when the Communists took power. This particularly hurt the Catholic Church, which had not localised enough of its hierarchy. Without many local bishops it could not ordain priests, which meant that many local Catholic communities could not administer sacraments beyond baptism.

The Cultural Revolution was a period of savage persecution of all religions, (although the intense anti-Christian phase had begun in the late 1950s). Priests and nuns were held in cages, like zoo animals, in cathedrals, and the public encouraged to come in and mock them. When China finally turned towards reform in the late 1970s, it loosened up a bit and this is when the huge Christian expansion took place. In 1982 the Communist Party issued an encouraging document, characteristic of that golden age of Chinese liberalising, known as Document 19. It denounced the 'leftist errors' of the Cultural Revolution and allowed normal religious activities.

The 1980s saw a huge expansion in Evangelical and Pentecostal Chinese churches. Christianity moved from the countryside to the cities. But any freedom in communist China is always temporary and provisional. I remember interviewing a leader of the Marxism–Leninism–Mao Zedong Thought Institute in Beijing in 1985 who explained to me why mass campaigns and repression would never return to China. He asked me, however, not to use his name. As I left, his assistant explained to me that the senior man did not want to be in trouble during the next mass campaign for saying something too forward leaning. After the Tiananmen Square massacre in 1989 things tightened up again, though nowhere near as severely as during the Cultural Revolution. The Protestant house church movement kept expanding.

The first decade of this millennium, the noughties, was very good for Christianity in China. The Protestant groups that did well in cities in the West did similarly well in Chinese cities, and with many of the same methods of outreach. City churches, often meeting in rented accommodation in office buildings, or in venues such as old cinemas, would hold Christmas celebrations, charismatic musical services and the like. Young people would come along, enjoy the music, enjoy the fellowship; some became Christians. At this point, going on straight-line projections, some thought China would eventually have, in absolute numbers, more Christians than any other nation. Some senior churchmen in the West even held out a particular dream for Xi Jinping. Reportedly, he had privately expressed admiration for some elements of Christianity. There was a fantasy that he might be China's Constantine, the fourth-century Roman emperor who converted to Christianity and paved the way for the Christianising of Europe.

Boy, was that ever one dream that didn't come true.

Since 2016 the Chinese state has become steadily more repressive. A substantial number of Protestant pastors and local church identities from unregistered churches, as well as priests and bishops from the underground Catholic Church, have been jailed. New, more restrictive, regulations were announced in 2017 and formally came into force in 2018. Numerous local party bosses had already taken actions against Christian churches in their own regions, shutting or amalgamating churches, ripping down crosses and forbidding their public display, and while the legality of these moves was unclear, they were never reversed.

Even harsher restrictions were announced in 2020. Beijing officially recognises five religions—Buddhism, Daoism, Islam, Catholicism and Protestantism. The constitution notionally guarantees freedom of religion. But its terms are vague and it has had no effect in slowing down persecution.

In 2017, Xi told a Communist Party Congress that 'the leadership should persist in advancing the Sinicisation of our country's religions'. The mantra of Sinicisation has been the hammer the Party has used to hit Christianity, but also to hit even Buddhism, which came initially from India but has been in China for more than 1800 years.

In 2018 the Vatican signed an agreement with Beijing, later renewed, which would theoretically amalgamate the underground Catholic Church—which had numerous priests and bishops in jail, some for many years and some now presumed dead—with the officially recognised Patriotic Catholic Association, which is officially tolerated but still heavily circumscribed. The agreement allows Beijing a say, a veto, over who the pope can appoint as a bishop. This is not what Catholic Church law requires but it was the situation which prevailed in many east European countries during the Cold War. And something like it applies in Vietnam. Some Catholic leaders believe that while deeply unsatisfactory, it's better than not being able to appoint bishops at all, that it's a worthwhile gamble.

The Vatican and the Communist Party want opposite things from this deal. The Vatican wants more bishops and therefore more priests. In the long term it wants a normalised civic status for Chinese Catholics. There has been no sign of either of these developments taking place. The Communist Party, on the other hand, views the agreement as a way of taking greater control of the underground Catholic movement.

The Protestant Christians are also divided into the official Three Self Movement as opposed to the independent, unregistered, mainly house church congregations. The term 'three self' refers to self-governance (no foreign allegiance); self-support (no foreign money) and self-propagation (no foreign missionaries). No foreign influence—all control in Beijing—is the big theme. It's important to be clear here. The Communist Party wants not just to exclude foreigners, it wants positive control of religion to be in the hands of the Party. But it is certainly allergic to foreign influence and it uses the suggestion of foreign influence to give public legitimacy to its coercive actions.

Some patterns in Christianity recur again and again across the centuries. In the New Testament Acts of the Apostles, St Paul, in Athens, is accused of 'advocating foreign gods', just what Christians are accused of in China today. Christianity's first big act in China came with the arrival of the Jesuit missionary, Matteo Ricci, who first went to China in the sixteenth century. An extraordinary man, he was the first Westerner to master Chinese language and culture. He won the acceptance of the emperor's court for his knowledge of science and astronomy. He argued that Christianity was compatible with the *Analects of Confucius* and converted a number of influential Chinese officials to Christianity. Confucius' *Analects* are mainly ethical and deal with moral philosophy and matters of education and good government. They make very little mention of the transcendent or the metaphysical. They are indeed mostly compatible with Christianity. Similarly, Ricci thought that a good portion of the Chinese custom of ancestor worship could be adapted to fit in with the Christian idea of the communion of saints (the unity between living Christians and the dead who are saved).

But subsequent emperors saw Christianity as essentially a foreign religion and became uneasy when it started to attract large numbers of converts. In 1724 Emperor Yongzheng granted an audience to Jesuit missionaries, Ricci's successors, and questioned them: 'You wish to make the Chinese all Christians, and this is what your law demands. We know this very well. But in this case what would become of Us? Should We not soon become merely the subjects of your kings? The subjects you have made already recognise nobody but you, and in a time of trouble, they would listen to no other voice than yours.'

A couple of years later, the same emperor would issue a famous edict which said: 'China has her Chinese teachings just as the West has Western teachings. Western teachings do not need to be practised in China.'

This is more or less just exactly what Xi Jinping has decided, 300 years later. The dialogue between Yongzheng and the Jesuits eerily anticipates the dialogue between Beijing and the Vatican in our own time. Nonetheless, the eighteenth-century emperor never wholly suppressed Christianity; nor has Xi.

At one level, the idea that Christianity must Sinicise to be successful in China is not entirely unreasonable. Chinese Christians don't wish to impose Western norms—many of which are now so gross that Western Christians don't like them themselves—on China. Nor do they have much wish to interfere in Chinese politics. But Sinicisation of religions in China today means explicit support for the doctrines and leadership of the Chinese Communist Party and an acknowledgement of the superiority of Party doctrine to any religious doctrine. Churches have famously been forced to hang pictures of Xi Jinping. Even Buddhism, which is integral to Chinese culture and is generally apolitical, has had its traditional statues suppressed at many temples. Those temples most favoured have a photo or statue of Mao. Schools have had to eliminate their Buddhist symbolism and heritage.

The Chinese Communist Party is itself a quasi-religious institution which cannot allow a heretical religious body to co-exist, to compete by offering an alternative credibility structure.

Kevin Carrico, a Chinese studies academic at Monash University, when I speak to him, explains: 'Marxism, or communism, is very much a religious belief system that views other religious belief systems as competition. Religions are the way people try to understand and make sense of the world. Marxism does that and does command an all-embracing loyalty. Marxism is an attempt to bring heaven to the world. Christianity has a narrative that people who suffer in this life are rewarded in the next life. The similar Marxist idea is that the proletariat which has been exploited will be rewarded when communism is fully realised. It's a competing monotheism but the Communist Party is God.'

It is sometimes said that the Chinese are the only great civilisation which never discovered God. But it's far too simple to think that Chinese culture was previously unreligious and lacked all sense of God. Geremie Barmé, perhaps Australia's most brilliant contemporary Sinologist, told me: 'China has had a concept of a monotheistic entity from very early on. They tried to combine the numinous, abstract workings of heaven and integrate these with the emperor and his court. The emperor incarnates the principles of the workings of heaven. The last dynasty called themselves the Celestial Dynasty. There have been a lot of Communist era attempts to meld the Party with the sacred workings of heaven. The Communists will always regard Christians as competitors for the hearts and minds of the Chinese. When they ask: do you believe in Marxism–Leninism?, they use the same word for 'belief' as in, do you believe in a religious faith? [Russia's] Josef Stalin, who had been a seminarian, introduced many aspects of Eastern Orthodoxy into communism, which the Chinese inherited, such as confession, and seeking redemption.'

In other writings Barmé has speculated that Xi and the Party see their role in part as giving transcendent meaning to the lives of ordinary Chinese. As it's sometimes said, the religion of Chinese people is China. The Communist Party believes that it embodies the essence of China. Thus Xi's frequent use of concepts and language of struggle, his warnings to his fellow Chinese that the future will be full of conflict and struggle, are not done just to evoke a sense of external enemies and national solidarity, but to impart transcendent purpose to the lives of Chinese.

However, long before Christianity came along the Chinese had an abundance of gods. As Johnson records, in 1911 Beijing had a thousand temples. From the fourteenth century, the government decided that each city should have a temple to its own city god. There is something of the attitude of ancient Rome to religion here. The gods were expected to perform by warding off bad fortune. Distinguished men of affairs could be deified, raised to a pantheon of gods. Chinese religion was diffused throughout society. It was predominantly folk religion.

Official thinking, at the level of the emperor and his court, was preoccupied with the harmony of heaven and the harmony of society. The emperors used the ethical teachings of Confucius to bolster their own position. As Ryckmans (using his pen-name, Simon Leys) comments in his translation of the *Analects*: 'Imperial Confucianism only extolled those statements from the Master that prescribed submission to the established authorities, whereas more essential notions were conveniently ignored—such as the precepts of social justice, political dissent, and the moral duty for intellectuals to criticise the ruler when he was abusing his power.'

The cult of ancestor worship was widespread, to honour ancestors, to make them comfortable in the afterlife and to seek their protection from misfortune for their descendants in this life. Although the metaphysics are not stressed and not very developed, the practice does imply the continued existence of ancestors after they have died. As Johnson argues, Chinese folk religion was weak on theology. Instead it was ritualistic and performative. And it was fluid and inclusive. Christianity had a big impact on modernising Chinese thought overall, not just on religious thought and practice. However, many Chinese fitted it into an existing cosmology.

As Barmé explains: 'In the morning, you're a Confucian, in the afternoon you go to [Christian] church and in the evening you practise Daoist meditation.' And of course Buddhism, which was and is the religious system with the most followers, has its own complex metaphysics.

In another dialogue between Emperor Yongzheng and another set of Christian missionaries, this time in 1728, the emperor criticised the Christians for having a negative view of Buddhist teaching and theology. The Christians, using other words, said in effect that Buddha did not understand who the real God was. The emperor replied sharply: 'What do you mean by enemies? They are no enemies at all. Buddha is not an enemy of God. He has created heaven and earth, has neither beginning nor end, and is infinite. We are not talking of the mortal Buddha who had a father and a mother, but of another invisible Buddha, principle of all things.'

Leaving aside the emperor's view of Buddhism specifically, his fascinating and sophisticated remarks illustrate one of the key insights of G.K. Chesterton's most brilliant and important book, *The Everlasting Man*. Chesterton argued that there is almost a human instinct about monotheism, that even many seemingly polytheistic religious traditions acknowledge that above all the gods and deities and forces that they enumerate, there is a supreme, guiding spirit, or a fundamental creator, to wit, God.

The Chinese are no more immune from the hunger for God, no more immune from God himself, than any other human beings.

So the Communist Party will always have its work cut out for it to prevent Chinese minds and hearts turning to God. As you might expect, given the ideological assertiveness of Xi Jinping's government, a wide range of actions has been taken to hamper Christianity. The most famous Protestant pastor, Wang Yi, who had built up a huge following around his church in Chengdu, was sentenced to nine years in prison in 2019 on charges of subverting state power and conducting illegal business operations. Dozens of his leading followers were also jailed. Wang Yi's movement had set up schools, he had hundreds of people attending his services, he was building a national network and he expressed views about the morality of abortion. This was all way too much for the Chinese authorities, who cracked down very hard.

That crackdown became widespread. Video cameras were installed in and around registered churches for the authorities to record everyone who participates and to hear what the pastors are saying in their sermons. From early 2020, churches were positively required to support and spread Communist Party teachings, something of a contradiction given that the Communist Party is formally atheist. Registered churches were forced to amalgamate. It became impossible to get permission to build a new church. It also became illegal for people under eighteen to attend church. Private or religious school education became illegal. Bibles could be sold at churches but not in regular bookshops. And it became illegal to sell Bibles online. Communist Party members may not belong to a church or express religious belief. The authorities try hard, not always entirely successfully, to suppress religious content on the net.

The underground Catholic churches and Protestant home churches never really operated in secret, given how extensive surveillance is in modern China. The government mostly knew about them but tolerated them up to a point so long as they remained very small and absolutely apolitical. But it would not be difficult for the government to become even more restrictive or indeed to try an almost complete shutdown, though this would certainly lead to greater anger and polarisation in China.

The government has effectively taken three sets of measures against Chinese Christians. The first is organisational. By changing the bureaucratic, institutional arrangements governing religion, it has made compliance harder and the range of permitted activities narrower. The second change is ideological. It is not enough for churches not to oppose the government: they must actively support Communist Party ideology. And the third is technological. The government uses to the full its enhanced capacity to monitor, to spy, to surveil. The Chinese state devotes enormous resources to watching its own citizens and there is no one it watches more closely than Christians.

It is trying to create a Great Wall of Heaven, but Heaven has ways of its own, and walls have never been enough to keep it out. Christianity in China is a long, long story. Nothing is harder than to predict its future.

The purpose of Christianity is to preach the Gospel, but this always has social consequences. Chinese Christians would like to help the government with charitable works, care for the aged and the otherwise marginalised, for example. The communist government is mistaken to be suspicious of these overtures. Communists can be like political Freudians in their misinterpretations—not everything is about politics. Sometimes a cigar is just a cigar; sometimes an act of charity is just an act of charity.

If Christianity ultimately succeeds in China, it won't turn China into a Western democracy. It will, though, make China a better China, a kinder, gentler China. That would be a victory for the Good News.

CHAPTER 11

If God is not Chinese,
he's not God

Man has places in his heart which do not yet exist,
and into them enters suffering, in order
that they may have existence.

Léon Bloy

[Chinese religions] are an important portion of the natural
dowry with which God has endowed me in preparation
for my marriage with Christ. I often think of myself as a
Magus from China who lays before the Divine Infant in
the arms of the Blessed Virgin the gold of Confucianism,
the musk of Daoism and the frankincense of Buddhism.
At a single touch by His hands, whatever is false in them
is purified, and whatever is genuine in them is transmuted
into supernatural values.

John Wu, *Beyond East and West*

George Yeo is the smartest man I have ever met in Southeast
Asia. Government, business and think-tank circles in
Southeast Asia are full of formidably smart people. In 40 years
in journalism, I've interviewed a lot of them. I never met anyone
there, or in fact in any region, I thought smarter than Yeo. His
analysis was always so acute that one of my few appearances
in the Wikileaks cables involves American diplomats cabling

accounts of the interviews I did with him. These were hardly secret, but the US diplomats involved realised that Yeo's analysis of the big trends in Asia and the world was the best, and they wanted their colleagues to read it.

For many years Yeo was a superstar of the Singapore Government. He held many ministries from information, health, trade and industry, to surely the peak of his career as Singapore's foreign minister, which post he occupied from 2004 to 2011.

I have interviewed him, engaging with him in a long dialogue intermittently over the course of more than 30 years. Yeo's distinctive ability was to place contemporary events meaningfully into the flow of culture and history. But he also always wanted to engage with ideas at whatever level you were looking for. He was generous with his time, I think in part because he enjoyed the engagement.

A Singapore Government is always full of over-achievers, but in terms of historic knowledge and, above all, imagination, Yeo was the over-achiever's over-achiever. Degrees from Cambridge and Harvard with the highest honours, then a stellar career in the Singapore Air Force before politics, set him up for the kind of national service that Singapore often draws out of its best people.

He could have made any amount of money in corporate life, and he went on to a good post-politics career in business. But his interest was always to grapple with ideas and with governance. He didn't want to speculate about history as an academic, but nor did he want to act as a politician without working on history, understanding the framework of his times, working to bend history's arc in a decent direction.

I've never known him pick a big trend wrong. During the 1997 Asian economic crisis he notably kept his head. The trends towards East Asian economic growth and power were not reversed by this crisis, he told me then, at a time when many Western analysts were decrying the Asian economic miracle, thinking it was finished. No, at worst the crisis meant these trends might be delayed by a few years, perhaps by a decade. He was right about that.

Yeo, like Singapore itself, is an eclectic, creative mix of divergent cultural influences. While fully conscious of his Chinese cultural heritage, he has always recognised the contribution of Western ideas and values to Singapore, and to what emerged as the East Asian economic miracle. History was never either/or for Yeo; it was rather plus plus.

Because I knew he was a Christian, I once or twice tentatively asked Yeo about his religious outlook and found he was as relaxed and forthright about that as about everything else. Very occasionally we would discuss the role of Christianity in Asian culture, and what it was like to be an Asian Christian, when the pantheon of Christian saints and heroes seems to feature relatively few Asians.

I had the chance to play a very small role in Yeo's own relationship with the Vatican. One day in 2013 I got a phone call from Cardinal George Pell, whom I had known well for many years. Pope Francis had asked Pell to clean up the Vatican's finances, which were opaque and, as it turned out, in parts, corrupted. To do this, Francis appointed Pell the Secretary of Finance for the Vatican. Pell in turn wanted to appoint a committee of the financially most literate and best Catholic lay people from around the world to oversee the reform of the Vatican finances.

'Do you know a Catholic in Asia who would be suitable for the job, who is a devoted enough Catholic that they might be willing to do it?' he asked me.

If I could think of such a person, he wanted the name fast because speed was of the essence. It really only took 30 seconds to nominate George Yeo. Pell asked about Yeo's background—is he a good man, am I confident in his character, does he know something about finance, is he a seriously committed Catholic? Do you think he might do it if asked? Pell requested I keep the conversation confidential at the time.

Pell took my recommendation and then operated through the Singapore Archbishop, who rang Yeo's wife to get his phone number and then asked Yeo if he could pass on the number to another bishop. Of course you can, Yeo told him, but who is the other bishop? That, for the moment, was confidential.

Yeo tells me how it went from there: 'Cardinal Pell rang me. I did not know him from Adam and thought that his name was Dell before he clarified that it was P for potato. He explained the proposal for a Vatican Commission to recommend reform of the administrative/financial system and asked if I would agree to be a member of it. Being a careful man, I asked for a copy of the proposal and for a week to think it over. He said there was no paper; he had told me everything he knew; and I had two days to decide because the announcement would be made in a few days.

'As I was working for Robert Kuok [a Malaysian business magnate], I needed to inform him first. Knowing that he had negative views of the Catholic Church because of bad experiences in his youth, I did not want to ask for his permission. So I asked for his blessing by email, which he quickly gave. I also rang my wife, who was on vacation in Europe. She chided me for even thinking about it. Of course I had to accept. I then went to see my bishop for his blessing and advice. He said to me: "George, you'll be disappointed with the Vatican." I was taken aback by his remark. Later I realised he was preparing me psychologically for my work.'

Yeo was the only non-European on the commission and with no disrespect to the other fine participants in that commission, that regional and ethnic skew shows up a weakness in the Vatican. Pell later told Yeo that Pope Francis himself had wanted a Chinese on the commission.

'I was that Chinese,' he says.

Yeo by then had big responsibilities in business and this appointment meant he had to fly to Rome once a month and undertake serious work: 'It should have been exhausting, but it was a labour of love. I found it exhilarating. But there were also worries and occasional fears. We knew we were doing something important for the Holy Father but also encountered fierce pushback.'

The task was not completed by the end of Yeo's five-year term, but in Yeo's view there was real progress. He compares the process to the *Boléro* orchestral work: 'the same tune goes round and round but with each cycle, new instruments are drawn in. It ends only when the entire orchestra participates.' Yeo didn't add, but might have, that it ends much more loudly than it begins, surely an apt metaphor for Vatican financial reform, which at times has been explosive, ugly and very, very loud indeed.

But all this is the public Yeo. Privately, his own journey in Christian faith has been deep, lifelong, thoughtful and shadowed by personal tragedy. When you see a high achiever like Yeo from a distance you think he must have the perfect life. But no life is perfect from the inside and Yeo's life has been complex and full of challenges.

When I speak to him, Yeo is in his mid-sixties, though he seems as youthful as ever. He has seen the outward expressions of Christianity change a good deal in his lifetime: 'I was born a Catholic, baptised at birth. During my school years I attended mass and received the sacraments. I remember my mother having to wear a black lace head covering when she went to church. The old missal [mass book] was printed in Latin on one side and English on the other.'

Yeo's father converted to Christianity when he was a boarder at St Joseph's, a school run by the De La Salle order of brothers. Later he fell away from belief. In 1937 Yeo's father went to China for his own father's funeral. Under the customs of the day, he should either marry within 100 days of his father's death or wait three years. So Yeo's father married in China. A month later the Japanese invaded China and Yeo's parents rushed back to Singapore.

Yeo's mother was born in Chaozhou, a city in Guangdong province. She left China at the age of nineteen and was not able to return until 1978 when, as a grandmother, she returned to see again her own parents.

Like everyone in Singapore, the Yeos did not have an easy time during World War II: 'During the war, my second brother died. After the war my third brother developed febrile convulsions and died in my father's arms. My father decided to baptise him. My father returned to religion and the whole family became Catholic.'

In order to break the spell of misfortune which seemed to have fallen over them, those of the family born after the war were not given Chinese names, a decision Yeo's mother regretted. Later they reclaimed Chinese names. Yeo had seven brothers and one sister. He never knew the two brothers who died, as he was born well after them.

It is truly said that you are only ever as happy as your unhappiest child. This was true for Yeo's parents: 'My eldest brother developed schizophrenia in his late teens, which was a great trial to my parents.'

Naturally the Yeos did everything they could for their afflicted son: 'My mother, who knew no English, spent six months in London with him. My parents brought him to Fatima and Lourdes in search of a cure. He did not get better. But my father became dedicated to the Fatima rosary movement. As a teenager, I attended meetings on my father's behalf when he got tired of the meetings. That's how I first got to know the Eurasian community in Singapore. My brother's schizophrenia was part of the cross we bore as a family, but it was especially difficult for my mother. For a mother never stops loving and hoping. In my parents' will the estate was to be devoted to looking after my brother for as long as he was alive. Only after his death was it to be distributed to the rest of us.'

Throughout his youth, Yeo was absorbed in his Christian beliefs: 'I was quite fervent in my religion up to my pre-university days, at one point attending daily mass. After my first year as an undergraduate at Cambridge I departed, and for a few years lost my faith. The explanation of religion by Marx and Engels was seductive. But in my maturity I realised that you can't explain everything. The most important things are often not within our control. There is something much bigger than us, which gives our lives meaning.

'[My faith] became a different kind of faith, less ritualistic, more philosophical. I developed a different understanding of love, Christian love. When we are bound together in love, there is potentially nothing in the universe that our collective brain cannot one day understand. It is in love for one another that our divine nature becomes fully manifest. I see spirituality encoded in our genes. It's a necessary accompaniment to intelligence. The mirror which enables us to see ourselves also tells us that it must all end in death, which, without hope, can only crush our spirit. That which makes us intelligent, which gives us forethought, also makes us spiritual. Spirituality is not an end point; it is a journey, a search. It makes our life on earth a spiritual quest. In our DNA, bound up with the coding of our intelligence is the coding of our spiritual enquiry.'

For a brief period at university, atheism had won Yeo: 'Karl Marx's thesis fascinated me. I read Engels' essay on family and religion. For a while I was inclined to the view that religion was an opiate. Pope John Paul II was anti-communist. He was partly responsible for the fall of the Berlin Wall. Pope Francis came from the opposite end of the political spectrum. Accused of being a communist, he replied that he was not one but had good friends who were. Francis said that communism adopted the Christian message but took God out of it. Without the human being at the centre of the ideology, it became evil. The individual should always be at the centre of things. The individual should be the subject, not the object.'

Having gone back to Christian belief, Yeo has never wavered after, and he and his wife have been on a deep journey in life and faith: 'My wife was an Anglican when we married and she remained an Anglican for thirteen years. In 1986 I had a near-death experience with a bad case of adult measles. Inspired by John Paul II, my wife told me not long afterwards that she wanted to become a Catholic. I asked her to think it over carefully and not convert because of me. I didn't want, after our next quarrel, for her to regret it.

'On Easter Vigil, 1997, she was admitted to the church. A few months later our youngest son was diagnosed with leukemia. It seemed as if our whole world collapsed then. He had two and a half years of chemotherapy, then a relapse after two years of remission, then two more years of chemotherapy, then a second relapse, this time with an additional blood cancer because of the chemo drugs. The prognosis was dire.'

George Yeo and his wife, Jennifer, like George's father before him, did everything they could for their son. They found a ray of medical hope in the US: 'St Jude Children's Research Hospital in Memphis, Tennessee, accepted him for a bone marrow transplant, but we had to find a bone marrow donor. We could not find a blood match among his siblings, which was unlucky because the chances of a sibling matching is one in two, and he had three siblings.

'We couldn't find a match in the whole of Singapore. Nor Hong Kong. Eventually we found one in Taiwan through a Buddhist foundation called Tzu Chi, which does wonderful philanthropic work around the world. My son had his bone marrow transplant in November 2004. It worked eventually and he is now [2020] a final-year medical student. His long years of illness kept us close together as a family.'

Yeo is grateful for all this, profoundly grateful. I have always thought the first response, and the natural attitude, for any Christian is gratitude. It's an attitude I find among serious Christians again and again. Nonetheless, it was a tough period: 'My wife and children were in Memphis for nine months while I was a new foreign minister. I remember visiting them seven times during that period. Although my son was not covered by medical insurance in the US, we did not have to pay for his treatment. St Jude is a research hospital using experimental drugs so they did not want parents making decisions on the basis of treatment costs. As most families in Singapore would not have the opportunities my son had, my wife established the Viva Foundation for children with cancer to bring medical expertise from St Jude and elsewhere to Asia.' The Yeos later extended their foundation to Hong Kong and mainland China.

Illness, and God's mercy, were not finished with the Yeo family. In 2017 his wife developed a terrible sinonasal undifferentiated carcinoma tumour, which grew from the sinus into the cranial cavity and destroyed, among other things, her sense of smell.

This was a pure emergency and after diagnosis Yeo took his wife to Houston for treatment. This kind of severe cancer requires that everything, including the kitchen sink, be thrown at it. After chemotherapy and radiotherapy the physicians expected they would need to go into the cranial cavity and the face to remove the remaining cancer.

His being a former Singapore Government minister didn't exempt the Yeos from US visa requirements, so: 'After the second infusion of chemotherapy we flew to Mexico City to get our B-1 visas. Singapore's visa-free access was only good for 90 days. We had a day free to pray the rosary and receive the Eucharist at the Basilica of Our Lady of Guadalupe. Next day we collected our passports and flew back to Houston. My wife had an MRI scan to assess how much the tumour had shrunk. It had completely melted away. My wife is very well now. We feel that God has extended her life for a purpose.'

His Christian faith is at the centre of Yeo's life and family, and, indirectly at least, of his work as well. Yeo and his wife pray together every night. He prays privately before important events, often before speeches. His wife organises weekly rosary events, which he always joins. Lifelong regular prayer is a good recommendation for any Christian. Yeo is certainly comfortable in his skin as a Christian. Yet many Asians have seen Christianity as a Western import, an element of colonialism, a foreign god brought by a foreign people. How does Yeo weigh the cultural interaction between Christianity and East Asia?

'I had a conversation with a fellow MP in Singapore who was Chinese-educated,' he recalls.

'She remarked innocently that Christianity is full of foreign faces. When your God is not Chinese and your saints are not Chinese, the subjugation is total. It's like when Cortez arrived in Mexico. The Aztecs had a belief about gods returning from the sea. It made it much easier for the Spaniards to prevail despite their small numbers. There is a feeling among some leaders that Christianity is a foreign religion which facilitates colonisation. The [historic] persecution of Christians in Japan sprang from such mortal fear among their leaders.

'Look at Buddhism in China. It's seen as almost a Chinese religion. It feels Chinese, though of course intellectually the Chinese know it came from India. Today, if you remove

311

Buddhism from Chinese civilisation, it's like removing a colour from a painting.

'God expresses himself in the deepest identity of human beings. The image of Our Lady of Guadalupe—Pope Francis reflected that it is of Mary as a Mestizo. God therefore is Mestizo. He [Francis] once said that God is a Rohingya. At a seminar I gave to a Chinese audience, I said that God is Chinese, which created a ripple of mixed reaction among them. If to Chinese people God is not Chinese, then he is not God.'

Yeo is not pessimistic about the future of Christianity in China. Rather he is excited by it: 'I go back to the writings of Matteo Ricci [the first Jesuit to win favour at the imperial court in Beijing in the sixteenth century] and the early Jesuits. They were astonished to find in China a civilisation ordered differently, one where a moral order was sustained without religion. This later influenced the thinkers of the French Revolution. The Jesuits brought back to Europe two important ideas from China. The first was that you should have exams in the selection of bureaucrats. The second was that you could have a moral order without clerics.

'Deus, God, was very difficult to translate into Chinese. Francis Xavier took the name of a minor Japanese deity for God. Not surprisingly, that was quickly abandoned. The Chinese believed in heaven above and men below—Tian and Tian Xia. The emperor was the son of heaven—Tan Zi. Matteo Ricci made God the lord of heaven, Tian Zhu. The religion of Tian Zhu became his translation of the Catholic Church into Chinese, a term used today. The translation of Christian ideas into Chinese was not merely a translation of words and phrases but the interpretation of deep philosophy from one civilisation sphere to another.

'At the philosophical level there is much in common between the philosophy of Daoism and Christianity. There is a sense of transcendence. There is a sense of awe. We are little cycles within bigger cycles. There are mysteries. The more we understand, the greater the sense of awe of the things we don't understand, and of our own impermanence. The Gospel of John, which was philosophically Hellenic, has a strong Daoist flavour to it, especially at the beginning.'

Christianity has been central to Yeo's conception of himself, to his identity: 'When I joined the People's Action Party [Singapore's ruling party], which is a Leninist party, I was asked to write an account of my beliefs. I said there were two sides of me. One is Chinese, which is both Confucian and Daoist. The other is my Christian side, which believes in the divine quality of love. Universal love sits uncomfortably in the world of Confucius, where relationships come first. Buddhist compassion, which is a form of universal love, gradually transformed Chinese society and softened it. When asked why God created the universe, Pope Francis gave a startling reply. He said that it was out of love.'

And after this life, the next life? 'I'm not sure what the next life will be like. I wonder what it will be like to meet God face to face. It is a mystery. God is Chinese, God is Rohingya, God is Mestizo, God is in Greg, I hope God is also in George, when we are reunited with him in our deepest being. We don't know, and we have doubts of course, but life has no meaning without this mystery. It is this mystery which gives our life transcendent quality and purpose.'

CHAPTER 12

New missions, new fire: Christian leaders

The spirit of the Lord is upon me, because he has
anointed me to bring good news to the poor,
to proclaim liberty to captives, and to restore sight
to the blind, to set the downtrodden free,
to proclaim the Lord's year of favour.

Luke 4:18–19

Catch on fire with enthusiasm and people will
come for miles to watch you burn.

John Wesley

St Patrick was not an institution builder in society, but a
Gospel planter among the locals. Our task is not to reinforce
crumbling structures on fractured ground, but to find
new ground to build new communities.

Catholic Archbishop of Melbourne Peter Comensoli

Sammy Rodriguez is a successful Hollywood film producer whose movies gross in the tens of millions of dollars. He is also a political adviser, who has given personal and policy advice to United States presidents of both parties. He is a speaker at presidential inaugurations. He is a TV personality. He heads a national body with more than 40,000 member organisations. He is a cultural conservative, he is also a civil rights activist. He is a bestselling author.

But in a sense I am listing only the bits and pieces of his activities and leaving out the most important part, the key to everything else. Sammy Rodriguez is a Pentecostal, Evangelical pastor. He is the president of the National Hispanic Christian Leadership Conference, with its 42,000 churches. This is the largest Hispanic Evangelical Christian organisation in the world.

The seemingly strange shape of his activities may be a sign of one type of church leadership to come. Because Pentecostalism in its modern form is such a young movement, it has always been contemporary (its distinctive beliefs are outlined briefly in the section on Scott Morrison in Chapter 9). For a church, it's pretty good at dealing with contemporary institutions like Hollywood and social media. The Pentecostals lack the magnificent institutional inheritance—hospitals, hospices, schools, universities, professional social care networks and the like—of older denominations like Catholics and Anglicans. This very lack of old institutional structures leaves them with a certain nimbleness in dealing with contemporary structures. And they are very energetic. They are always having a try. They have to build new institutions because they don't have any old ones.

In this book I have consciously taken a 'mere Christianity' approach, honouring every Christian tradition (and every Christian) that can recite the Apostles' Creed and mean it. I have no interest in comparing favourably or unfavourably one Christian denomination with another. Everybody has some bit of brilliance or innovation they've discovered, and everyone has their difficulties. But here and there I try to highlight something that might be worth wide consideration. We can all learn from each other. The Rodriguez style of leadership, highly individualistic as it is, merits examination because of the way he engages and confronts contemporary technology and communications, which have generally proven very difficult for Christians.

Rodriguez is based, with his church, in Sacramento, California, and I am in Melbourne. COVID means a trip I planned to the US is impossible so we catch up for a long discussion over Skype. He is in his early fifties, full of energy, happy to share his time and his story.

He came to ministry in the oddest way. His family, Puerto Rican in origin, was religious but his parents were not pastors. They attended a Pentecostal church aligned with the Assemblies of God. A strange selection of unconnected people he met in his youth—preachers, conference leaders, speakers at Christian youth events, choir masters—kept telling him he was going to be a preacher and he was going to pray over presidents.

As a kid he was a maths nerd, a *Star Trek* geek and a mild religious sceptic. But so many people told him he'd be a preacher, he couldn't ignore it. He took it as a sign from God and delivered his first sermon at the age of fifteen. He discovered he had a gift. At nineteen he married the sweetheart he'd met when they were eleven. At twenty, he decided to finish his maths degree but attend Bible college simultaneously and become a pastor: 'I was thinking computer engineering. I did not deny I had a gift for preaching. I wanted to nurture that with humility and grace.'

He thought he could be a computer engineer professionally and preach at weekends. But God apparently wanted all his efforts. He is a product of the Pentecostal movement and now a leader of it: 'We all go through the existential queries—why do we exist? Is there something beyond us? But experiences define us, we all have experiential needs. What Pentecostalism does is take the cognitive interpretation of God—what we perceive God to be intellectually—and gives it vitality. We hunger for spirituality, we hunger for mysticism, for the reality beyond what we can see. I believe we are making great inroads. It's the Holy Spirit's job—he fuels the church. There are signs and wonders and giftings.'

Rodriguez sees this as leading to much more unity among Christians than ever before: 'The Spirit of the living God is moving. I believe the Holy Spirit is the quintessential unifier. It's the will of the Holy Spirit in order to answer Jesus' prayer: Father make them one.'

One thing to like about Pentecostals is that while they trust in the spirit, they work like everything depends on them. Rodriguez runs his own church in Sacramento, but he is involved in countless activities and ventures across the United States, and across the world. He has an invigorating formula for his own particular vocation: 'Billy Graham has always been my north star—the quintessential Evangelical evangelist. I saw a film where Billy Graham was preaching. But then I saw Dr Martin Luther King's I Have a Dream speech. Something said to me—Samuel, your mission is to reconcile Billy Graham and Martin Luther King. The church has essentially been divided between the followers of Billy Graham and the followers of Martin Luther King. We need to combine righteousness and justice; truth and love; what I call the vertical and the horizontal.'

He thinks Christians can reshape the world, and he's impatient for them to get on and do it: 'The Western world is becoming more morally relativistic. There is an assault on truth in the culture and we'll continue to see that assault on truth. But my number one problem is not with the assault, it's with lukewarm Christianity, which is willing to sacrifice the truth on the altar of expediency, which is always a comfortable Christianity.

'There are still enough Christians in the world, 2.5 billion, maybe 3 billion. Between Protestants and Catholics it's still nearly half the world's population. It's still the world's largest faith narrative. It should wake up and advance an agenda of truth and love. Do not keep our Christianity private. This idea of private Christianity is counter to the teachings òf Jesus. He publicly died on the cross so we could publicly live out our Christian faith for him.'

This is a stirring call to action by Rodriguez, who speaks with that characteristic Pentecostal high-energy, high-speed delivery, his words often come in a rush, with concepts and facts and numbers and appeals all tumbling over each other, all perfectly coherent, but words and ideas struggling and jostling to stand side by side rather than in the orderly lines which constitute conventional sentences. You can see it would be easy to be swept up in his enthusiasm, and this is no small thing. He is being, I suspect, a bit overly optimistic about the total numbers of Christians, rounding up rather than rounding down. Most estimates put Christianity at about a third of the world's population. But his overall point is surely right.

And, he adds, while Christianity is certainly under challenge in the West (meaning Western Europe, North America, and Australia and New Zealand), that is not remotely true in the rest of the world: 'There's an explosion of Christianity coming out of Africa, Latin America and Asia.'

But Rodriguez is hardly going to let Western culture itself slip away from Christianity without a fight, in the US, or anywhere else.

Here is where his role as a film-maker comes in. The broad culture in most Western nations has become at best unsympathetic to Christianity and at times downright hostile. Christianity is a universal religion which came from the Middle East. The majority of its believers today are not found in Western nations. But Christianity did uniquely shape Western civilisation. The trend by Western intellectuals to reclassify Western civilisation as a thing to hate, despite its occasional virtues, as opposed to a thing to love, despite its many lapses, involves a simultaneous, explicit rejection of Christianity and its truth. Once the background culture was pro-Christian, so there were many signals to believers and non-believers alike reinforcing Christianity. Now the background culture tends to ignore, ridicule, attack or patronise Christianity. This is demoralising for Christians and makes it much more difficult for the Christian message to get a hearing in the minds of those unconvinced, unschooled in Christianity, or with little or no background in it.

Christians should not just complain about this. They need to create the culture themselves. This is something Rodriguez does by producing mainstream Hollywood films which have a Christian theme. Having the Latino connection is surely a big factor in this. Latinos, or at least very many of them, still openly believe in Christianity and openly practise their religion. That's why *Jane the Virgin* could be such a pro-Christian TV series. That in the United States more of them vote Democrat than Republican is no bad thing. Christianity, in so far as it overlaps with politics, has to live, and inspire people, on the moderate centre left and the moderate centre right.

A well-made Christian film, with lots of Latino characters, has a good shot at securing at least a sizeable chunk of the Christian viewership in the US, which is still something like 200 million people. And of course if the film is genuinely well made it will get viewers beyond just self-identifying Christians, and it will also earn money beyond the United States. And if it's even a reasonably sized project it has a chance of securing mainstream Latino stars. Eva Longoria, a genuine Hollywood Latino star, has been associated with Rodriguez's movies.

Also the Pentecostal ease with dealing with Hollywood and money and celebrities and all the rest is important. It's hard to imagine a Catholic or Anglican bishop hooking up a movie deal with Hollywood, just knowing how to talk to the folks involved and how to get a project going.

One of Rodriguez's films is *Breakthrough*, which was released in 2019. It had a budget of $14 million, which is small by Hollywood standards but by no means minuscule, and it generated worldwide box office revenue of more than $50 million. This was in every sense a mainstream film. It was released by 20th Century Fox. It got an Academy Award nomination for best song. Most of the actors in the film are not Latinos, but the central character, John Smith, is a Guatemalan boy who has been adopted by American parents. The film explores the cultural identity issues. The plot pivots around the boy falling through a sheet of ice and being submerged for 15 minutes before being rescued. A complex story of prayer and faith and family tensions ensues and finally John recovers. It's based on a true story and it contains a number of unapologetically miraculous episodes. The critical consensus was that this is a very good movie, a reasonably predictable plot but sustained dramatic tension, fine performances, engagement with contemporary issues, good music—it's a winner.

Several things about the film are worth reflecting on. The experience of seeing the film would be beneficial. It reinforces the Christian message for the believer, and it gently asks some questions of the non-believer. There are wider effects as well. One pro-Christian movie is not going to change the culture. But there's nothing like persuading Hollywood that there's money to be made in giving Christianity a sympathetic hearing.

Says Rodriguez: 'That's what I do. The Billy Graham pastor preaches every Sunday. The horizontal pastor is a movie producer, a civil rights leader, a political adviser. We've done three movies with a faith perspective with 20th Century Fox. These are mainstream films with Hollywood studios. They also are films with a Christian perspective. And they get great worldwide distribution. That's all part of the agenda—reforming the culture and leading a new generation to the saving grace of Jesus.'

This question of leading the new generation to Jesus is one of the most vexed in all Western Christianity. Even the most successful Christian denominations and movements face a steep challenge in passing on Christian belief from one generation to the next. Tens of millions of Christian young people all over the West are an example to their elders in their passion and commitment to the Christian faith. But it was once the genius of Christianity that it was a faith of the ordinary as well as the passionate, it was a faith of the rank and file, the regular folks, as well as the devout. The ambient culture in the West has now become so hostile to Christianity that it requires a positive act of assertive counter-cultural individualism and contrarian self-definition for a young person to embrace Christianity, certainly to embrace it publicly.

In any event, whatever the reason, parents are having a lot of trouble passing on Christian belief to their kids.

Despite the general success of Pentecostals in recruiting younger folks, Rodriguez does not deny this problem for a second: 'There is a generational disconnect, there is a glitch in the matrix from one generation to the next. Is it being addressed? Yes. Are we addressing it in a viable and sustainable way? We don't know yet. All church leaders and movement leaders are meeting to discuss this. The prescription? With this generation it's all about content. We have to generate content that will lead to conversation which results in cultural reformation.'

Rodriguez repeats the formulation: 'In the 21st century, it's all about content. For the millennial generation, and the generation after that, it's all about content. That includes videos, YouTube, audio, podcasts, sermons, movies, books— there has to be content that will lead to a conversation that will lead to a reaffirmation of faith. Back in the 20th century we talked about being born again, about having a conversation with someone that will lead them to Christ. In the 21st century you can't get to that conversation unless there's content first. That's what I do.'

Rodriguez is involved extensively in politics. He is a conservative, and strong on life issues and traditional Christian views of morality and the like. He was involved with both Barack Obama's White House and Donald Trump's. He thinks the Democratic Party has gone too far to the left and parts of it have become anti-Christian.

However, Rodriguez does not create comfort altogether on the left or the right. He excoriates the left on cultural issues. But he is strong on the civil rights of immigrants and would-be immigrants. Not only that, he thinks that some of his friends on the right don't realise that Christianity in the United States is reinvigorated by Christian immigrants from Latin America, Africa and Asia. He is against illegal immigration and wants the US to have secure borders, but he is against deporting undocumented immigrants unless they have criminal records. He is against separating families. He may well have played a role in Trump de-emphasising immigration as he sought Latino votes at the 2020 election.

I respect Rodriguez's political engagement, but I don't think his political positions are the only ones open to a conscientious American Christian. But it is surely a fantastic thing that Rodriguez and his movement are engaging their society so broadly, especially across areas where Christians have not in recent decades been doing that well. The spirit moves him, and he moves the world, at least a little.

And a little, really, is a lot.

* * *

The scene is rocking. It's the most racially diverse gathering I've ever encountered in London. Lots of Afro-Caribbeans, plenty of Asians, lots of white folks, too, and almost every other variety you can imagine. Singer and guitars and a big, big sound. Boom! Boom! Boom! After the 'concert', the big crowd, as diverse in age as in ethnic origin, spills out onto a precious patch of green in central London, there to enjoy an informal lunch of many ethnic cuisines—curries, paella, chilli con carne, pizzas and ice cream. There's no cost, though you can make a donation if you like, and as far as I can tell everyone does.

I am attending the Sunday morning service of Holy Trinity Brompton, in Knightsbridge, one of the most dynamic and important Anglican parishes in the world (though the good folks there would never make such flattering claims about themselves). The big feature of the service is the music. But the spiritual highlight is the legendary pastor, Nicky Gumbel, interviewing the Christian musical couple Matt and Beth Redman. Gumbel and the Redmans are stars in the world of British Evangelical Christianity. One of Gumbel's books, *Questions of Life*, sold more than a million copies. The Redmans have both written books of Christian testimony and they are sell-out musicians in the US and Britain.

In 2019 I spent a few months based in London as a visiting fellow at a British university, and I spent some of my time investigating what was happening to belief in Britain. The big story of 21st-century Britain—as big as Brexit or COVID— is the radical loss of belief and meaning. It is a transforming social dynamic. But there are also important, if still tentative, signs of a counter-trend.

Right next to Holy Trinity Brompton, its good neighbours live in the Brompton Oratory, the historic and also, in its way, world-famous, Catholic church. Just a little before the rocking and rolling at HTB, the Catholic priests at Brompton Oratory celebrated the old Tridentine mass. Not only is this mass conducted in Latin, the liturgy follows the ancient rites formalised by the Council of Trent in the sixteenth century. The Tridentine mass was replaced with an updated liturgy in vernacular languages by the second Vatican Council in the 1960s. Brompton Oratory is liturgically conservative, though most of its masses use the modern rite in English rather than the Tridentine rite. The music at the Tridentine masses is sublime, exquisite, solemn and contemplative, a piercing it might seem of the soul itself with transcendent beauty. I have been to both sorts of masses a few times at the Brompton Oratory and they too are all strikingly well attended.

It seems that HTB and the Oratory next door are poles apart, but I don't think that at all. The sacred music that a community uses is mainly a matter of taste. The two churches strike me as not much different at all on the things that really matter. One, with its ancient Latin liturgy, looks shockingly counter-cultural. The other, hip and groovy, seems to be riding the wave of contemporary culture. But the worship and the music in both churches are based squarely on the words of the Bible, Old Testament and New, and the message of the Christianity is essentially the same. Both forms of Christianity are growing, in London and elsewhere.

Holy Trinity Brompton uses contemporary cultural style, but it does not endorse contemporary culture in total, any more than Brompton Oratory does. Beth Redman, in a dialogue that

I found convincing, thoughtful, impressive and direct, recounts how she has gone off Twitter and scaled back her Facebook. Partly this is theological—the Bible says do your good works in secret. Partly it is, like everything in this tradition, experiential. She found that even when she was trying to pray, her iPhone distracted her. She was inclined to check it. So she chucked it. She also tells people to be careful of the films and television they consume, to be careful of the evil they put in their heads. She and her husband had much else to say about more profound issues of life. But I was struck by the good sense and uncompromising nature of her social media advice. It offers a clue to the genius of this style of Christianity. It is as hip and groovy and contemporary as you like, but it doesn't shirk tough messages that in other contexts may sound wowserish.

The question is whether the two Bromptons and all the other signs of life in contemporary British Christianity are really signs of hope, maybe of a turn at last, or are they really more like crowded lifeboats bobbing around in the wake of a sinking ocean liner?

Whether you are religious or not, the pivot point of history that Britain and Western Europe have reached is awe-inspiring, epochal and little understood. Britain and Western Europe have abandoned the faith of their fathers, even more the faith of their mothers, and with it, incidentally, so much of their cultural and civic inheritance, so much in fact of their traditional view of what it means to be a human being.

According to social research, towards the end of the 2010s, among 18- to 29-year-olds in France, there were as many practising Muslims as there were Catholics. As many young Muslims go to mosque in France as young Catholics go to mass.

In London, paradoxically the most religious part of the UK, of a total population of eight million, just over four million self-identify as Christian, and 2.4 million self-identify as Muslim, although as the decade turned into the 2020s, Christians at last seemed to be holding their numbers. According to survey results from 2017, some 7 per cent of 18- to 29-year-old Brits identified as Anglicans while some 6 per cent identified as Muslims.

This is not to criticise Muslims. There are three reasons their numbers have grown so fast. They have been a big part of the immigration cohort for a long time. They have more children than non-Muslim families do. And they are much more successful in passing on religious affiliation to their children. It is not necessary to be in any way anti-Muslim to recognise that this represents an epic shift in the cultural identity of Europe. Other religions are also growing in Britain, among them Hindus, Sikhs and even, off a very low base, Orthodox Haredi Jews. All of these groups are more successful than European Christians in maintaining their religious affiliation across generations.

There is one significant point of context which mitigates these trends a bit, but only a bit. For a long time, Christianity was a nominal affiliation for large chunks of European populations. Secularisation, the loss of God, has meant in part the end of nominal Christianity in Europe. Nick Spencer, a researcher at the London religious think tank Theos, told me: 'For the last generation or two, Christian identity and ethics have ceased to be the default position. That's been replaced by a default liberal outlook—me and my choices.'

There is a long debate over whether secularisation is a process that has progressed over centuries—from the Renaissance de-emphasising the divine in art, through the wars of

Christianity to all the savage disruptions of the twentieth century—or something much more sudden. The classic account by Callum Brown, *The Death of Christian Britain*, argues that the process was much more sudden. It was kicked off by the cultural disruption of the 1960s, the sexual revolution and everything that followed. Brown's book suggests that Christianity reached a high point in Britain in the first part of the twentieth century, but the proportion of Christians was still not very far below those highs as late as the 1950s. There had even been some revival of Christian sentiment and practice in the 1940s and 1950s.

There is some evidence that the decline of Christianity in Britain has hit bottom and may be turning around. If that is so, it is in part at least because of the efforts of Gumbel. Although, as Sammy Rodriguez would have predicted, the immigration to Britain of Christians from central and eastern Europe, especially disproportionately religious Poland, as well as Africa, the Caribbean and Asia, has also helped Christianity in Britain.

Gumbel's father was a German Jewish refugee, who was secular. Gumbel's mother was nominally Christian. Gumbel graduated from Cambridge University and became, like his father, a successful barrister. But he had converted to Christianity as an undergraduate as a result of reading the New Testament. After a few years at the bar, he went to train at Wycliffe Hall in Oxford with a view to becoming an Anglican clergyman. Although he did not found it, he has run the Alpha program since 1990. Alpha is a phenomenon, one of the most successful Christian formation and evangelisation efforts in modern history.

It is an approach to teaching the basic Christian faith, mainly to non-Christians. These days, however, so many nominal Christians have so little knowledge or experience of Christianity, and contemporary Western culture provides so few positive signs or clues to it, that the distinction between non-Christian and nominal Christian when people first come into contact with Alpha can be pretty slight. Around the world, perhaps something more than 25 million people have taken the Alpha course in one form or another. In some countries, such as China, no numbers are kept for Alpha attendees. Inevitably it's an estimate, but it's in that order. Within Australia alone, a half million or so have taken the Alpha course.

About ten days after I attend the service at Holy Trinity Brompton, a friend arranges that I might go and see Gumbel at his home, which is just near the church. Whatever his success selling books, his own home is modest. Of course anything in this part of London would notionally be worth a fortune. But it is situated where it is so as to be next to the church. And while it's respectable, it is by no means flash. Rather it has a comfortable, well-worn, thoroughly lived-in feel about it. He makes me a cup of tea and we walk through to his study, which is book-lined and a little ramshackle, and contains more than one chair that doesn't bear very vigorous use.

Gumbel doesn't think Christian decline is inevitable, ongoing or irreversible: 'If you take the Church in the UK, people think it's a steady decline. But actually, it's back and forth. In 1750 the Church had declined to almost nothing. There were ten thousand sex workers walking the streets of London and sixteen people at St Paul's Cathedral at Easter. Then along came the Wesleys [John Wesley was an Anglican minister who founded the Methodist congregation] and William Wilberforce [a Christian politician who campaigned successfully to end slavery] and it [Christianity] builds all the way to 1910. Since 1910 there's been a decline. But even within the cycles there are reverses. When Billy Graham came there was a blip of growth. The question is: are we at the end of the decline? The old [Christians] are still dying but the young are still coming forward. There's been a huge rise in Anglican ordinands [people studying for the Anglican ministry].'

Another Theos researcher, Paul Bickley, pointed me to research which shows that religious communities of 'experiential difference' are flourishing. The term 'experiential difference' means really two things—the idea that there is something different about being a Christian and you experience this difference within the community where you worship, and second, a sense of some kind of transcendent experience of God.

Gumbel's movement of Anglicans has been involved in 'church planting' in Britain and around the world. Where a church is about to close, or there is a need on a housing estate or in some other community, the HTB network, as it is sometimes called, tries to step in with volunteers and energy and passionate commitment and see what it can do.

A decade ago, HTB founded a seminary, a college to train new ministers. In many churches, certainly Anglicanism and Catholicism in the West, for hundreds of years the typical way to train to become a priest was to go away for several years to a residential college and study theology and philosophy and the like. HTB's college offered a new model. For a few days a week, students for the priesthood studied, but for a couple of days a week they worked in a parish, and on Sundays participated fully in the life of the parish. All the while, they lived at their homes. This has now become one of the biggest and most successful Anglican training colleges in Britain.

Gumbel tells me of his plan to create a 'Peter stream' to train ministers. The two great leaders of the early Church were Peter and Paul. Paul was an intellectual, as virtually all Anglican and Catholic and many other denominations' ministers are trained to be. But there are many devoted followers of Jesus who, like Peter, are not intellectuals. They certainly know enough to know what the faith is. But they won't compose Oxbridge-style essays about fine points of theology and philosophy. Is it right that the Church doesn't use their skills for ministry?

So why has Alpha become such a worldwide success? 'One thing, I think, is the genuine community. There's food, people are welcomed, it's non-confrontational, everyone's loved for who they are. It's organised around a series of talks, each followed by group discussions in which the Alpha leaders don't provide direction but facilitate discussion of the talk just held. At a certain point, there's a weekend away. People are searching for meaning in life, and purpose. The talks are organised around that. The first asks: what is the purpose of life? The second is: who is Jesus, why did he die? It's all around forgiveness. The next is about faith—who do you trust? The weekend away is about the Holy Spirit. It's an opportunity to experience God. This generation is much more interested in experiencing God than learning facts about God. There is an evening on healing . . . healing and mindfulness are very in now. Alpha is running in all parts of the Church—the Reformed

Church, the Pentecostals, the Catholics, Methodists, Baptists, Salvation Army. We're Church of England. That's very good because we're less of a threat than anybody because nobody really knows what the Church of England believes.'

Gumbel is being self-deprecating here. We shouldn't let him get away with too much modesty. Although Gumbel is a dynamic pastor and preacher and, in Alpha, the fashioner of a great Christian movement, he is still, after all, an Oxbridge-educated Englishman of his generation and traffics effortlessly in irony, understatement and a courtesy which can almost be a courtliness. The Anglican tradition is one of the pillars of global Christianity, and where it is well led and growing, it is as dynamic as any part of Christianity.

Finally, I ask Gumbel what a person loses if they lose the knowledge of God. In a long, animated, fluent conversation, it is the first time he pauses.

'I was not brought up as a Christian,' he says slowly. 'I know the difference between belief and not having belief. Ultimately, you can lose everything. A person obviously can find purpose outside of the faith, but I don't think you can find ultimate purpose and meaning outside of a relationship with God.'

Another pause: 'And if Jesus did rise from the dead, there's hope, and meaning. And love.'

* * *

Peter Comensoli, the Catholic Archbishop of Melbourne, has a fine Italian/Australian name. Comensoli—say it slow and celebrate how the rich Italian syllables roll around each other, spilling out to the final, characteristic vowel. And Peter, the leader of the first Christians after Jesus' resurrection—that's a great name for a bishop to bear. The Archbishop has a particular devotion to his ecclesiastical namesake: 'I like Peter, he's sometimes an idiot like me, but he learns and trusts.'

But Comensoli has another namesake too. His late cousin, also Peter Comensoli, was a priest in the Wollongong diocese. He was also a paedophile who went to jail for sexually abusing two altar boys, and was later convicted of other similar offences. The clerical sex abuse crisis has been the worst thing Comensoli has ever had to deal with as a Catholic priest and bishop. For all Catholics, it is a matter of shame and sorrow. I believe the Church has been overwhelmingly a force for good in all of its human history. But it encompasses 1.2 billion people and some of them have done terrible things. Wickedly, some of them have used the authority of the Church to do such things.

Comensoli now heads the biggest Catholic diocese in Australia, covering a million Catholics. It is bigger even than the diocese of Sydney because Sydney has been divided into a number of smaller dioceses. It is indeed one of the bigger Catholic dioceses in the world. Comensoli has huge work ahead of him. He wants to communicate what C.S. Lewis called the 'deep magic' which gives meaning and purpose to people's lives, and he needs to do this in a culture which doesn't find archbishops interesting, and is increasingly indifferent or hostile to Christianity.

He is animated to answer this challenge, on fire with energy and enthusiasm, but one thing to like about him is that he is also a moral realist. Shortly after his appointment, in a major oration, he declared: 'I cannot deny that I also stand here amid the darkest days of our proud history in this city.'

Just as the city emerges from lockdown in late 2020, I go into central Melbourne to talk to Comensoli at his office, near St Patrick's Cathedral. Like the greatest city churches, it combines leaf and stone in the throbbing heart of a big city, rest amid the mayhem, calm in the pandemonium. The cathedral office this day has a sepulchral air—almost everyone is still working from home. One kind priest on the cathedral staff is just doing a coffee run as I arrive and furnishes us with the necessary caffeine.

Comensoli has grown a beard over summer. It's a good look, manly and authoritative. Catholic bishops in general could benefit from looking a bit sparer, a bit tougher. For surely, tough times are coming.

Comensoli is committed to supporting the victims of abuse and making sure such circumstances cannot arise again. How did it happen in the first place? 'I offer these thoughts with hesitancy. The peak period of the bulk of the abuse followed some years after the peaking of numbers entering the seminary in the 1950s and 60s. Then the peak of abuse was in the 70s and 80s. The so-called sexual revolution is traced to the 60s and 70s. It had an influence on everyone. You can trace a lot of the malaise of life to things that were abandoned then. The priesthood was seen as an institution of power and authority. There was a lack of human formation. Formation was coming from an Irish model that had an element of Jansenism about it, a disregard for the body. There was a lack of understanding of psychosexual formation and living your life. There was a club mentality of power and entitlement.'

Jansenism was a tendency in French Catholicism, which was later defined as heresy, and which tended to regard the human body as inherently evil. It demanded a highly ascetic lifestyle as the only legitimately Christian way of living. History shows us that when you set impossible standards, no one can meet them and many abandon the effort altogether.

Was the problem also related to a loss of a sense of the sacred among priests? 'It doesn't necessarily come about from a loss of the sacred, but from a profound sense of doubt about the purpose and the effects of God in our lives, of whether there's any benefit to what you're doing.'

As a young priest, Comensoli learnt about his cousin's offending only when it hit the media: 'I was a hospital chaplain [at the time the case was proceeding]. I found myself as an initial reaction very hesitant to admit who I was. For a period of time it was very challenging. Then after a time I got angry—I'm not an abuser, I didn't do this. One of those Peter abused was a classmate of mine at the seminary. I saw my cousin a few times leading up to the case and saw him in prison once. I've forgiven him but I couldn't bring myself to be with him and talk to him. A lot of this has to do with my brothers. They were scarred by this and fiercely protective of their kids. I worked through these things myself, I believe.'

At the same time Comensoli has to continue to deal with the legacy of these issues, he has the bigger challenge of proclaiming the Gospel in Melbourne, and more broadly in Australia.

How did he end up a priest in the first place? 'Ours was an ordinary Catholic family. We were always practising [their religion]. The faith was there. We went to mass on Sundays, got our formation at Catholic schools. Mum's sister became a nun. About Year 10 I started thinking about the priesthood but I was still interested in girls. But there was a persistency in God, like the drip, drip, drip of rain. I was part of a team of young people in the youth group Antioch. This was a significant formative dimension of my life. Antioch was couched in the image of the Body of Christ—Antioch as a youth community. Every Antioch group had a married couple—marriage as a vocation was very strong. And it had a parish structure. Antioch shaped my understanding of the priesthood. I believe in the image of a "married" priesthood.'

Let me hasten to say this does not mean Comensoli is opposed to priestly celibacy. He explains: 'One of the images Jesus uses is of himself as the bridegroom of the Church. It is also evident in the sacrificial nature of the cross and the sacrificial nature of marriage. The priesthood comes out of the life of Christ. During that period I was interested in girls and had one near-serious relationship. What gets me over the line for celibacy is that I could never imagine myself with just one other person for life. I could certainly imagine myself as a father.

'When I left school I got a job at a bank and was doing Commerce part-time at Wollongong University. I did that for four years and got two-thirds of the way through a degree. The idea of the priesthood was always there. The thought of it wouldn't go away. It was nearly an itch. I went to the seminary with the idea of getting it out of my system. I didn't go there with the deep sense of committing myself forever to the priesthood, though I believed in that.

'I hadn't had any experience or knowledge of abuse. I wasn't aware of it.'

I can bear out the authenticity of Comensoli's experience in that last remark. Like him I went to the nuns and then the brothers for school, like him I was involved in a wide array of

Catholic youth groups (so many that I can barely remember all their names). I went to a Redemptorist junior seminary for a year to see if I might become a priest, I even worked for a few months for *The Catholic Weekly* in Sydney. And in all that time I never heard a whisper of clerical sexual abuse, nor could I even have imagined such a thing happening.

Comensoli is relatively young by Catholic bishop standards (56 when I talk to him) to be in charge of such a big diocese. It's a job that needs many qualities, but perhaps none more so than energy and passionate belief. Comensoli identifies his priorities as: local communities; marriage and family life; young disciples; and the poor, the broken and the wounded.

His analysis of the place of the Church in society offers striking resonance with the views I've heard from Sammy Rodriguez and Nicky Gumbel in their different but comparable societies: 'The Church has had a sense of its place in the city. With the great Catholic institutions, the Church has loomed large in the political world, in the civic world. All these things in the big Church have broken. We've experienced an earthquake in sexual abuse and in the cultural changes of the West. So then you're on very unstable ground. We need to pitch for new grounds. Where? In households, in communities.

'Our parishes must be neighbourhoods of grace. We need to pitch for a land where we can rebuild and plant seeds. Evangelisation is a person-to-person, family-to-family business. We've relied on the institutions but they're broken, on broken grounds. We need to emphasise the local, the small, the intimate, the household, the domestic. That takes us back to the Acts of the Apostles. It so often references household churches, not the great institutions of empire.'

Like Rodriguez and Gumbel, Comensoli gets it that Christianity is now going against the cultural grain: 'Yes I do have a sense of this being counter-cultural. I'm aware of being an outsider. We are yeast and yeast is a foreign body, but it does good things. And we are incarnational in our Christianity, enmeshed in people's lives. We're not abstract theories. Jesus came to certain people at a certain time and in a certain place. Now he is to come to this people in this place at this time.'

Comensoli is serious when he talks about changing the way the Church operates. Take the question of training priests: 'I have begun a process about this. The idea that you'd withdraw from ordinary life for seven years and live in a collegial life with other fellows [that's basically the way it's done now], that's not really forming you in the life of a diocesan priest living in the community. We are diocesan priests, so how should our formation prepare us for that? The system of formation in its seminary structure has a pretty ancient pedigree. The Archdiocese of Paris since the 1980s has had those in formation living in small houses in parishes, going to universities.'

This sounds as though Comensoli might be moving towards something like a deinstitutionalisation of priestly training, small group houses and active parish work throughout. If so it is strikingly similar to the approach Gumbel has pioneered in training Anglican clergy in London. It's all about bringing the priesthood closer to the people. And yet Comensoli himself remembers three great benefits from his own seminary training: 'It was a wonderful education; I made some great friends and I had a very good spiritual director.'

So this will be a question of balance. You certainly want to avoid exclusive or unhealthy clericalism, but you do want priests still to be well-trained intellectually, to have a positive *esprit de corps*, and to make those peer friendships which will help sustain them through a lifetime of priesthood. At the same time you want them closely involved with real life, real families, rank-and-file Catholics and especially people in need.

Comensoli has been happy in the priesthood: 'I don't see the priesthood as this terribly hard life. I disavow that attitude to my fellow priests. It can become a woe-is-me attitude. I'm not saying that it can't ever be tough, but marriage and family life is inherently tougher.'

I wonder if, like Gumbel in a different context, Comensoli is not being a bit too modest here. The modern Catholic priest is not well loved in the culture, acquires no possessions and wealth to console himself about security in old age, moves from post to post, and, while forming many human friendships, is denied the natural warmth of a family. And he is available, always, for the work of God and the demands of the distressed. For the true priest, this should be more than compensated for by the love of God and the chance to serve God by serving his people. And there is the chance for the priest to know God more fully in prayer. Yet it can be a tough, tough life. Often a priest effectively lives alone in a presbytery, with fewer people finding his work important, much less critical to their own lives and families. Every priest in the West now is called to be a missionary priest, to bring the Good News to people in a deeply unsympathetic culture.

One point Comensoli makes to me in passing is that the Catholic Church is intensely Biblical these days. Mass every Sunday involves four readings from Scripture—an Old Testament passage, a series of verses from the Psalms, a Gospel reading, and a passage from another part of the New Testament, the Epistles. Most of the prayers the Church promotes—certainly the Our Father [Lord's Prayer] and the Hail Mary—are drawn directly from the Gospels.

Comensoli's own prayer life revolves around his daily mass and reciting the Divine Office. The Divine Office is the prayers the Church sets aside for different times of the day. They are used primarily by priests and mostly drawn from the Psalms. Comensoli adds: 'I like praying through Mary and I do that every day.' (Praying through Mary means asking for Mary's intercession with God; it doesn't mean praying to Mary as though she were God.)

He describes Melbourne as the 'saint whisperer' among Australian cities. Mary MacKillop, Australia's first Catholic saint, was born there. So was Eileen O'Connor, the founder of Our Lady's Nurses for the Poor, and Mary Glowrey, a nun who was also a doctor and pioneered medical services, especially for women, over nearly 40 years working in India. The Church is investigating the cause of sainthood for both these women.

Comensoli doesn't recall any deep temptation to atheism in his life: 'Everyone goes through this questioning about atheism. God finds us and it's us being open to being found. My philosophical head continues to puzzle about eternal life. I believe in eternal life. Trying to reason it out, what it's actually like, is challenging.'

Comensoli strikes me as a moderately gregarious, upbeat kind of person, understanding fully the dark side of the Church in the terrible child-abuse episode, but full of passion and commitment for spreading the message of Christianity. In one of his YouTube mini-sermons he reflects on Thomas Aquinas's observation that heaven 'is the friendship of God'.

'I'm a sinner,' he says. 'Saints are sinners who've been found by God.'

It's a good hope for a bishop, for any Christian, to one day be that 'good thief'—a sinner found by God, through grace and forgiveness to enjoy God's friendship.

* * *

Thank God for the Salvos!

All my life I have known that refrain. It is surely one of the most powerful messages any Australian Christian Church has ever broadcast. I never knew any members of the Salvation Army personally, but in my youth and young adulthood I spent a lot of time in pubs. The only recognisable Christians you'd ever see there were the Salvos, rattling their tins to raise some money. They tended to be long, lean, stringy blokes, always friendly, always cheerful, and as far as I could see no one ever really turned them down. If you wouldn't give a few bucks to the Salvos, you were a pretty miserable species of human being—that seemed to be the common thought in any pub.

And all of us in those pubs all those years ago wanted to do something for the Salvos—just open our wallets to them, nothing more than that—for a couple of reasons. The idea I had of them was that they would work with anybody. They'd never turn anybody away. There was a sense that if you had nowhere else to go, no one else to turn to, the Salvos would have some attention for you still. They might not be able to turn your life around and solve all your problems, but they'd help the poor, the sick, the alcos, the wretched. Of course they did other things too, but the sense was the Salvos were there for people. There seemed to be a special association between Salvos and drunks, Salvos and alcoholics. There are a lot of drunks in pubs, and a lot of alcoholics.

The other thing was, the Salvos weren't scared of pubs, they weren't uncomfortable there, they didn't need gentility around them. They famously don't drink themselves, but they show up. The most important part of Christian solidarity is to show up. Like all Christian denominations, the Salvos have had their troubles, even their scandals, but I can hardly imagine a Christian group with a better name.

The Salvation Army was founded in London by William Booth in the 1860s. It grew out of the Methodist movement. It quickly developed an idea of salvation that was both spiritual and physical. It wanted to save people from the devil, save them for the Lord, like all Christian denominations, but it also wanted to save them from violence and drugs, from alcohol and poverty, from abuse and neglect.

Lyn Edge, the Salvation Army's Secretary of Mission for Australia, tells me that one of her tasks is to make sure the church is operating with the whole person, to help to save people now in this life and to help to save them in their spiritual relationship with God. Yet she doesn't like really even to accept that duality. God, she has frequently written, works not with fractions but with wholes, that is, with whole people.

Edge is an energetic, competent, friendly person, theologic- ally well qualified but exuding that air of practical priority, practical preoccupation, which the Salvos project. She seems concerned more with the society around her than the fate of the Salvation Army as an institution. Nonetheless, she proudly embodies its traditions. She grew up in a Salvation Army family in Bankstown, in the middle of Sydney's working-class and multicultural western suburbs: 'I was nurtured in a faith-filled family. I had working-class parents who loved the Lord and were the salt of the earth. My dad was a truck driver, my mum worked in administration. They worshipped as soldiers in the Salvation Army church.'

The Salvos fairly early on adopted a system of military rank and organisation. When I meet Lyn Edge, she is wearing a crisp white top that recalls the navy more than anything. Their officers are the equivalent of other denominations' ordained ministers. Worshippers in their corps, or churches, are soldiers if they've taken certain commitments, such as no drinking or smoking, or adherents if they just come along and are part of the community.

Edge and I meet in a noisy coffee shop, on a sweltering summer's day, in suburban Melbourne, where Edge now lives. Her career has taken her to different parts of the world. She left school early, went to work and for a time grew very doubtful in her faith. But in her early twenties, as a surely misnamed 'mature-age student', she quit work, lost an income, moved back home with mum and dad and went to university to study social work. Her faith revived in that period.

She became a social worker and went to work first for Wesley Mission and then the Salvation Army itself, before deciding to train to become a Salvos' officer, or minister: 'My professional life moved into social work and my personal life of faith was growing. The question was how could I bring them together? My decision was a clear decision to be a good steward of who I was, what resources I had, to live out who I was meant to be.'

So after two years of theological study and ministry preparation, in 1996 she was assigned to Glebe, in inner Sydney, to work with students and plant a church. There was a committed Salvation Army couple there, and one or two others: 'It started with us meeting privately for a while and then working out: what did Glebe look like, what were the needs, where could we help. Then we did have Sunday services and people just came along. I felt a need to help uni students, and then we moved to helping overseas students. There were a lot of lonely people there, who were having their professional needs met but that was all. We offered networks of relationships, places to belong. We ran English classes, then after that we ran an Alpha course [the Christian instruction courses pioneered by Nicky Gumbel, as related earlier in this chapter]. We said to people, there's no pressure to stay for this. But they wanted to stay. The Alpha format is so good, there's a meal, there's an open discussion about Jesus and the life of faith. Someone presents some ideas and then there's a really respectful discussion of those ideas. And it only goes for ten weeks, people are not signing their lives away. Many people came to faith through Alpha courses. I don't buy the idea that Australians are not open to faith. People are losing faith in institutions, in all institutions, the police, boy scouts, the judiciary, the Salvation Army. But many millennials I find are up for a challenge. If you ask them to come and live in Wilcannia for a year, they respond. Maybe they won't live in Wilcannia for their whole life but they'll come and help for a year.'

She was asked to work the same magic in Paris, but while that didn't go exactly to plan, she spent several years there working with disadvantaged people, especially women in danger of becoming homeless. Then back to Sydney, lots of academic studies while also working in people's lives, and now she is Secretary of Mission, based in Melbourne, looking after the Salvos' activities in six key areas: homelessness; domestic violence; youth; alcohol and drugs; disaster relief; emergency response [finding people a place to stay and the like]: 'At our heart, we are a Christian church which expresses its faith through social and community provision.'

She is adamant that salvation has to encompass the here and now as well as the prospect of heaven: 'This is probably the movement of our generation. Our understanding of salvation is of body and soul. Our founder's hymn, "O Boundless Salvation", does mean that people are housed, they also have meaning in their lives, have a relationship with God. The idea of salvation got captured in the West as an other-worldly thing, but it can also be salvation from alcohol and drugs and despair. The Army is grounded in the lives of people and their lived experience.'

She is particularly inspired by the spirituality of the Old Testament. The Hebrew scriptures show God interested in every aspect of a person. Jewish culture of the Old Testament did not make a sharp division between the spiritual and the earthly. That is a dichotomy, she says, of Western civilisation.

The Book of Isaiah (65:17–25) contains a vision of this salvation: 'For I am about to create new heavens and a new earth . . . be glad and rejoice forever in what I am creating . . . I will rejoice in Jerusalem and delight in my people; no more shall the sound of weeping be heard in it, or the cry of distress. No more shall there be in it an infant that lives but a few days, or an old person who does not live out a lifetime . . . They shall build houses and inhabit them; they shall plant vineyards and eat their fruit . . . The wolf and the lamb shall feed together; the lion shall eat straw like the ox; but the serpent—its food shall be dust! They shall not hurt or destroy on all my holy mountain, says the Lord.'

But Edge is also clear that, while for the Salvation Army religion is not spirituality without care for the physical and emotional welfare of people, at the same time, as a religious community, it's not just social welfare without God either. It certainly doesn't remotely insist on people professing God in order to get its help, but it does believe in the metaphysical and transcendent truths of Christianity.

'Jesus never won a motivational speaker's award. He said follow me and die [to yourself]. Jesus is not my therapist. To build the kingdom of God is incredibly demanding.'

The Salvation Army is inspired by the passage in Matthew 25 where Jesus comes in judgement and separates the sheep from the goats. And the good people he praises are those who feed the hungry, welcome the stranger, shelter the homeless, clothe the naked, take care of the sick, visit those in prison. That's a pretty clear injunction to social solidarity. In that particular passage there is nothing about the need to profess belief, but there are plenty of other passages in the New Testament which do demand the love of God, the love of Jesus, personal morality, repentance of sins. So, as Edge says, 'it can't be either/or, it has to be both/and.'

One distinctive element of the Salvation Army is that it doesn't practise any sacraments, including baptism or communion. It doesn't oppose sacraments, but does not believe they are necessary for salvation, or for leading a Christian life. One explanation, which Edge recounts to me, is that many of the early members of the Salvation Army were reformed alcoholics and it was thought wiser not to have altar wine around them. Similarly, by never having wine on their premises, the Salvation Army provides a safe place for alcoholics.

It is fascinating to discover that this highly committed, motivated, energetic and notably self-sacrificing group of people in its early days had a disproportionate number of alcoholics in its ranks. This experience of the extravagant sinner (or at least the sinner whose travails are extravagantly public) becoming extremely active in God's kingdom recalls the book *Strangers to the City*, by Father Michael Casey, a Cistercian monk of the Tarrawarra Abbey in the Yarra Valley outside Melbourne. The Cistercian order of monks was founded nearly one thousand years ago and was basically a stricter, tougher, more demanding version of Benedictines. Casey wrote: 'The first generations of Cistercian monks were all adult recruits who were presumed to have pursued lives of youthful self-indulgence with sufficient zest to warrant a radical conversion. In the monastery they lived a rugged, macho existence with little comfort and a more than usual degree of bodily exertion.'

The lives of youthful self-indulgence which needed radical conversion and led men to become monks must surely have borne some resemblance to the lives of alcoholic despair which led other men, nearly one thousand years later, to service in the Salvos.

Like St Augustine, some of the most devoted Christians have come back from lives of extravagant sin and dissolution. They are, in Peter Comensoli's terms, sinners found by God. William Booth in the nineteenth century, and Robert of Molesme (the first Cistercian) in the eleventh century, both founded movements especially welcoming for sinners found by God.

Edge tells me that in her own prayer life she has come to highly value written and formal prayers, whereas the Salvation Army tradition is for spontaneous prayer. She is disarmingly self-deprecating about areas where she thinks the Salvation Army could do even better, and open to learning from other Christians, as they themselves should be open to learning from the Salvos: 'There are prayer movements in the Salvation Army, but it hasn't been our long suit. I've come to love written prayer. Our emphasis on extemporaneous prayer has left us a mile wide and an inch deep. There is a clear encouragement in the Salvation Army to a life of prayer. The new depth of understanding is in realising that prayer is something which has been going on as a movement for hundreds and hundreds of years. I'm discovering a prayer life, and the profound nature of some beautiful written prayers. I'm trying to develop a life of prayer, rather than having a prayer time, trying to keep a sense of God in life.'

Internationally, the Salvation Army is doing well in those places where Christianity is growing, such as Africa and Latin America. In the West, and in Australia, the Sunday congregations are declining, but the Salvos still have thousands of volunteers. Their footprint is not in decline. It seems to an outsider that the Salvos have a very high ratio of activists to members: 'If you're finding friends in the church, if you're getting loved, if they know it's your birthday and you get invited round for dinner, that's something good.'

The Salvation Army is perhaps the only church which has no different sections of its bureaucracy for its social work and its religious work—it's all the same work: 'In the West, there's a real discussion about us finding our place in society. It's a critical question—what does it mean to be the people of God in Australia today? If God is at work in Australia and I'm partnering with God in that work—of course the Salvation Army has its challenges—but I think we're well placed to have a cautious optimism.'

The Salvation Army does a lot of outcome measurement and one of the responses which has most stayed with Edge is the remark of one the Salvos' clients who said: 'I want someone in my life who isn't paid to be there.'

Thank God for the Salvos.

Epilogue

There is a promise that Jesus makes which is worth repeating. He tells Peter, standing in place of all the disciples, that he is the rock of the church, and 'on this rock I will build my church, and the gates of hell will not prevail against it'. (Matthew 16:18). Whatever else you might say about Jesus, there is no sense at all that he is a liar.

So what does it mean, this promise, that the gates of hell will not prevail against the Christian Church?

It means really that there's no excuse for Christians to stop trying their best, in their own lives and in public leadership. Jesus has promised that they will never be left alone and finally that they will not fail, though success might be hard to see in the mists and fog of our times. Jesus' promise most assuredly does not mean that life will be easy or their efforts lead to immediate and obvious outcomes.

The first part of this book has tried to look at the human stories of the New Testament, primarily of Jesus himself, but also of his closest family and followers—Mary, Peter, John, and that complete original, Paul. None of them had an easy life. Perhaps there is no such thing as an easy life—lives look easy mostly from a distance.

Even with Jesus in their midst, the first disciples could be discouraged, confused, terrified. And surely they made plenty of mistakes, as they tell us themselves. The idea of Mary as the chief source for Luke's gospel is immensely appealing. So, too, is the idea of Peter as Mark's source, for this explains why the episodes are included that cast Peter in such a bad light. The worst moment for Peter comes after his greatest expression of devotion.

Before Jesus was arrested, Peter told Jesus that he would never desert him. Peter was not boastful but surely sincere when he declared: Even if all fall away on account of you, I never will. Then he repeats the promise, stronger even than before: 'Even though I must die with you, I will never deny you.' (Mark 14: 31)

But then, before the cock crows twice, which may mean something as routine as a bugle call for a change of soldiers' shifts, Peter does deny Jesus. Three times. He's scared when a girl identifies him as one of the Jesus group. More scared when someone else does it again. And appalled when the group near him can recognise his accent. Then the cock crows and Peter realises what he's done. He breaks into bitter tears and runs off, weeping surely with a loathing and shame for his own weakness.

But while Peter has momentarily lost his courage, he has not lost his faith. He never altogether gives up on Jesus. Much more important, Jesus never gives up on Peter.

I think Peter instructed Mark to include this in his account in order to show that you can make terrible mistakes and yet you can still come back. There is no sin you cannot finally repent, no difficulty which can ever finally prevent you from seeing the face of Jesus, or prevent Jesus from seeing into the deepest parts of your heart.

Christianity has probably never been weaker institution-ally in the West than it is now, certainly not for hundreds of years. Yet these are typically the moments when Christianity does the most surprising things, the most extraordinary things. As Nicky Gumbel points out, the great Christian revival in Britain associated with the Wesleys followed a level of religious indifference which almost resembles the neo-paganism creeping into our own times. Who would ever have expected that the number of Chinese Christians would grow from a couple of million when the communists took power, to somewhere between 60 and 100 million, 70 years later? Who would have thought that Christianity would catch fire in Africa, long after the last colonisers had gone?

Christians in the West are not persecuted, but they are discouraged, the sentiment of the culture is indifferent or hostile. This is partly the consequence of terrible crimes committed by some Christians. But it is also a much wider cultural movement.

Some of Christianity's critics, and even some of its followers, would like it to go quiet for a time, not to rock the boat. But Jesus, in Mark's gospel, gave a very clear instruction: the Good News must be preached to all.

No matter how silly or awkward we look, no matter how silly we've sometimes made ourselves, there is still a need to tell people the Good News. People deserve the truth.

The moment the early disciples faced after the crucifixion was infinitely worse than any difficulties Christians face in the modern West. Yet they kept praying. What transformed them was the resurrection and return of Jesus.

But even that did not solve all their problems. It gave them a new spirit, a life transformed, a path of truth, a way forward. But still, as the Acts of the Apostles demonstrates, they had to raise the funds, send out the Apostles, endure all manner of hostility. They had to determine disputes within their number. Paul's Letter to the Galatians gives us an intimate glimpse of just such a dispute. Jesus didn't remove their difficulties and challenges, he gave them the strength and vision and purpose to meet those challenges. He stood beside them. Peter and Paul, and others of the first disciples, died as martyrs. Once Peter was scared when a girl thought she recognised him as a follower of Jesus, later he preached and set up churches and, according to the oldest Christian traditions, went to his death rather than deny his faith.

But for all the daunting troubles and persecutions, the early Christian community grew, and it brought with its growth joy and new life and abundance.

The people in the second half of this book, contemporary Christians, are as much Jesus' disciples as are those in the New Testament. This is one of the most thrilling realisations of Christianity. The same message, the same teachings, the same lessons and truths and inspirations, in some deep sense the same religious culture as that which nurtured Peter and Mary, or Paul or Mary Magdalene or John, or all the other early disciples, embraces and inspires Christians today. The continuity is astounding.

When, sometime after the resurrection, Jesus ascended to heaven, the early disciples had to not only follow Jesus, they had to model Jesus. For people who had not known or seen Jesus personally were most likely to form their sense of him through their experience of the real, living Christians they met.

The early Christians, for all their troubles, were happy and good. They didn't practice female infanticide, so their families had lots more girls and that naturally made them much happier.

They didn't run away during plagues but stayed to help. They made marriage a bond of love. They looked out for the poor. Everyone was welcome. Slaves became bishops.

So there is no mystery to the way ahead for Christians. They should do their best, proclaim the truth, try to be kind to people, expect to take some knocks. They know for sure they won't be labouring on their own, and as the old Psalm says: joy comes in the morning.

For Christ is risen.

Acknowledgements

This book has benefitted from the help of so many people, it's impossible to thank everyone properly. But I must express special gratitude to all the people I interviewed for the second half of this book. None was a volunteer. None was seeking publicity. They were all conscripts. One of the particular joys of journalism and book writing is that they give you an excuse to approach interesting people and boldly ask them to share their life secrets and most profound beliefs with you. Some of the interview subjects I'd known for many years, some I met only in the course of arranging and doing the interview. But each rewarded me with candour, grace and substance.

There were also a number of people who offered wise counsel in their areas of expertise and undertook the task of reading some parts of the manuscript along the way, greatly helping me to improve what I was writing and to avoid many mistakes. Among them were Karl Schmude, John Dickson, Brendan Purcell, Ross Fitzgerald, Joel Hodge and for the chapters on China, Geremie Barmé. Other Christian friends helped me in long conversations to work through insights on the New Testament, especially Rod McArdle, Christine Wood, Piers Paul Read, and in one memorable lunch, the great Larry Siedentop, whom I met through the generosity of John Dauth, who doesn't claim belief but certainly exhibits a deep expertise in friendship. Thanks too to Peter Rosengren, always an astute critic, similarly the brilliant Steve McAlpine and Rory Shiner in Perth, and Arthur Cairncross. On China, both Geremie Barmé, that peerless interpreter of Chinese culture and history, and my friend and colleague Rowan Callick, were of invaluable assistance. Working through what COVID meant for our society and for Christians, which I then compared with Christian responses to plagues in earlier epochs of history, I was the beneficiary of numerous journalistic conversations with Professor Jodie McVernon of the Doherty Institute, Professor Raina MacIntyre of the University of NSW and Dr Nick Coatsworth, former Deputy Chief Medical Officer.

The magnificent Campion College appointed me an Honorary Fellow which gave me various research and library privileges. Keziah Van Aardt, the Campion librarian, was infinitely helpful and resourceful in locating books, both through Campion's own collection and from other sources. For a period in 2019 I was a Visiting Fellow at Kings College London, which offered a wonderful vantage point on British society and a collegial environment. Nick Spencer and Paul Bickley of London's Theos Think Tank helped me a great deal with research and insight on the state of belief in Britain, while Dan Hitchens of the *Catholic Herald* was a deeply thoughtful and well-informed interlocutor on many aspects of Christianity.

None of the generous and kindly people on this list should be assumed to share any of the views that I express in this book.

As was my practice in *God is Good for You*, I did not stick to one translation of the Bible. All the main translations are faithful and broadly accurate. I was looking for qualities of clarity and even poetry, so I chose whichever translation of particular passages seemed to serve the purpose best. I have not cluttered up the book's pages with footnotes. The books I draw on are referred to in the text and figure in the bibliography.

I want to pay a particular tribute to my publisher at Allen & Unwin, Tom Gilliatt. When I am writing a book, he becomes a kind of life counsellor to whom I bring all problems, which he duly solves. In this case he helped me work a series of ideas into a book. Sam Kent was the book's editor and she was patient and kind, worked to demanding deadlines and had a great eye for detail.

Finally, I must thank my wife, Jessie. Without her generous partnership nothing would have come of the ideas behind this book. My debt to her is incalculable.

Bibliography

Andrew, Brother, *God's Smuggler*, London: Hodder & Stoughton, 1968

Barton, John, *A History of the Bible*, London: Allen Lane, 2019

Bauckham, Richard, *Jesus and the Eyewitnesses*, Grand Rapids: Eerdmans, 2006

—— *Jesus*, New York: Oxford University Press, 2011

—— *Gospel of Glory*, Grand Rapids: Baker Academic, 2015

Benedict XVI, *Jesus of Nazareth*, London: Bloomsbury, 2007

Berger, Peter L., *A Rumor of Angels*, Harmondsworth: Pelican, 1970

Blainey, Geoffrey, *A Short History of Christianity*, Melbourne: Viking, 2011

Bonavia, David, *The Chinese*, Harmondsworth: Penguin, 1981

Brown, Callum G., *The Death of Christian Britain*, London: Routledge, 2009

Bruce, F.F., *The New Testament Documents*, Leicester: Inter-Varsity Press, 1992

Buchan, John, *The Thirty-Nine Steps*, London: Pan, 1970

Callick, Rowan, *Party Time*, Melbourne: Black Inc., 2013

Camus, Albert, *The Plague*, Harmondsworth: Penguin, 1967

Carpenter, Humphrey, *J.R.R. Tolkien*, London: George Allen and Unwin, 1977

—— (ed), *The Letters of J.R.R. Tolkien*, Boston: Houghton Mifflin, 1981

Casey, Michael, *Fully Human, Fully Divine*, Liguori: Liguori/Triumph, 2004

—— *Strangers to the City*, Brewster, MA: Paraclete Press, 2013

Cather, Willa, *Death Comes for the Archbishop*, London: Heinemann, 1927

—— *My Ántonia*, London: Virago, 1980

Chesterton, G.K., *The Everlasting Man*, New York: Doubleday, 1955

Cosgrove, General Sir Peter, *You Shouldn't Have Joined: A memoir*, Sydney: Allen and Unwin, 2020

Dickson, John, *A Sneaking Suspicion*, Sydney: Matthias Media, 1992

—— *If I Were God, I'd End All the Pain*, Sydney: Matthias Media, 2001

—— *A Doubter's Guide to Jesus*, Grand Rapids: Zondervan, 2018

—— *Is Jesus History?*, Sydney: The Good Book Company, 2019

Dickson, John, *Bullies and Saints*, Grand Rapids: Zondervan, 2021

Donnithorne, Audrey G., *China in Life's Foreground*, Melbourne: Australian Scholarly Publishing, 2019

Douthat, Ross, *The Decadent Society*, New York: Avid Reader Press, 2020

Dowling, Jane N., *Child Arise!*, Melbourne: David Lovell Publishing, 2015

Edge, Lynette & Morgan, Gregory, *Partnering with God*, Eugene: Wipf & Stock, 2017

Farrington, Tim, *The Monk Downstairs*, New York: Harper Collins, 2002

Fleming, Peter, *The Unexpected Light*, Melbourne: Morning Star Publishing, 2017

Frame, John M., *Systematic Theology*, Phillipsburg, New Jersey: P&R Publishing, 2013

Frankl, Viktor, *Man's Search for Meaning*, New York: Simon and Schuster, 1962

Graham, Billy, *Angels*, London: Hodder and Stoughton, 1977

Greene, Graham, *The End of the Affair*, New York: Viking, 1951

Guinness, Os, *Last Call for Liberty*, Downers Grove: Inter-Varsity Press, 2017

Gumbel, Nicky, *How to Run the Alpha Course*, London: Kingsway Communications, 2004

Hodge, Joel, *Violence in the Name of God*, London: Bloomsbury, 2020

Holland, Tom, *Dominion*, London: Little Brown, 2019

Bibliography

Johnson, Ian, *The Souls of China*, London: Penguin 2018

Johnson, Paul, *Jesus*, London: Penguin, 2010

Kolakowski, Leszek, *Religion*, London: Fontana, 1982

Kreeft, Peter J., *The Philosophy of Tolkien*, San Francisco: Ignatius, 2005

Lee, Hermione, *Willa Cather*, New York: Vintage, 1991

Lewis, C.S., *Fern-seed and Elephants*, London: Fontana, 1975

—— *Surprised by Joy*, Glasgow: Collins, 1995

—— *Mere Christianity*, London: Collins, 2012

Leys, Simon, *Chinese Shadows*, New York: Viking, 1997

—— *The Analects of Confucius*, New York: Norton, 1997

Lloyd, Michael, *Café Theology*, London: Hodder & Stoughton, 2020

Lu Hsun, *Selected Stories of Lu Hsun*, Beijing: Foreign Language Press, 1978

—— *A Brief History of Chinese Fiction*, Beijing: Foreign Language Press, 1982

Maritain, Jacques, *Natural Law: Reflections on theory and practice*, South Bend: St. Augustine's Press, 2001

McAlpine, Stephen, *Being the Bad Guys*, Sydney: The Good Book Company, 2021

McKnight, Scot, *The Real Mary*, London: SPCK, 2007

Pearce, Joseph, *Literary Converts*, London: Harper Collins, 2000

Pitre, Brant, *The Case for Jesus*, New York: Image, 2016

—— *Jesus and the Jewish Roots of Mary*, New York: Image, 2018

Read, Piers Paul, *Alive*, London: Secker and Warburg: 1974

—— *Polonaise*, London: Secker and Warburg, 1976

—— *A Married Man*, London: Secker and Warburg, 1979

—— *The Free Frenchman*, London: Secker and Warburg, 1986

Robinson, Marilynne, *Gilead*, London: Virago, 2005

Siedentop, Larry, *Inventing the Individual*, London: Penguin, 2014

Stark, Rodney, *The Triumph of Christianity*, New York: Harper Collins, 2011

Strobel, Lee, *The Case for Christ*, Grand Rapids: Zondervan, 1998

——*The Case for Christmas*, Grand Rapids: Zondervan, 2005

Tolkien, J.R.R., *The Lord of the Rings, The Fellowship of the Ring*, London: HarperCollins, 1991

—— *The Lord of the Rings, The Two Towers*, London: HarperCollins, 2001

—— *The Lord of the Rings, The Return of the King*, London: HarperCollins, 2002

Warren, Rick, *The Purpose Driven Life*, Grand Rapids: Zondervan, 2002

Waugh, Evelyn, *Brideshead Revisited*, London: Penguin, 1951

—— *Men at Arms*, London: Penguin, 1952

—— *Officers and Gentlemen*, London: Penguin, 1955

—— *Unconditional Surrender*, London: Penguin, 1961

Weigel, George, *The Fragility of Order*, San Francisco: Ignatius, 2018

Wilson, A.N., *The Book of the People*, London: Atlantic Books, 2015

—— *The Healing Art*, London: Penguin, 1980

—— *Paul: The Mind of the Apostle*, London: Norton, 1998

Wright, N.T., *Paul: A biography*, New York: HarperOne, 2018

—— *Surprised by Hope*, London: Society for Promoting Christian Knowledge, 2007

Index

Index

Index

Index

Index